The Pleasures of Structure

The Pleasures of Structure

Learning Screenwriting Through Case Studies

Julian Hoxter

Bloomsbury Academic
An imprint of Bloomsbury Publishing Inc

B L O O M S B U R Y
NEW YORK · LONDON · NEW DELHI · SYDNEY

Bloomsbury Academic

An imprint of Bloomsbury Publishing Inc

1385 Broadway	50 Bedford Square
New York	London
NY 10018	WC1B 3DP
USA	UK

www.bloomsbury.com

BLOOMSBURY and the Diana logo are trademarks of Bloomsbury Publishing Plc

First published 2015

Library of Congress Cataloging-in-Publication Data
Hoxter, Julian.
The pleasures of structure : learning screenwriting through case studies / Julian Hoxter.
pages cm
Summary: "Helps develop a much deeper understanding of story structure, using case studies with short practical lessons which all emerge organically from the example at hand" — Provided by publisher.
Includes index.
ISBN 978-1-4411-3082-2 (hardback) — ISBN 978-1-4411-0139-6 (pb)
1. Motion picture authorship.   I. Title.
PN1996.H7334 2015
808.2'3–dc23
2014039939

ISBN: HB: 978–1–4411–3082–2
         PB: 978–1–4411–0139–6
         ePub: 978–1–4411–6426–1
         ePDF: 978–1–4411–9385–8

Typeset by RefineCatch Limited, Bungay, Suffolk
Printed and bound in the United States of America

For all the Bobs

Contents

Preface

This is the second book I have written about the craft of screenwriting. The previous volume, *Write What You Don't Know: An Accessible Manual for Screenwriters,* offered a broad, introductory overview of the screenwriting process.[1] It also provided a simple, but detailed model of movie storytelling to help readers develop their own screenplays. Happily, *Write What You Don't Know* has been pretty successful. It has been adopted as a textbook at a number of US and Canadian universities and film schools and has also been published in a Chinese language edition. As a result, I was given the opportunity to write a sequel.

This present volume is the result. It is simultaneously a partner to the previous book and a stand-alone volume. Where *Write What You Don't Know* was a broad introduction, *The Pleasures of Structure* teaches through a series of core case study examples that explore and explain features of movie story structure. If you have already read *Write What You Don't Know,* you will find that the content of this book reinforces and develops ideas and models introduced therein. If you haven't read it don't worry, you don't have to be familiar with the other book to get value from this one. I would be remiss, however, if I didn't encourage you to get a hold of it anyway. There's much in the way of helpful advice in there, plenty of detailed examples, and more than a few jokes—good and bad—to keep the read flowing. However, I introduce everything that needs to be explained from the first book in the pages that follow this preface.

As its title suggests, *The Pleasures of Structure* starts from the premise that in creative screenwriting nothing is more important than story structure. I am hardly unique in suggesting this. Within the screenwriting industry, William Goldman's mantra that "SCREENPLAYS ARE STRUCTURE" (capitals in the original) is well known and many other writers and teachers work from the same broad assumption.[2] Of course, part of the attraction of books like this is the confidence with which we authors make that kind of blanket assertion about the way screenwriting works. Think of us like a gang of "Robert McKees" in *Adaptation,* laying down the lore to you, a sorry bunch of neurotic "Charlie Kaufmans," crippled by your writerly uncertainty as you struggle towards

---

[1] Julian Hoxter, *Write What You Don't Know: An Accessible Manual for Screenwriters* (New York: Continuum Books, 2011).
[2] William Goldman, *Adventures in the Screen Trade: A Personal View of Hollywood and Screenwriting* (London: Abacus, 1983), 195.

dramatic clarity and meaning. At least that's one—reductive and formulaic—way of telling our story.

A key criticism laid at the door of the screenplay manual is that books like this merely reify assumed mainstream industry standards and transmit them as a formula to be copied. Thus the worst clichés of Hollywood storytelling are transmitted, largely uncritically, to succeeding generations of aspiring writers who don't have the gumption to think for themselves or to work creatively around (and indeed away from) the examples of their peers—to say nothing of standing on the shoulders of giants. Of course there can be a certain amount of truth in that charge, assuming that we manual writers are stupid enough to believe in the unassailability of our formulas (some are) and that you readers are gullible, craven or unimaginative enough to think that copying is the same thing as creating (and, just possibly, some few of you were until you read that last sentence). This kind of criticism also sometimes implies, erroneously, that there is no substantive difference between form and formula.

This book adopts a somewhat contradictory attitude to the idea of a story formula. On the one hand it is important to recognize, very much in the spirit of the title of this book, that *formulas can be fun*. They have always made our favorite movie genres pleasurably *generic*—in the very best and most creative sense of that term. Genre stories provide opportunities for far more narrative complexity than the simple idea of patterning incidents on the surface of movie storytelling might suggest. In genre screenwriting formulas are where, unashamedly, the writer often begins. However, as we shall see in this book, there is more to genre than the generic and the case studies that follow will offer some evidence of this. On the other hand, there is nothing worse than sitting in front of your screen to watch a movie and feeling like you have seen this tired old format too many times before. That's another way of saying that good writers are inspired by established paradigms and poor ones are trapped within them.

Of course the structure of movies is about much more than formula. Indeed, even the standard paradigms of movie structure (my version of which we will be working with in the pages that follow) are flexible and dynamic enough to enable a very wide range of storytelling possibilities. Art makes trouble and paradigms can be pushed. This book will give you lots of examples of how very different screenwriters and filmmakers are making that trouble and doing that pushing.

Once you get past the easiest pejorative and reductive connotations you may have attached to the word "structure," you may come to embrace it as the very life—the essence, the beating heart and the joy of stories and their telling. Structure is something to be reveled in, not resisted. It organizes your ideas and enables creativity. Structure opens untold new opportunities for writers, even when they are working with patterns of storytelling established thousands of years ago—and I don't just mean by **Aristotle**.[3]

Readers of *Write What You Don't Know* will find familiar terms here, and we will work from the same structural model. I call it the "W" for reasons that will become obvious shortly and, although I have renamed its story **beats** in this book for ease of use, it works exactly as it always has. The W is a friendly and straightforward way of thinking about how screenplays work. It doesn't apply to every conceivable movie story type, but it helps to explain most, from the spectacular mainstream **tentpole** film to the gritty, **character**-driven independent drama, with a lot of interesting stories in between.

Here's an example from my own teaching to show the breadth of our model. I use the W as a straw man to explain certain kinds of storytelling thinking in the industry in my introductory lecture class at San Francisco State University, CINE356 Fundamentals of Screenwriting. One variant of the in-class final asks students to outline and discuss the structure of a recently released film that will be screened for them on the day. They are to follow the W as far as possible, noting and commenting on divergence when and if it occurs. The students don't know which film we will screen in the class so, even if they happen to have seen it before, they come to it fresh on the day.

To date, my unseen case studies for the CINE 356 final have included *Bridesmaids* (2011), *True Grit* (2010), *Låt den Rätte Komma In / Let The Right One In* (2008), *Winter's Bone* (2010), and *The World's End* (2013). All of these very different movies, from diverse genres including different breeds of comedy, horror, western, and independent drama, follow the W pretty much exactly. Occasionally an individual beat is underplayed, switched around or disguised in some way and needs a bit of thought on the part of the students (hence, of course, the exercise) but, through all of them, the basic model of story structure holds.

The common criticisms of the screenwriting industry tend to assume that alternative approaches to screenwriting are, almost by definition, more radical or somehow more valid expressions than the films produced closer to the familiar mainstream. There is a tendency among some critics of screenplay manuals to fall into empty or reductive value judgment by default. The truth is that most screenwriters and filmmakers today are highly cine-literate. They are members of the second and third post-film school generations, very familiar with mainstream as well as alternative or subaltern forms. They often work between paradigms, depending on their inspiration or the needs of a given project. Many of my students are just as keen to explore different

---

[3] Names and terms that have entries in the critical glossary of screenwriting at the end of the book are given in **bold** the first time they appear.

approaches to storytelling in the short films and microbudget features that they produce as they are to write engaging genre screenplays or historical dramas. The same is true of my own peers from film school in the early 1990s.

In my own work I write books (both practical and scholarly), write and consult on independent features, and also write genre screenplays and novels. In working between these registers—and in finding creative and intellectual fulfillment from all these writerly activities—I am hardly unique. This book is for those of you who are also open to exploring those diverse pleasures for yourselves. It is a book about flexible thinking and, thus, the broad creative potential of story structure. But what about that other common criticism of the screenplay manual, that it sells the unrealistic fantasy of "breaking in" to an industry that can almost never be broken into? Turn the page . . .

Introduction:
American Screenwriting Today

It is very hard to "break into" Hollywood as a screenwriter. It never was easy and, given the current state of the movie industry, it is especially difficult at the time of writing this book (2014). I would certainly be guilty of selling you screenwriting snake-oil if I didn't tell you upfront that you are very unlikely to do so—at least without a strong track record. Note this well in what follows.

A simple reason why Hollywood screenwriting is a hard career path to launch yourself upon right now is that the major studios just don't buy many screenplays anymore. There may be a whole screenwriting industry (of which this book is clearly a part) geared up to sell you the elusive elixir of success but, realistically, the opportunities to sell a script—even a good script—to the corporate entities that we all still think of as Hollywood are very limited. The so-called spec market, in which screenwriters try and sell their original screenplays, has been very weak for years. Looked at through conventional metrics, although total **spec screenplay** purchases by the major studios have risen somewhat since the 2008 writers' strike, the total number of screenplays being purchased in Hollywood is still way down from the recent highs of the late 1980s and early 1990s. According to *The Scoggins Report,* 124 screenplays and 85 **pitches** for a total of 209 were sold in 2013, against totals of 213 in 2012 and 238 in 2011.[4]

These sales figures may come as no surprise to you, however they tend to shock film school students when I tell them the hard truth. For my own interest I always ask my groups to guess—or report if they happen to know—the total number of spec sales in the last year. Typically, their guesses range from around 500 to several thousand, which tells you how well the fantasy of the viable "spec route" into Hollywood is still being sold to them by the screenwriting industry.

Of course, most of the few spec screenplays that are sold each year will never get through the **development** process—in other words they will never get made. This has always been the case, but now an even more significant proportion of the studios' release slates for a given year are being generated through projects generated in-house. Many of those projects are adaptations

---

4   https://specscout.com/yearendscorecards, accessed May 26, 2014.

of intellectual properties (IP) originated in other media: novels, comic books, games, memoirs and other non-fiction, journalistic articles and so forth. In Hollywood, the search for the next big tentpole movie is ongoing and, where once those tentpoles were designed to hold up the "tent" of a studio's profitability to cover the risk of producing smaller movies, increasingly the studios are just erecting taller and taller poles with less and less risky canvas to hang upon them.

One consequence is that development is also skewed towards fewer tentpole or blockbuster-friendly genres. During the writing of this book, in 2013 and early 2014, the breakdown of spec sales by genre was still trending strongly towards Thriller (34), Action Adventure (32), Science Fiction (20), and Comedy (17). The number of Drama scripts sold (10) was significantly lower, just one above Horror for the year. Indeed, these genre biases have been broadly consistent over the last five years.

For those screenwriters who do in fact sell, or work in Hollywood, the contracts they are given have also become more restrictive in recent years. There have always been traps and get-out-clauses like **one-step deals** and unwritten requirements such as free pre-writes, but these are now more the norm.[5] The upside is that some less-experienced writers are being given opportunities to work on big-budget movies, the downside is that their deals allow the studios to remove them from those projects early and to bring their favorite script-doctors and rewrite specialists in to take over sooner. In a period of severe budgetary pressure this allows the studios to save money by commissioning or purchasing cheap first drafts, then paying A-list writers rewrite fees rather than their more expensive rates for full screenplay drafts.

Of course Hollywood studios are not the only institutions making movies. There are still indie movies being made and some scripts are being sold. However, the great indie renaissance promised by the rise of the Sundance Film Festival and of once independent distributors such as Miramax in the early 1990s, was swiftly transformed into what is often called "Indiewood," as the studios bought out or otherwise co-opted much of that iteration of independent filmmaking. Indiewood itself also retrenched from the late 1990s, leaving a smaller group of institutions releasing fewer "niche" and "prestige" mainstream-indie movies as a partial replacement for what used to be the studios' drama product.

In the last decade, many of the best movie writers who don't specialize in tentpole genres have taken their talents to pay (HBO) and basic (AMC, FX)

---

[5]   At time of writing, some studios are promising to back off from one-step deals per their statements and the WGA, but the situation is still in flux.

cable, online (Netflix, Amazon) and even network television, where the most creative dramatic writing is now located. Despite its quest for ratings and subscriptions, contemporary American television (defined thus loosely) is now so much more a writer's medium than the institutions that produce Hollywood movies. Successful TV showrunners have remarkable creative freedom and there is even a clearer career structure for aspirant writers. As Aaron Sorkin (*The West Wing, The Social Network*) noted recently: "If Herman Mankiewicz, Billy Wilder, Preston Sturges and Budd Schulberg were alive today, they'd be writing on TV."

Where independent cinema is truly flourishing—where there are many more opportunities for screenwriter-filmmakers (note that construction well) than ever before—is at the low and microbudget end of the production spectrum.[6] Supported by affordable digital production technologies, online funding and distribution opportunities including crowdsourcing, and an expansion in the film festival circuit, it is easier than ever before to make a movie and to get it seen. Moreover, at the microbudget level, filmmakers are more likely to have the added creative autonomy born of economic control. You may not have much money to make your movie, but you are likely to be able to spend it how you wish. For example, the creative and professional development of filmmakers linked to mumblecore, the major microbudget non-movement-movement of the last decade, is testament to the potential of these new circumstances for aspiring filmmakers today.

Remember also that microbudget does not just mean mumblecore. Shane Carruth made his remarkable science fiction debut feature, *Primer* (2004), for around $7,000 and his second film in that genre, *Upstream Color* (2013), for a reported $100,000. The point is that there are now unprecedented new opportunities for all kinds of creative filmmaking and for screenwriters to tell the kinds of stories they want to tell—as long as you don't need much money to tell them.

Although I work in independent film alongside my teaching and will certainly cover independent screenwriting in what follows—and indeed independent films will comprise a number of our case studies and examples— this book is not only focused on the alternatives. Rather it is about developing your understanding of the starting points and accepted principles of screen storytelling. For present purposes, however, we will be concentrating on helping you to understand the defaults of movie story structure and using

---

[6] One way of defining microbudget screenwriting is according to the Low Budget Agreement from the Writers Guild of America West (WGAW). This document applies to writers working on films budgeted at $1.2 million and below. Most microbudget movies come in far below this level however.

examples from independent film, not simply to break those defaults but also to explore their remarkable flexibility.

Where you see yourselves as working screenwriters, now and in the future, is an open question. However, from the perspective of 2014, the routes that are now open to you to realize those ambitions are simultaneously broader and narrower than they were for the generation that came before you. The opportunities are broader on the creative fringes, which you may choose to inhabit for their own sake or as wedges to gain access to the Hollywood "center." They have contracted at that center, however—and this begs the question: is Hollywood still the center of American filmmaking? In terms of public recognition, exposure and economic power the answer is, of course, still yes. However, since the turn of the millennium Hollywood has been simultaneously clinging ever more desperately onto and moving beyond (arguably being moved beyond) old definitions of a cinema culture located in movie theaters. That's what tentpole movies are about by the way, propping up falling audience numbers in a culture experiencing the ongoing phenomenon of media convergence—of transitioning between old and new screens.

For a long time it has been Hollywood movies that have set many of the defaults for Western cinematic story structure. Independent films of different kinds variously lionize it, adapt it, ironize it, undercut it, despise it, aspire by copying it, and pretend to ignore it—sometimes at the same time—but they are all working in its long shadow. This book and its preceding volume both start from the assumption that it is still important to understand how Hollywood's stories work before you attempt to compete for the chance to work in that idiom or chart your own course alongside or away from it.

Another reason why you need to know this is because it will be assumed by your fellow professionals that you are using a recognizable structural model for your own stories—typically some iteration of what is called the **three-act structure**. Coming to your writing blind, industry **script readers**, agents, producers and other professionals will expect that it is going to conform to what they think movie stories should be like. If yours is different, and you want to be taken seriously by insiders with green-light power, you need to convince very fast on the page or to have a successful track record of difference that they are buying into—like you are this year's indie maverick with buzz.

Even when I am consulting on more experimental independent films I find it useful to be able to offer clear and succinct "Hollywood versions" of a story choice to the filmmakers with whom I am working. In so doing I am giving them a starting point around which they can set up a grid of potential alternatives. The logic of redemptive character arcs and three acts is at once a comfortable basis for discussion and a challenge for filmmakers to transcend. In my experience, even the most alternative filmmakers make educated reference to movie norms in their creative discussions. But don't worry, our W model of movie story structure is designed to be very flexible and you will be able to use it as a basis for a very wide range of stories.

If you want to operate completely outside the box in your screenwriting, all power to your avant-garde elbow. Whatever route you choose, write your own movies. Make your own movies. Get them out there. Put them online. Enter your films and screenplays in festivals and competitions. Build your personal creative track record. Use this book to keep your thinking on track, or to remind you of the kind of storytelling you *don't* want to fall into. Either way you are using this book constructively and that makes me happy!

Lesson Break: Screenwriting Studies

This book is a screenwriting manual, not an academic monograph. Its purpose is to help you develop skills and to understand key ideas that inform creative screenwriting practice today. It is also informed by recent scholarship in the cadet branch of cinema studies that researches the history and practice of screenwriting from a scholarly perspective. In recent years, screenwriting studies has offered important interventions in the academic study of cinema history and production. Leading scholars in the field such as Ian MacDonald, Claudia Sternberg, Steven Maras, Steven Price and Kathryn Millard (as well as the work of the *Journal of Screenwriting*) have done much to reformulate the critical and historical discourse around screenwriting and to explore and explode many of the most persistent myths about how writing works both within Hollywood institutions and outside them.

Much of the work being produced in this emerging academic discipline is absolutely germane to the thinking and development of budding screenwriters. Screenwriting studies tends to be broadly industry focused. In particular, the research and scholarship that is being undertaken around contemporary screenwriting is deeply valuable to anyone who wants to understand and engage with current thinking and practice in the craft. The critical glossary that forms the final section of this book includes some entries that speak directly to this scholarly work and I would direct you to it as a starting point for further investigation and reading. Its traces may also be detected, both directly and indirectly, in the body of what follows. For those of you who are inspired to explore some more of this groundbreaking material, the following books might be of initial interest:

Steven Maras, *Screenwriting: History, Theory and Practice* (London: Wallflower, 2009). Maras' influential book set the agenda for much of what came after in screenwriting studies.

Steven Price, *The Screenplay: Authorship, Theory, Criticism* (Basingstoke: Palgrave, 2010). A groundbreaking critical investigation of the screenplay.

Steven Price, *A History of the Screenplay* (Basingstoke: Palgrave, 2013). An excellent single author history informed by the latest scholarly work.

Andrew Horton and Julian Hoxter eds., *Screenwriting* (New Brunswick: Rutgers University Press, 2014). A volume in the *Behind the Silver Screen* series. Scholarly essays on key periods in the history of screenwriting.

Section One

Principles of Movie Storytelling

NOTE: This section introduces key concepts in screenwriting. Some of the material develops ideas first introduced in my book, *Write What You Don't Know*, but in condensed form and using entirely new case studies. For new readers, this is the part that gets you up to speed with how many screenwriters think before we launch into the detailed case studies of movie structure that form the key central section of this book. We will cover important topics here, such as *internal story logic* (the wardrobe), *parallelism*, and *screenplay style and format*.

The blacklisted Oscar-winning screenwriter, Dalton Trumbo (*Roman Holiday* 1953, *The Brave One* 1956), wrote both fast and brilliantly. That's a very hard act to sustain. Trumbo developed a writing process that worked for him, although sometimes it alarmed unprepared colleagues when he showed them his work in progress. For example, Kirk Douglas recalls how, during the scripting of *Spartacus* (1960), Trumbo explained his method in a note attached to his first screenplay draft: "The only way I can write a script is from beginning to end, dialogue only. Then I make first corrections. Then I do the script—that is, fill in shots and description and action."[7]

As Trumbo's example demonstrates, writing is a very personal process. Indeed, I would argue that it can be among the most personal and private activities any of us engage in, along with masturbation and defecation—activities for which you can not, as yet, officially win Academy Awards. If we are doing it right, our ideas rise up to us from the deep places. We do our best to snag them in the mesh of our creativity, but we all throw our nets with a unique cast. In other words, every writer writes in their own way and a lot of that "personal process stuff" can't be taught in a book like this. We all discover tricks that get us to write, just as we develop individual strategies to help us unstick when we are blocked.

---

[7] Kirk Douglas, *I Am Spartacus! Making a Film, Breaking the Blacklist* (New York: Open Road Integrated Media, 2012), 58.

We writers approach storytelling from different starting points. Some of us begin with an idea for a character, others with an image, others with an urge to "turn" a familiar genre or story type to our own ends. Others still set out to explore a social, cultural, political, or historical issue that intrigues or vexes us in some way. A teacher can suggest that these are all valid approaches, but you will each have your own individual "inspirational libraries" that are open only to you. However we come to them, we tease at these beginnings, and fret over them and worry them to pieces, but it is only when we attach structure to them that they become stories.

The origins of story, part one: Evolution, storytelling and selective advantage

All stories have structure.

Well of course they do, and wasn't that just about the most redundantly obvious statement imaginable? A story without structure wouldn't be a story at all, merely, as the anthropologist Mary Douglas might have put it, a chaotic accumulation of wild words. Structuring a story is the process of creative sense-making, ordering and organizing that transforms words into art (or *Transformers*), giving them drive and purpose and placing them firmly within culture.

It is structure that gives stories weight and meaning. It is structure that binds them to our imaginations and allows them to resonate with us as insight and commentaries, as lessons, as explorations of human experience and potential as well as all kinds of other creative adventures. It is structure that gives our characters *intention* and thus a reason for existing—because for characters to be engaging they must *act with a purpose* and thus also be embedded in story structure. Acts have consequences, consequences create causality and causality inserts structure . . . and so it goes. It is structure that allows us to assess your characters' development, growth or dissolution. It is also, most importantly, a means of influencing the way your audience responds to your story. As Dancyger and Rush argue, "structure is a pattern designed to focus the questions we want the viewer to ask as the story unfolds."[8] Structure drives everything that is meaningful in storytelling. In sum, structure is fundamental to the success of your stories because, in every way imaginable, for your audience *structure = pleasure*.

---

[8]   Ken Dancyger and Jeff Rush, *Alternative Scriptwriting: Beyond the Hollywood Formula*, 5th edition, (New York: Focal Press, 2013), 366.

When you strip away all of the inevitable historical accretions of particular national or culturally specific literatures, at the most universal level we discover that every story deploys some kind of a causal chain of events tending towards a given goal. This has been a given from the beginning of human storytelling through to the present day and it is well understood in the movie industry. As Dore Schary, Head of Production at MGM, suggested in 1950, "... everything that happens must be arranged in a logical sequence of cause and effect so that at any point in the script [the screenwriter] can say, 'Given these people, under these pressures, what is happening here is inevitable.'"[9]

The work of the story is undertaken by a character (or characters), typically with human psychology, and its causal chain is eventually resolved in respect of that character's goal. The evolutionary psychologist Michelle Scalise Sugiyama argues that this universality of narrative—of telling and of understanding stories—is an ancient cognitive phenomenon and that long ago, for reasons of natural selection, human beings evolved into effective processors of narratives. She writes:

> ... all normally developing humans acquire the ability to process and generate stories: studies of Western children indicate that the ability to tell stories emerges spontaneously between the ages of two-and-a-half and three, and children as young as thirty months can distinguish between narrative and non-narrative uses of language. In contrast to reading, writing, and arithmetic, no special education is required for narrative competence to develop, nor is there any evidence that oral literacy is acquired through contact with other cultures; although subject matter is often exchanged between groups, the practice of storytelling itself arises independently among even the most isolated peoples. Nor does any type of culture have a monopoly on narrative sophistication: the stories of hunter-horticulturalist societies are no less observant, insightful, or artful than those of agrarian or industrial societies.[10]

Sugiyama suggests that storytelling emerged as a response to the demands of our long evolutionary history as hunter-gatherers. Stories efficiently perform socializing and educative functions that bind groups and transmit knowledge and best practice in both oral and written traditions. A group that transmits such knowledge effectively across generations reinforces it and has the potential to build upon it, thus gaining selective advantage. Of course,

---

[9] Dore Schary and Charles Palmer, *Case History of a Movie* (New York: Random House, 1950), 29.
[10] Michelle Scalise Sugiyama, "Narrative Theory and Function: Why Evolution Matters", *Philosophy and Literature* Volume 25, Number 2, October 2001, 233–250

stories can also be used to impose common purpose through social control. In this way, stories also transmit injunctions, laws and other standards of behavior and thus bind power in the storyteller or in those for whom she speaks or writes. Many key survival tasks including finding food, avoiding danger and all manner of collaborative social interactions require what Sugiyama calls "cognitive access to one's surroundings." Storytelling is one important way in which such access is similarly mediated and disseminated to all members of a group.

The Hugo Award winning science fiction author C. J. Cherryh (*Downbelow Station*) makes a similar link between biology and environment in an interesting discussion of world building on her determinedly old-school website. Cherryh, whose own academic background is in archeology, argues that "culture is how biology ... makes its living conditions better."[11] That's another strong evolutionary argument for the pleasures of storytelling.

As human societies have developed, our stories and our rituals of storytelling have forgotten or disguised their primal evolutionary functions as—and beneath—their surface function as entertainment. To open with a simple example, we don't go to see *Spiderman* movies for hints about how to survive as hunter-gatherers beset by packs of hungry wolves and dependent on correctly anticipating the migratory patterns of caribou or buffalo. However we are still given an evolutionary lesson or two for the price of our admission, whether the writers plan it or not. In *Spiderman*, of course, we learn something about the desired relationship between the moral individual and the collective: "with great power comes great responsibility." This principle is repeated for us by the story's structure until—well until we remember that line as a kind of mantra, a signal that we have also learned a little of Spiderman's lesson.

Audiences tend to respond positively to structural repetitions with variation because, as we shall see, much of the enjoyment they will get from your story comes from how you work its structure. In so doing you will establish a kind of contract with your audience, encouraging them to think in certain ways and working on their expectations variously to confirm them and to surprise them as your movie plays out. You may not set out in your writing to teach anyone anything in the form of a simple lesson—nothing sounds more redundant than that, right? You certainly didn't plan to further the evolutionary development of your species through a little indie movie

---

[11] http://www.cherryh.com/www/worldbuilding.htm accessed June 2 2014.

about halting first love. Although, without pushing it too far, a story that has some bearing on a young adult's ability to select a competent reproductive partner might also tip towards selective advantage. This is a great big can of worms, but you can see how it goes. Whatever kind of story you tell us, then, a lot of very basic *what it is to be human* work is going on under the surface of your structure.

This is not by way of telling you to make all your stories stuffy and didactic, nor even into radical post-Brechtian lehrstücke. Nor is it a way of telling you simply to obey the rules. On the contrary, some of the best filmmakers take great delight in playing games with the fundamental expectations we have of movie storytelling and of the lessons of classical Hollywood causality in particular. Whenever I watch one of my favorite films, *Repo Man* (1984, scr. Alex Cox), I revel in Alex Cox's subversion of conventional causality with a "lattice of coincidence" that drives the storytelling. In that genre-bending post-punk B movie Cox, a very smart guy and a UCLA alumnus who knows the rules too well to take them entirely seriously, sticks two fingers up at the lessons his film school professors taught him. More importantly the attitude fits the movie and that buys him all the unconventional structure he could want.

Iconoclastic experimentation notwithstanding, stories are a fundamental legacy of our human uniqueness and being a storyteller links you to a practice that has played a major role in our survival and success as a species. We will come back to this link between stories, their structure and thinking like a human when we discuss **ring compositions** and **parallelism**. For now, just hold this single idea in your mind: the pleasures we derive from the structure of our stories speak as much to our biology and psychology as a species as they do to the concerns of a given individual or culture at a given historical moment.

The origins of story, part two: Written culture, ring compositions and the principle of parallelism

As I have already argued, our understanding of the structure of stories is predicated in large part on the lessons of thousands of years of literary and pre-literary history as it speaks in and through our contemporary cultures. In the Western theatrical canon, for example, the legacy of Sophocles, Marlowe, Shakespeare, Webster, Molière, Goethe, Ibsen, Strindberg, Turgenev, Wilde and many others besides informed the expectations we have for how drama should work both before and after the invention of cinema.

The history of screenwriting—still a young art among longer-established forms to be sure—offers both a break from and a continuity with the dramatic canon of the pre-cinematic era. It is a break inasmuch as a new medium necessarily creates its own new rules. It offers a kind of continuity in that screenwriting looked—and still looks—to broader traditions of storytelling to make sense of itself and to speak to its audiences in a dramatic language they will understand and respond to. In recent years we have often thought about the influence of television, comic books, video games and other contemporary media on cinematic storytelling, but in the early years of the twentieth century filmmakers adapted the forms and traditions of theatrical melodrama in a direct attempt to attract more upmarket audiences to motion pictures. The adoption of melodrama was neither *natural*—for who was to say what this new medium of cinema could and should be—nor intrinsically or essentially *necessary* to the art and craft of cinema. It is important to note that there was no built-in or pre-ordained final or perfect form to the development of cinematic storytelling. The history of screenwriting, like the history of cinema, is not a teleology. Once the link with melodrama was made, however, it stuck.

Although there is much more to movies than melodrama, contemporary films still deploy its tropes to keep us in our seats, and the happy—or cathartic, or "redemptive"—ending still plays strongly. Ask yourself, what was *Gravity* (scr. Alfonso Cuarón & Jonás Cuarón, 2013) under all the spectacle other than a simple, redemptive melodrama, set in space? As I write these words it has received ten Oscar nominations and grossed around $678 million worldwide, so the old tricks clearly have some life left in them.

Beneath the veneers of style and setting, and despite advances in technology, the way Hollywood filmmakers (and most American independent filmmakers besides) tell their stories hasn't changed that much since the classical period of the Hollywood studio system. Indeed, in terms of the key principles underlying its structure, it hasn't changed that much since human societies first developed written culture and began to record their stories. The late **Syd Field** may have brought the "three-act structure" to a wider public in his influential book *Screenplay* (1979), but many of the other principles of movie storytelling go back at least as far as the *Torah, Gilgamesh* and the *Iliad*.

Other writers on the craft of screenwriting have looked to the past for inspiration. For example, Christopher Vogler offers a well-known model for screenplay structure based on lessons appropriated from the heroic "monomyth" paradigm developed by Joseph Campbell. Similarly, the talented screenwriter Pamela Gray (*A Walk on the Moon* 1999, *Conviction* 2010) uses and teaches "The Heroine's Journey," her own engaging version of Campbell's hero's journey re-worked for female **protagonists**. As readers of *Write What*

You Don't Know will already be aware, I am also interested in looking back through ancient literary history to learn lessons about contemporary screenwriting. Unlike Mr. Vogler, however, I am less concerned with the structures of heroic myth per se. What intrigues me about the very first written stories, heroic or otherwise, is how they speak to and reveal the most basic *needs* that drive human storytelling into its first forms.

To be specific, I am suggesting that we can learn much about what we humans have always needed from our stories from what are called ring compositions. Ring compositions are among the earliest narratives preserved in written form. They mark, in part, the transition from oral to written traditions, and they developed in many cultures without contact with one another across the world. In other words ring compositions turn up *independently* in different cultures, as they begin to record their own stories, myths and laws in writing. If human cultures have all told stories in this way, then surely that must tell us something significant about what stories are for and how and why we enjoy them and get different kinds of value from them. If storytelling does indeed have an evolutionary function, if it does offer selective advantages, then commonalities in the way stories are structured across independent cultures should speak to this also. Additionally, I would argue that the lessons ring compositions teach us are more universal and far less prescriptive than those taken from heroic myth. As we shall see, their historical distance from us notwithstanding, ring compositions organize their stories along principles that will be very familiar to those of us trying to organize our own screenplays today.

Briefly, a story written in the form of a ring composition develops in a linear fashion, from exposition to resolution, its events unfolding one after the other in familiar causal sequence. However, the story "turns" around a clearly defined center—or **Midpoint** as we say in screenwriting. After the midpoint, each beat (significant moment) of the story pairs up in some way (thematically, visually, linguistically or otherwise) with a corresponding beat in the first half of the story. In this way the story proceeds *both* as a linear development and as a series of parallel thought exercises. What is set up at a given place in the first half of the story is resolved distinctly as the second half bends back towards thematic resolution.

Screenwriters are already familiar with this principle of parallelism, even if most of them have probably never heard of ring compositions. The idea that whatever you set up must be resolved is central to the principles of narrative economy and coherence. We are told that, after primary exposition, an **inciting incident** occurs in a movie that impels the protagonist into their story task—something important happens that motivates them to take action. This incident carries with it the expectation of an unknown, yet already essential resolving incident to come (Robert McKee calls it the "obligatory moment," and I'm borrowing his terms here). In a revenge drama, for example, the original crime or injustice (inciting incident) demands payback (obligatory moment). At the time this crime is committed we do not know what form that obligatory revenge will take, but we are certain that it will come. What's more, we are in two senses—one temporal and the other pleasurable—*looking forward* to it.

Another term that speaks to the importance of parallelism that you might come across in conversation with screenwriters, or in books on dramatic writing is "Chekhov's gun." This is the idea that once something is revealed in a drama it must be used, as the Russian playwright Anton Chekhov wrote in a letter to Lazarev (A. S. Gruzinsky) in 1889: "One must never place a loaded rifle on the stage if it isn't going to go off. It's wrong to make promises you don't mean to keep." The rifle may be thought of literally or metaphorically—a revelation could "discharge" with lethal force in a **scene**. If something is necessary to the drama, establish it and pay it off; if it is not necessary, remove it. After all, even red herrings pay off their foreshadowing in stories.

This kind of creative thinking across your story would have seemed entirely logical and appropriate to Homer, to whom key events such as the fall of Troy or Achilles' death are, after all, fixed and predestined by fate and the Gods. But parallelism works at every narrative level and has to do with more than destiny. It is also one of the most fundamental pleasures of any kind of storytelling because it links into our basic human thought processes at a very deep level. After all, we human beings hold pattern recognition as a key component in our evolutionary skillset. Parallelism, then, is storytelling at our species center.

I don't propose to revisit any more of my discussion of ring compositions here.[12] I will just offer the following simple lessons that, those narratives remind us, are neither time bound, nor the product or property of individual human cultures. Rather they are the closest we come to accessing the universal human language of storytelling.

Most importantly, ring compositions teach us that *stories are full of symmetry.*

1. *Stories begin with exposition.* They introduce us to their purpose and **theme**.

---

[12] For more information on ring compositions, see my brief discussion in *Write What You Don't Know*, 140–147. For a much fuller, scholarly investigation of the subject, see Mary Douglas, *Thinking in Circles: An Essay on Ring Composition (The Terry Lecture Series)* (New Haven: Yale University Press, 2010).

2. *Stories end with resolution.* They re-address their purpose in some way, reflecting on the events and lessons of the story.
3. *Good stories often turn in the middle.* There is symmetry to the arc of a story and the middle is a key point at which we take stock of our progress on the journey. As characters learn and experience, they are enabled to make more important decisions. The most important decisions turn mere protagonists into heroes and heroines. By the midpoint, they should be ready to enact an important stage in this transformation.
4. *The most important structural principle of storytelling is parallelism.* Audiences work with what they are given. They anticipate change and development and they enjoy being given work to do. We don't just read, or view, stories along a linear track; we continually work back and forth, evaluating what we have already been told and shown and wondering about what is yet to come, in order to make sense of it all. This process should be *fun* (under a broad definition of the word), as much for you the writer as for a reader or the paying moviegoer in her seat. *Structure, my dear reader, is pleasure.*

These lessons are as important as three acts, character arcs, beats, backstories and all the other terms I and other writers will throw at you. Of them all, the most important is parallelism, but we will go on to discuss them in detail as the book develops.

Here's a diagram of a simple ring composition in screenwriting terms. The *linear read* is down the left, across the middle and back up the right. The *experiential read* works back and forth from the linear to the parallels as set-ups and payoffs play out across the track (the number of beats in this example is arbitrary).

	ESTABLISH THEME	
↓ EXPOSITION	←---------------→	RESOLUTION
↓ SET-UP	←---------------→	PAYOFF ↑
↓ SET-UP	←---------------→	PAYOFF ↑
↓ SET-UP	←---------------→	PAYOFF ↑
↓ SET-UP	←---------------→	PAYOFF ↑
↘	MIDPOINT TURN	↗

Now write a screenplay . . .

Case Study: Parallelism in *The King's Speech*

David Seidler did write a screenplay, and *The King's Speech* won him a screenwriting Oscar in 2010. In this, our first case study, we will explore the power of parallelism in storytelling by considering how the single motif of public speaking implied in the movie's title is used throughout the film. Parallelism is one of the simplest principles of storytelling. Like many simple propositions, however, works of great subtlety and complexity can be woven out of it. There is much more to be said about screenwriting and *The King's Speech* than this, of course, but for now let's just focus on how David Seidler works his central motif.

In creative writing an interesting story often starts from a simple premise and explores it through repetition with variation and through comparison. In this way one thing can mean many things and have different emotional value and moral weight when viewed from different perspectives, or through the lens of a different character, or given the space of experience. These repetitions and comparisons are where the principle of parallelism becomes the creative concrete that binds your audience into your storytelling. This case study uses one specific example, but the principle of building your story around a simple thematic idea with complex potential is a very good way of starting your structural thinking.

The movie's title already suggests a double meaning in the word "speech" from the specific (one speech) to the general (a man's ability to speak). However, the story keeps showing us ways in which "speech" means different things to different people at different times. This is important because *The King's Speech* is, in fact, a tale not of one but of many speeches. Speeches are used as markers of both character and crisis, indicating significant personal and political developments. In other words, these parallels are the key devices that the writer has used to reinforce the significance of the story and to keep us on track with its progress.

In *The King's Speech*, speeches of different kinds ask the audience to engage in critical comparison. These comparisons mark *change* and, in turn, change signals story development.

Set in England in the 1930s, the movie tells a simple story about a very private man, called Bertie by those near to him. In public he is also the Duke of York, second son of King George V, and he will eventually become King George VI. Poor Bertie has a terrible stammer and he **needs** to develop an effective public speaking voice in order to lead his country through a period of historic crisis. As the story unfolds, events both foreign and domestic are propelling this reluctant monarch towards his crown in the era of radio, a time in which the spoken word is transcending the written as the most important and persuasive mode of public discourse. In order to address his speech impediment, Bertie reluctantly turns for help to Lionel Logue, an unconventional Australian speech therapist. The film recounts their relationship as Bertie struggles to overcome his problem and to lead the British Empire through the Second World War.

The use of multiple speeches—multiple instances in which the key motif of the story is repeated with variation—follows common, and age-old storytelling principles. In simplest terms, the movie's title tells us what to look out for: *speeches*. When we see and hear public speeches, therefore, we are already attuned to pay special attention to them. We expect them to be important. We are ready to ask straightforward questions of these scenes and **sequences** and to *remember and compare* each instance of speechmaking with and against those that have come before.

So far this is simple stuff, right? We, the audience, pay attention to what we already know the subject of the movie's story to be.[13] However, in *The King's Speech*, the Oscar-worthiness of the script comes, in part, from how David Seidler deploys narrative complexity around and within that simple follow-the-lead-of-the-title principle. For example, in the movie the ability to speak in public doesn't just mean one thing. Speech—and speeches—develop a number of interconnected thematic threads throughout the story, for example:

1. *Speech as duty.* To lead, we are told, a modern king now needs to be heard. It is Bertie's duty as king to have an effective voice. He accepts his duty and all the personal struggle it brings with it.
2. *Speech as psychology.* In his sessions with Bertie, Logue discovers that unhappy, even abusive, childhood experiences may well have contributed to his client's speech condition. In this way, the surface impediment represents deeper trauma: *plot (events) reveals story (motivations)*.
3. *Speech as maturity.* In the context of this psychological **backstory**, there is a sense in which Bertie's struggles to overcome his stammer mirror a process of growing up—both as a man and as a potential king.
4. *Speech as democracy.* There is also a sense in which the "proper" forms of verbal communication—those forms bound by tradition, class, deference and protocol— are embodied in Bertie. They are embodied in him, but uncomfortably so perhaps, for his destiny is to become a transitional figure, harbinger of a new kind of monarchy. We are shown

---

[13] There's a reason a simple but eloquent title is often an important marker of a successful movie. Again, *Gravity* is a big clue to what's going to be important—there's even a double meaning in there somewhere! Calling a film *The Verdict* asks *us* to pass judgment, along with the jury in the movie, so we duly assess and reassess the moral progress of Paul Newman's alcoholic lawyer in his slow rehabilitation both as a man and a professional.

how Bertie is "loosened up" and appropriately deflated by the eccentric colonial, Logue—the first "ordinary" person Bertie has ever really got to know. At first he kicks against this imposition on proper manners—even unwisely firing Logue for his presumption at a key moment in the middle of the story—but in due course he learns his lesson.

5. *Speech as a weapon.* The movie gives us a glimpse of the aggressive power of speechmaking with a newsreel clip of Hitler speaking. Churchill's liminal presence in the story also suggests the true power of the British oratorical response to come, but Bertie's speech to the Empire at the end of the movie is a quiet sort of weapon in its own right. Propaganda of all sorts is designed to influence opinion and bring its listeners into line behind the speaker's goals. Despite its obvious lack of Churchillian confidence and oratorical flourish, Bertie's speech is played as a binding force that calms and provides a sense of moral rightness and common purpose to the people of the British Empire as they go to war. In this way the story suggests that it is no less important a propaganda weapon than Hitler's, only expressed as a condensation of Englishness.

Over the course of the film, Bertie develops a much more informal friendship with Logue becoming, in the process, the kind of king he needs to be to unite his people against the global threat of fascism. In this way, through his relationship with Logue, the king is democratized and demystified. His climactic speech will have the power to unify. His progress towards a cure for his stammer mirrors this modest, reformist social development.

So the motif of public speaking means more than one thing and the parallels established and paid off in the script all address one or more of these meanings. Here are some key examples:

First parallel – speeches as exposition and resolution

The film opens with Bertie giving the closing speech to the British Empire Exhibition. He fails terribly, almost unable to get the simplest words out. Both he and his audience are embarrassed and Bertie appears woefully unqualified for any public role. Fortunately, as the second son of King George V, his destiny does not point to the throne at this point in the story.

This opening beat works *in parallel* with the film's climax in which Bertie, now King George VI, gives his first radio address in wartime. While he is hardly natural or truly fluent in his delivery, he is able to get through the speech and (as we see in an accompanying montage) to communicate with his people. *In comparison* with the opening beat, the transformation is certainly remarkable.

This first parallel demonstrates the scale of Bertie's (and Logue's) achievement. On the surface it simply shows his mechanical improvement as a public speaker but, having joined him on his journey through the story, the audience understands that this outward success also speaks [*sic*] to the far more transformative psychological development he has undergone in becoming a more confident and self-aware adult.

Anticipation: when we see Bertie fail at the start of the story we—the audience—are already looking forward (in two senses again) to the moment when he gets it right. We feel for him and support his struggle for change. Moreover, we know that second moment is coming, and the script is written explicitly *to* that knowledge.

Second parallel – public speech versus private speech

Having shown us Bertie's abject failure as a public speaker, Seidler is careful to offer us an internal parallel within the first act of the screenplay to show that, in the privacy and comfort of his domestic world, he has already found his own voice. We see Bertie telling a bedtime story to his daughters. His voice catches occasionally, but he manages rather well and is funny, affectionate and eloquently paternal in a way that, only being shown his public voice, we would never suspect.

This scene is important in prefiguring the learning process when he comes under Lionel Logue's care later in the story. Logue is convinced that Bertie can find his voice and now we have already seen evidence that he does, indeed, have the capacity for it.

Anticipation: going forward, that privileged knowledge defines the audience's role as *encouragers*, rather than merely *wonderers*—the audience are firmly inscribed as members of Team Bertie. We know the private Bertie that can match with the public George VI and we will him to succeed rather than wondering if he truly can have a voice.

Third parallel – speeches as political alternatives

The third pair of speeches comes towards the ends of the first and second acts of the story respectively. These points in a movie typically mark the moments in which a protagonist first accepts the challenge of the story and, finally, is in a position to enact or accomplish it. The second act gets the protagonist from acceptance to ability. In other words, it changes them.

The first of these beats, at the end of act one, is the very competent radio address given by Bertie's father, George V. This serves as an example for Bertie of how a king should communicate. Indeed, George tells Bertie that "this devilish device [radio] will change everything" and makes his example explicit in encouraging and even bullying his son to improve his speaking.

George's radio speech works in parallel with a short newsreel clip of Hitler addressing the crowds at Nuremberg that arrives at the end of act two. Bertie watches it after his own coronation and it speaks to the power of public speaking, but also offers a frightening alternative to a potentially incompetent king. To over-simplify somewhat, this parallel is telling Bertie: if you can't be like your father in this respect, the Nazis could win.

Anticipation: we educated audience members know from the start that Bertie will be king and that war is coming. The historical plot line that pulls Bertie inexorably towards his public destiny is what movie people—and especially screenwriters—like to call the movie's *clock.* It circumscribes the story and gives the search for a solution to Bertie's stammer a deadline. It adds the question of whether he will sort it out *in time* to the other questions we ask of the characters and their struggles. We understand, therefore, that the newsreel scene comes at a point in the story in which Bertie can no longer avoid the necessity of solving his problem. War is approaching and, as Bertie himself acknowledges after watching Hitler speak, that however vile his message may be, "he seems to be saying it rather well."

Fourth parallel – speeches as markers of progress

The fourth pair of speeches mark early progress in Bertie's condition. In the second act, as he is starting to work with Logue, Bertie does make some early progress. He is surprised, upon hearing a recording of his own voice reading Shakespeare, that he has the potential to be articulate in public. Later in the angle we see him give a speech in a factory and, although it is stilted, there are small signs of hope for the future.

Anticipation: progress markers are all about encouraging your audience to think ahead of the pace of your storytelling. If he's like this now, we reflect, how far does he still have to go to succeed?

Fifth parallel – speeches as dramatic reinforcement

A quick parallel occurs soon after the story's midpoint. Bertie's older brother, David (King Edward VIII) abdicates so as to be able to marry for love, opening the way for Bertie to become king. We hear an extract from David's famous speech on the radio, before Bertie is required to offer a brief public statement. Bertie fails again.

Anticipation: This is a straightforward reinforcement parallel. We know what is at stake by now, but this pair of scenes drives up the tension right after Bertie has fired Logue, making us wonder how he is ever going to find his voice now. This is a common tactic at this point in movie storytelling. Typically, the midpoint is followed by immediate evidence of the weighty consequences of its action. In this case Bertie has just derailed his own potential for progress by firing Logue, so we duly see the danger of that action in his continuing inability to communicate in public.

Parallels and *pleasure*

The enjoyment of the audience is invested in pulling for Bertie's eventual success. The structure of the story plays to that investment and the individual pairs of parallel story moments deepen and reinforce that engagement. They are central to our enjoyment of the drama—once again, *structure = pleasure*.

Using the same basic diagram of a ring composition we saw above, but addressing several of the core speech beats of *The King's Speech*, we come up with a simple structural guide to the core of the movie's story that looks like this (beats that include public speeches are in bold):

	SPEECH IS DUTY	
↓ **FIRST SPEECH, FAILURE**	←----------→	**KING'S SPEECH, SUCCESS**
↓ **GEORGE V'S MODEL**	←----------→	**BERTIE AND HITLER** ↑
↓ LEARNING MECHANICS	←----------→	TRUST THE TEACHER ↑
↓ **SLOW PROGRESS**	←----------→	**BERTIE FAILS AGAIN** ↑
↓ GEORGE V DIES	←----------→	DAVID'S ABDICATION ↑
↘	BERTIE FIRES LOGUE (MIDPOINT CRISIS)	↗

Of course, you will not be writing *The King's Speech*. However, when you do sit down to plan out your next screenplay, think back to this simple case study and try and build a thematic net that suits your project but that gets your audience to do the same kind of work with the core of your own story.

Remember also that all stories use parallelism, even elliptical tales that are all about people going nowhere much. At the beginning of the recent mumblecore movie, *Hannah Takes the Stairs* (2007, scr. Joe Swanberg, Greta Gerwig, Kent Osborne and contributions from the cast), we find Hannah in the shower with her current but soon to be ex-boyfriend. At the end of the movie she is taking a day off work and playing trumpet in the bath with her latest crush. The story follows Hannah, a drifting college grad, going through a repeating cycle of short relationships without finding real purpose or fulfillment. The parallel between these two scenes shows us that Hannah at the end is very much like Hannah at the beginning, and that's the point. Well maybe now she's having more fun in water, but that's not much in the scheme of growth. It is a parallel that chronicles a lack of progress but that, in doing so, still marks structure of a kind.

Another recent indie movie bookends with a parallel that signifies small, but significant character change. In Fred's car at the opening of *Palo Alto* (2013, scr. Gia Coppola, based on the stories by James Franco) teenager Teddy allows himself to be browbeaten by his buddy Fred over his answer to one of Fred's endless series of annoying hypothetical questions. At the end, just before the final sequence of shots that locates the main characters at their emotional exit points, Teddy has the sense to have had enough of Fred's crap when the same conversation—the same low-key bullying—repeats with minor variation. Teddy demands to be let out of Fred's car and walks away. We leave an angry Fred driving down the freeway the wrong way into oncoming traffic. Teddy's equivocal growth is measured in a number of ways in the movie, but it is in this final parallel payoff, in this final recognition that Fred is no good for him, that we understand his loose arc has resolved.

As qualified pattern recognizers we are so attuned to parallelism in our stories that it is one of the most flexible tools available to you as a writer. It is also a way of reinforcing story and character without being literal or "on the nose"— as the examples from *Hannah Takes the Stairs* and *Palo Alto* demonstrate. Your readers and audience will interrogate patterns of activity by your characters and infer connections and complexity from those patterns without your having to specify it or refer to it in dialogue. That makes parallelism powerful.

We will go on to consider a more complex model of story structure shortly (the aforementioned "W"). However, the pattern of storytelling parallelism, inherited from our ancestors and so instinctive—so close to our most primal human thought patterns—will always live within it. Indeed, whatever structural model you end up working with, you will not be able to escape working with the primal pleasures of parallelism. We will return to specific examples in due course.

The skeleton of a story: Internal story logic

I have already suggested that every story deploys a kind of cause and effect chain. This is the first level of internal story logic in which one idea or event in the story has a rational connection to the events that precede and follow it. More than this, stories manage their causal development through the interaction of specific structuring elements. I don't mean only the surface incidents in the story itself here as much as I do the pieces that go to make up the often invisible skeleton that lies under your story and articulates it smoothly in the telling. Sometimes the work of these elements is obvious, but often their operation goes on without us being directly aware of it as we watch a movie.

We are all familiar in general terms with words like *story*, and *plot*, and *arc*, and *theme*, but to organize our storytelling effectively we need to be clear about what these words really mean. They all have more specific definition in screenwriting. Undoubtedly you have heard them used casually and you will find them referred to often in what follows. In screenwriting their interaction drives the internal logic (the skeletal structure) of your story. I will discuss each of them briefly and then offer a quick illustrative model to show how they are all essential to a well-articulated story and how they interact.

Theme – what your story is actually about

Good stories have themes. Themes bind everything together and give your story a single, unified purpose. Once you have picked a theme for your story it doesn't change. If your theme changed, you would be telling a different story. Although a single story may have a number of subsidiary themes, it should have one central thematic driver that pushes your protagonist into action and helps us judge their progress.

Dore Schary wrote of theme in terms of developing the *emotional line* of a movie (in this case *The Next Voice You Hear*, 1950, scr. Charles Schnee): "It was pretty well established by now that the emotional line of the story would be fear, mortal fear which would key the reawakening of our characters to the freedom from fear which awaits them in God."[14] The American screenwriting industry has also been extolling the virtues of a single, clear theme for almost as long as there have been movie stories to tell. For example, in their book *Writing the Photoplay* (1913) Esenwein and Leeds were already advising writers that there should be "a single main theme, one main line of development, in every well-constructed story – and only one."[15] Typically, screenwriters try and express their theme in a single word that expresses the purpose of the story specifically and unequivocally.

---

[14] Schary and Palmer, *Case History of a Movie*, 59–60.
[15] J. Berg Esenwein and Arthur Leeds, *Writing the Photoplay* (Springfield MA: The Home Correspondence School, 1913).

In conventional screenwriting terms a theme is the idea goal that lies behind your protagonist's desire, or need to act. Your story's theme can be a lesson which your protagonist must learn, only played as lightly as possible in the context of your story world. If your story offers a problem to be solved, or a challenge to be overcome, it is the theme that determines the way in which your protagonist will approach that problem and how we will assess their growth (change) in doing so. If your story is less strongly plot driven, it should offer another kind of thematic exploration—the theme might describe the part of their personality or life experience with which your protagonist is struggling or trying to come to better terms with. Here we might think of Hannah's immature decision-making in acting on all her crushes, for example. Perhaps your story speaks its theme quietly, but without a central theme to bind it there is no clear focus for motivation and your story has no center.

Good themes tend to offer either experiential or conceptual frameworks for debate and action. A story's theme might explore a political, cultural or social system or condition, like *faith*, or *racism*, or *family*. On the other hand a good theme can speak to universal emotional and personal conditions such as *love*, or *friendship*, or *grief* or *mourning*. Other examples of common movie themes might include any of the following: *loyalty, revenge, betrayal, duty, parenthood, survival, power, democracy, freedom, acceptance, success, maturity, childhood* . . . the (evolutionary) list goes on.

Remember, those words may be simple, but the stories built around them need not be. How many different and moving stories have you seen based around the theme of love, for example?

Arc – your protagonist's progress in addressing your theme

The arc of your protagonist is the journey they take through the story. When you know your theme, you establish a measure by which their progress along their arc or path can be judged. While your theme won't change, the attitude of your protagonist—and indeed of all your other characters—to your theme most certainly will. Sometimes people need to be convinced to change or to accept the importance of an issue. In that case they may start your story in a negative relationship to the theme, the work of the story being to change their opinion and, thus, their actions. A revenger might start a movie in forgiving mode, only for a terrible event to push them into darker motivation.

Conversely, your protagonist might start a story closely aligned to a theme only to grow up and take a more mature view as events and experience teach. A character might start your movie all too in love with love. Hard life lessons and one too many unrealistic, failed relationships might change their view. Because characters change their relationship to themes, because arcs bend, screenwriters often acknowledge this by referring to their interactions with theme as a **transformational arc**. A well-drawn character will reassess their attitudes due to experience and a well-crafted story will embed those changes at the heart of its structure.

Note that *all* of your principal characters should have clearly defined attitudes to the theme of your story. It is through your protagonist's interaction *with them* that she will address her theme after all. The other characters earn their keep by taking action to help, hinder, distract, advise and so forth—but their actions only have weight in your story if they do so while addressing its theme. If you and I are friends and our attitudes to love and romance are very different, it is likely that the kind of advice we would give each other, when one of us is having relationship problems, would be very different. Indeed, no matter how close our friendship is in other ways, this difference could be the cause of disagreement or even more serious conflict—and conflict is at the heart of drama.

Lesson Break: Theme Versus Arc

A protagonist's problem isn't static. At least, while it is static thematically it develops positionally. This means that their theme never changes but their attitude to their theme develops throughout and, most importantly, *because of* their story.

Most typical Hollywood and indie stories follow their protagonists through key thematic positions. Let's take an easy example and say our theme is "love." First your protagonist might reject love (bad past experiences), then they meet the person of their dreams and accept it. Then they either lose it and have to work harder to prove themselves worthy of it (girl meets boy, girl loses boy, girl gets boy back) or they give it up for the greater good, or in favor of a "more deserving" case of some kind, in a noble sacrifice. Because this is Hollywood, they usually get it back again at the end as a reward for being a good girl or boy. This kind of resolution is often referred to (sometimes pejoratively) as a "redemptive ending." Think of the structure of Nora Ephron comedies like *When Harry Met Sally* (1989, scr. Nora Ephron), or *You've Got Mail* (1998, scr. Nora Ephron, Delia Ephron).

As previously noted, many screenwriters call this sequence of positions or attitudes in relation to their theme a character's "transformational arc" or just "arc." For a really clear exegesis of this common structuring strategy pick up a copy of Donna Michelle Anderson's (DMA's) elegantly simple *1–3–5 System*.

Think about it, if your story did not take your protagonist through a series of positions in relation to their theme it would be having no effect on them. That would mean it was going exactly nowhere. Not all movie stories work this way of course. Not even all mainstream Hollywood stories—they all work their protagonist's arc, but not always in the reject → accept → sacrifice sequence.

Hiccup's protagonist's arc in *How to Train Your Dragon* follows the most common variant on that model. He starts out as an outsider who completely buys into Viking culture and **wants** desperately to be a part of it. He then goes through a learning process that exposes the ignorance upon which his culture is based. He even gets the chance to gain the acceptance he so desperately seeks but finds deeper truths in himself and passes up those opportunities. Later he gives up the chance for easy acceptance and risks everything in order to help the dragons.

Hiccup's arc in DMA's schema is: *accept → reject → sacrifice.*

Plot – how we see progress in the story world

Plot is what we see on screen. Plot is events. Plot is expressed in the overt meanings of the dialogue we hear and the actions our characters take. Plot is surface. Events occur and they mean something literal or obvious in the moment of their occurrence. A man gets hit by a car. A woman throws her cheating lover's clothes out of her apartment window. Two children find a dead body. A country declares war on its neighbor. A young girl sees dancing horses at the circus. In their different ways these are all *plot events*.

These events, and myriad others like them, may be interesting, exciting, frightening, and spectacular, but to be truly eloquent in your screenplay—no matter how beautifully they might be described—they need also to have meaning on a personal, human level. In other words they mean more to us when we understand what they mean to your characters. That understanding takes us from plot to *story*.

Story – what your plot means to the characters experiencing it

If plot is surface, then story is depth. **Story** is the subtext of dialogue, the emotional and thematic weight and meaning of the events and actions we see on screen. Just like it says above: story is what your plot means to the characters experiencing it. Screenwriters talk of story advancing in *beats*—in significant moments when we feel your characters moving forward—or sometimes backward—in their search for ... whatever your script has them searching for! (Clue: it might just relate to the theme.)

When we know the man who gets hit by that car—and we understand the desperate emotional state that led him to risk crossing a street full of fast moving traffic—his fate can only be more meaningful to us. When we know how much the woman has put up with from her abusive partner and what a huge expression of personal courage and growth it is to finally throw his clothes—and, by extension, him—to the curb, our cheers and tears can only get louder and . . . wetter.

In the early days of screenwriting—or, perhaps more accurately, of "photoplay writing"—the term "plotting" was commonly used to describe the structure of movie storytelling. Over the years, the distinction between the terms "story" and "plot" has shifted in screenwriting language, but the importance of strong motivation as the driving force beneath a good story hasn't changed, as this quotation from Epes Winthrop Sargent's well-known early manual *The Technique of the Photoplay* (1913) makes clear: "most beginners are prone to regard connected incident as a plot . . . the plot is that which makes those connected incidents a story by giving those incidents some reason for being shown."[16] Many screenwriters still make this fundamental mistake today. Over and over . . .

The wardrobe

Readers of *Write What You Don't Know* will already be familiar with this analogy, but it is a quick and helpful guide to the working of internal story logic so I'll offer it again briefly here. Also this time there is a picture (see Figure 1) which will, as we all know, save us all exactly one thousand words of my explanation.[17]

- The *wardrobe* in this picture is your theme. It is sturdy and stable, unchanging, and everything it contains relies on that unchanging stability for support.
- The *clothes rail* is your protagonist's transformational arc. It is locked to your theme (screwed into the walls of your wardrobe). Attitudes will change along the story arc, but the important attitudes will be to your unchanging theme.
- The *hangers* are story beats. They mark change and development and hang off the clothes rail—the character's arc. Without the theme to lock the arc to (without the wardrobe to lock the rail to) they would have no support and fall.
- The pretty *clothes* are plot events. They hang off story beats (clothes hang on hangers) for additional significance.

---

[16] Epes Winthrop Sargent, *The Technique of the Photoplay* (New York: Motion Picture World, 1912).

[17] My friend, the talented animator, artist, teacher and ex-Disney imagineer Ken Cope provided the illustration.

Figure 1 Wardrobe analogy, by Ken Cope

So the wardrobe supports the clothes rail which supports the hangers and these, in turn, hold up your clothes. In screenwriting terms, the theme supports the arc which supports story beats and these, in turn, hold up your movie's plot.

Putting flesh on a story's bones: Narration and pleasure in the telling of the tale

In a 2005 interview with Catherine Bray for *Hotdog* magazine, Joss Whedon (*Serenity* 2005, *The Avengers* 2012) summed up the importance of structure and of the writer's commitment to preparation:

> Structure means knowing where you're going; making sure you don't meander about. Some great films have been made by meandering people, like Terrence Malick and Robert Altman, but it's not as well done today and I don't recommend it. I'm a structure nut. I actually make charts. Where are the jokes? The thrills? The romance? Who knows what, and when? *You need these things to happen at the right times, and that's what you build your structure around: the way you want your audience to feel.* Charts, graphs, colored pens, anything that means you don't go in blind is useful. (Emphasis added.)[18]

What he's really saying is that *structure is about giving pleasure through discipline.*

Beat [sic].

Sure, that was a very cheap joke, but it serves to remind us that audiences want and need a certain amount of being ordered about by storytellers. Sitting in our cinema seats, or in front of our domestic screens, we often want to feel the strong, guiding hand of the writer ...

                    IMPLIED YOU
        Even if it's wearing a velvet glove?

                    FRIENDLY ME
        Oh joy . . .

                    IMPLIED YOU
        Well, your readers really liked me
        in *Write What You Don't Know*, so I'm
        back. Ta da!

                    FRIENDLY ME
        That's. Nice.

---

[18] http://www.aerogrammestudio.com/2013/03/13/joss-whedons-top-10-writing-tips/ accessed May 31, 2014.

                  IMPLIED YOU
Isn't it? Besides, one of your
tenure reviewers — congratulations,
by the way — wrote that the "use of
screen-writing dialogs as a meta-
teaching voice is clever and
original and is another great asset
to keeping the reader interested,
laughing, and most important,
wanting to pour through the book."
And he's a lot smarter than you. You
do want the people to pour through
this book, don't you?

                  FRIENDLY ME
I suppose . . .

                  IMPLIED YOU
Course you do. So now I'm a
recurring character with a two-book
arc. Snarky ellipsis at me all you
like, but I'm sticking around.

Beat.   [Don't overdo this, by the way.]

                  FRIENDLY ME
As I was trying to say, we demand
contradictory things from our stories.
We want them to be somehow universal
and unchanging and at the same time
as varied and unique as possible.

                  IMPLIED YOU
That's so Genre Studies 101.

                  FRIENDLY ME
Well. Yes, I suppose it is.

                  IMPLIED YOU
Impressed you, did I? I've been doing
some reading on hiatus. Whedon is

```
          just saying that we need to put
          ourselves in the minds of the
          audience and keep asking ourselves
          what they need.

                    FRIENDLY ME
          That's right . . . It's the
          difference between structure and
          narration.

                    IMPLIED YOU
          Yeah, yeah, between the tale itself
          and the telling -- foreshadowing,
          revelation, all that good
          stuff . . .

Friendly Me throws Implied You a hard glance.

                    IMPLIED YOU (CONT'D)
          What? Why are you looking at me like
          that?

                    FRIENDLY ME
          Are you done?

                    IMPLIED YOU
          Oh. Sure. Don't mind me. You carry
          right along there, Spanky.

                    FRIENDLY ME
          Sometimes . . .
                    (clears his throat)¹⁹
```

Sometimes the demands movie stories place upon their audiences are overt and insistent. For example, the writers of clever mysteries, puzzle stories, tales told elliptically and out of sequence and yarns about brilliant amateur detectives ask us very directly to earn our keep, to figure things out as we go.

---

¹⁹ Note that all instances of screenplay format in this book are approximations, conformed to page size and other publishing requirements.

In our minds, we work back and forth between important moments (parallels), and weigh important clues or information to make sense of what has happened, or what is going on right now or, indeed, to leap ahead and work out what may come next. Some of the most enjoyable moments of movie watching are the times when you figure out an important fact or plot point before our heroine and groan inwardly in anticipation of the impact that revelation is going to have on them and their story.

On the other hand, sometimes the feeling of encountering a story is more like being carried along a stream of gentle revelations, happily discovering little surprises as we float, and given buoyancy by a structure of which we are only marginally aware. There is still work for us to do, but as we watch, read, or listen to this kind of well-crafted story, we often half forget that we are being led down a carefully crafted path from first words to final.

Stories carry us with them then, but they also surprise us, enlighten us, delight us, teach us, puzzle us artfully, shock us, amuse us, frighten us, disgust us, admonish us, move us and, finally, entertain us. They do this through their structures, because in storytelling everything comes from and goes to structure. *Structure is creative order and that order is also creative potential.* It helps you tame those wild words and bends them to your will. In so doing it opens up the complex, contradictory, and sometimes even confounding pleasures of storytelling to your audience. Here again we can turn to Joss Whedon for more clarity and sense:

> *You have one goal: to connect with your audience. Therefore, you must track what your audience is feeling at all times.* One of the biggest problems I face when watching other people's movies is I'll say, 'This part confuses me', or whatever, and they'll say, 'What I'm intending to say is this', and they'll go on about their intentions. None of this has anything to do with my experience as an audience member. Think in terms of what audiences think. They go to the theatre, and they either notice that their butts are numb, or they don't. If you're doing your job right, they don't. (Emphasis added.)[20]

This book is about making sure your audience doesn't notice its collective butt is numb. It is about the pleasure of embracing the structure of movie stories in your writing. Many writers find approaching structure daunting. It can be, especially when you are writing your first screenplays. Many others just think of it as a chore that gets in the way of doing all the fun things you

---

[20] http://www.aerogrammestudio.com/2013/03/13/joss-whedons-top-10-writing-tips/ accessed May 31, 2014.

imagine your characters doing. The thing is, *characters are also structure*—at least they should be.

Tell me one important fact about a character in your screenplay and I'll ask, in return: "Why is that important for their story?" This is code for, "how does your character simultaneously create and fit within the story's structure?"

>   IMPLIED YOU
>   My heroine has green eyes.

Beat.

>   IMPLIED YOU (CONT'D)
>   Well, come on then. I gave you a
>   fact about my character.

>   FRIENDLY ME
>   Why? Why? Why . . . is that
>   important for their story?

>   IMPLIED YOU
>   Glad you asked. It's important she
>   has green eyes because the love of
>   her life lost his first wife in
>   tragic circumstances. His wife had
>   these beautiful green eyes, so now
>   he can't see a pair of green peepers
>   without getting all overcome and
>   mopey.

>   FRIENDLY ME
>   I guess she could wear . . .

>   IMPLIED YOU
>   Contacts? Way ahead of you. She's
>   wearing colored contact lenses as
>   part of her Halloween costume when
>   she first meets him. They hit it off
>   and walk around the streets just
>   talking and having these charmingly
>   unlikely cosmopolitan pranks, coming
>   upon well-composed and romantic

vistas and all that good stuff. He
opens up to her and tells her about
the green eyes and all. When things
get serious, she starts to panic
about how she's deceiving him. I
mean it's a comedy, right?

                FRIENDLY ME
She's a lovable idiot and the whole
thing gets out of hand. Her
deceiving eyes open a window to her
deceiving soul?

                IMPLIED YOU
Don't get cocky.

                FRIENDLY ME
Right . . . so yes, this really is
all about structure. It's *The Crying
Game* without the imminent penis and
. . . all the other good ideas.
Chance, then deceit at the start,
throwing forward to a moment we all
know is coming – parallels again —
when he sees her green eyes.

                IMPLIED YOU
Exactly. What will he do? Will she
tell him before he finds out? How
will she help him get over it and
move on? Can she ever be sure he's
looking into her eyes and seeing
her, not his past love?

                FRIENDLY ME
Those questions do speak directly to
the pleasures of structure.

                IMPLIED YOU
Right? I'm locking those key scenes
in right now. The title is:

Temptation. I've got the basic idea
worked out. I registered it with the
Writers Guild. Everything.

                    FRIENDLY ME
It's a bit of a stretch to build a
whole story around the color of
someone's eyes, don't you think?

                    IMPLIED YOU
Hey, you asked for one fact. I gave
you one fact. I have others. In fact
I have several. You don't make it
easy to help you.

                    FRIENDLY ME
I'm still getting over how you just
turned up again. Also you've . . .

                    IMPLIED YOU
Grown, both as a person and as a
writer?

                    FRINDLY ME
Grown. Yes. That's exactly what I
was going to say.

                    IMPLIED YOU
This is the sequel, so get used
to it.

The pleasures of this little idea about green eyes and deceit are all about
looking forward in the story to an as-yet-unknown point where one character
catches up with what *we* already know. That moment will have consequences,
and the writer may "play it" any number of ways, but we know it is coming in
some form and we are looking forward to it. It means our heroine has work
to do in anticipation, and expiation, and work means structure. For the writer,
the fact of her green eyes is part of her character development, but that makes
it always also about structure.

Of course a fully developed movie story would be a lot more complicated,
and yet the control of revelations, of story information, of **narration**, is

central to the way your audience responds to your characters and their struggles. *Structure = pleasure.*

Keeping the story flowing: Narrative economy and screenplay format

This section is about getting the most value from your structure in the limited number of pages you have to write your screenplay. As you already know, feature films typically run between 90 and 120 minutes. The long established rules by which screenplays are formatted ensure that one page equates closely to one minute of screen time. Thus a feature screenplay should be between 90 and 120 pages long.[21] As a screenwriter, your job is to get the most story possible into that finite page count.

Dore Schary describes the writing process as one of *distillation* and *combination*. His example is of an adaptation, however the craft process is basically the same for all screenwriting: "[The screenwriter] must, particularly, distill and distill and combine and combine, until each scene of his final script has brevity and power and quickness, telling whole pages of dialogue in a single momentary exchange ..."[22] Furthermore, the writing process involves "... discarding whatever does not sharply develop the character and move the story along the straight line to its goal, and relating everything to that line."[23]

We achieve this through *narrative economy*; by saying the most with the least. Of course, this is where structure comes in again. A well-structured screen story can be brought home satisfactorily at that length. It is also why we learn the importance of proper *format*. **Screenplay format** has developed and been refined over the decades to help you squeeze as much story as possible into your pages.

Let's work through a case study lesson that illustrates, both in broad terms and with detailed examples, the kinds of formatting choices screenwriters make as they write.

---

[21] Some microbudget movies are less than 90 minutes long. There are many reasons for this including the need to include less plot mechanics in small character films and freedom from the requirements of theatrical distributors. At the other end of the budgetary spectrum, many tentpole movies are longer than 120 minutes. These are often adaptations of longer sources, developed in-house and should *not* encourage you to break the 120 page limit for your spec screenplays.

[22] Schary and Palmer, *Case History of a Movie*, 29.

[23] Ibid., 28.

Case Study: Introduction to Screenplay Style

Many aspiring screenwriters find that one of the hardest principles to master when learning to write in screenplay style is *brevity*. It turns out that writing less can be more difficult than writing more. When I give the introductory lecture in my Fundamentals of Screenwriting class at San Francisco State University (SFSU), for example, I tell my students that their challenge is all about "... learning to write less, well." Please note the importance of the comma in that statement.

The **new spec format**, which is roughly Hollywood's default screenplay style, prizes brevity in description for a number of reasons (see glossary) but in almost any kind of movie script the need to tell as much story as possible in your 100-odd pages is of paramount importance. My experience of teaching screenwriting to students who come with little or no experience of creative writing, or whose previous experience has been confined to prose fiction, is that their understanding of writing succinctly is often very different from what is required of a professional screenwriter.

Quite naturally, many students assume that writing for a visual medium requires them to detail everything we might see and hear. What they should be doing, first and foremost, is telling a story. They have also been educated into believing in the unassailable importance of writing in complete sentences, with all attendant grammar and syntax intact. Seems reasonable, right? However, learning screenwriting is, in this sense, partly a process of unlearning, because screenplay style often ignores *some* of the rules of "good writing" that schools (should) teach.

The best way to understand how narrative economy works on the screenplay page is to read into the corpus of contemporary scripts. This is the quickest way to appreciate both the flexibility and the specificity of the modern style.[24] You will understand how individual and distinctive voices can express themselves eloquently within what can seem, in the abstract, like a restrictive set of stylistic principles. Another is to see a before and after comparison between a writer's over-written first draft and a cut down revision of the same material.

To this end, we're going to work with the very first screenwriting exercise one of my students, Nico Bellamy, produced in my Fundamentals of Screenwriting class. Nico—who kindly gave his permission for me to use his work (and his name) for this case study—has gone on to develop an engagingly comic style as a writer and filmmaker. His undergraduate thesis

---

[24] You should be aware of the differences between spec and **shooting scripts**. Most screenplays that are published or available in libraries and archives are examples of shooting scripts. They may vary in their formatting and level of descriptive detail from that found in a typical spec screenplay.

film won awards at SFSU and, at time of writing, Nico is taking his first professional steps in Hollywood. But he is now famous in my introductory class for his first, entertaining attempt to write a movie sequence.

As you will see, Nico's first draft is full of fun ideas. It demonstrates a genuine, wry appreciation of genre tropes and an admirable early commitment to expressing visual style on the page. All of these are promising, but there are also some formatting issues and, frankly, the script is completely over-written. With his permission, I edited the sequence to conform more closely to the norms of contemporary screenwriting, while doing my best to follow the tone, structure and dramatic intent of his original. In one of my first lectures in the class I compare the two documents, and we discuss what is lost but also what may be gained from my editing. What follows is Nico's first draft, followed by my own version.

Nico's draft

INT. A DARK SALOON IN THE MEXICAN DESERT – SUNSET

Enter DANTE SAN MONTEDANTE, a gigantic cloaked man with a mustache as dark as his soul, and as thick as his blood. As Dante's spurs scrape along the ground, tangled with the hair of his dead family, the population of the saloon promptly run, hide and take their own lives. He steps over the freshly dead patrons and moves to the bar, flipping his poncho as he sits down. He looks up and sees his reflection in the mirror behind the bar, which shatters from his gaze.

                    DANTE
              Cerveza. Now.

The DEAD BARTENDER's arm raises and pours Dante a beer. Dante snatches it out of the bartender's hand, gulps it down in two seconds, then smashes the glass on his own head. The bartender's hand falls limp again by his side. Behind Dante, a COWBOY enters quietly. Dante's ears twitch. He glances at one of the shards of his beer glass embedded in his hand and sees the cowboy's silhouette in the doorway, gun at the ready.

                    DANTE (CONT'D)
         Put the weapon down amigo.

                       COWBOY
              Dante.

The cowboy throws a wanted poster onto the
ground with a crude drawing of Dante's face on
it. It reads "Mysterioso: Wanted Dead or Alive
for Genocide. Preferably Dead."

                    COWBOY (CONT'D)
              I'm bringing you in.

                       DANTE
              Did your mother buy you that
              gun?

The cowboy's trigger finger starts to waver, and
a bead of sweat rolls down his forehead. The
drop hangs on the tip of his nose with
desperation before falling to the ground. As it
makes impact, Dante kicks his bar stool out
backwards into the cowboy, knocking him against
the wall and onto the floor. He spins around and
catches the cowboy's gun and aims down the
sights.

                    DANTE (CONT'D)
              Many have tried before you and
              failed. What makes you so different
              hermano?

Dante fires the pistol and hits the cowboy
directly between the eyes.

The pistol disintegrates in his hand to a pile
of dust. He slowly walks over to the cowboy,
leans down, and pulls out one of the cowboy's
teeth. He opens his poncho to reveal a necklace
of teeth in different sizes and shapes, takes it
off, and easily threads the string through the

new tooth. He puts it back on, puts a toothpick
in his mouth and pushes on the saloon doors
(which burst off their hinges and fall to the
ground), then walks into the . . .

EXT. MEXICAN DESERT - CONTINUOUS

An army of cowboys, some on horses, some
standing, aim with their various weapons at
Dante.

                    RANDOM BRAVE COWBOY
              You're surrounded! Surrender now!

Dante glances up directly at the Random Brave
Cowboy.

                         DANTE
              No.

He spits his toothpick out, which flies through
the army and eventually pierces through the
random brave cowboy's lungs. Everyone nervously
turns to look at him as he chokes out his last
breath and falls backwards onto the ground. The
men quickly turn back and start blindly firing
their weapons, filling the area with dust and
smoke. When they run out of ammo and the smoke
clears, Dante is nowhere to be seen, and a few
of the men lay dead, shot by bullets in the
crossfire.

EXT. AN OASIS IN THE MEXICAN DESERT - NIGHT

Dante sits against a boulder, gazing into
his bonfire. He spits onto it and the flames
burst outwards and higher than before. A snake
slithers menacingly towards Dante, but when
he looks down at it, it slithers away
backwards. Dante turns back towards the fire
and grimaces.

<pre>
                    DANTE
              Curse this place.
</pre>

Dante reaches into his pocket and pulls out a photograph. In it is Dante, sans mustache, smiling with his arm around a dog. Dante stares at the photo for a long time, then glances at the fire, then back at the photo. He closes his eyes and puts the photo back in his pocket. He stands up and looks off into the distance, over the mountains.

<pre>
                    DANTE
            Fido, mi amor, do not give up.
            I am coming.
</pre>

Dante walks off into the distance towards the mountains.

My revision

INT. DARK DESERT SALOON - SUNSET

We open on DANTE SAN MONTEDANTE, a gigantic cloaked man with a mustache as dark as his soul, as thick as his blood. His spurs SCRAPE along, tangled with the hair of his dead family . . .

The POPULATION run, hide and take their own lives.

Dante glares at his reflection in the mirror behind the bar. It SHATTERS from his gaze.

<pre>
                    DANTE
              Cerveza. Now
</pre>

The DEAD BARTENDER's arm raises, pours Dante a beer. Dante gulps it, then SMASHES THE GLASS on his own head.

A COWBOY enters quietly. Dante's ears twitch. In a shard of glass embedded in his hand he sees the Cowboy in the doorway.

                          COWBOY
              Dante.

The Cowboy throws down a WANTED POSTER:
"MYSTERIOSO: WANTED DEAD OR ALIVE, FOR GENOCIDE.
PREFERABLY DEAD."

                    COWBOY (CONT'D)
              I'm bringing you in.

                       DANTE
              Did your mother buy you that
              gun?

The Cowboy's trigger finger starts to waver, and
a bead of sweat rolls down his forehead. The
drop clings to the tip of his nose — falls . . .

It hits the ground — Dante kicks his bar stool
backwards into the cowboy — knocks him against
the wall. Dante spins — catches the cowboy's
pistol — aims down the sights.

                    DANTE (CONT'D)
              Many have tried before you and
              failed.

Dante shoots the cowboy between the eyes, then
crushes the pistol to dust in his hand.

He pulls out one of the cowboy's teeth,
threading it on a necklace of teeth he wears
under his poncho.

Dante puts a toothpick in his mouth. He pushes
through the saloon doors, which BURST OFF THEIR
HINGES . . .

EXT. SALOON, DESERT TOWN - CONTINUOUS

An army of COWBOYS, some on horses, guns aimed
at Dante.

>   BRAVE COWBOY
>   You're surrounded! Surrender
>   now!
>
>   DANTE
>   No.

Dante spits his toothpick, hard — it flies
through the army to pierce the Brave Cowboy's
lungs. Nervously, everyone turns to look as he
chokes out his last breath and falls backwards.

They turn, firing their weapons blindly, filling
the air with dust and smoke, hitting each other
in the crossfire.

They run out of ammo. The smoke clears. Dante is
gone.

EXT. DESERT OASIS — NIGHT

Dante sits against a boulder. He spits into the
fire. FLAMES BURST OUTWARDS. A menacing snake
slithers forward. Dante glares at it — the snake
slithers away backwards, fast.

>   DANTE
>   Curse this place.

He pulls out a photograph of himself, sans
mustache, smiling, his arm around a dog. He
gazes at it, lost in thought.

>   DANTE
>   Fido, mi amor do not give up.
>   I am coming.

Dante strides towards the distant mountains . . .

Now obviously we can argue the toss over what I cut and what I kept on
a micro level, but you should be able to see the major differences between
the two documents. Here are the *key lessons* to learn from this comparison
case study:

1. My version is about a half page *shorter*—at least it was in my original Final Draft document before I converted it to Word for inclusion in the manuscript of this book. Imagine how much space you would save multiplying that over the length of a feature screenplay. In fact, I'll do the sum for you: that's about twenty pages. This is important because *more space = more story*. However, I am less interested in length per se than I am in readability (see 2 below). In other words if it had come out at the same page length I wouldn't have been too worried.

2. My version is formatted to be a more enticing read, just from its layout on the page. Specifically, I *use more white space*, I *condense description*, and I divide it into *smaller paragraphs*. A script reader who sees a screenplay formatted like this after plowing through a big pile of over-written scripts is going to silently thank me. Trust me, this is a good thing.

   Screenplays are written to be read as fast as possible. The principle here is to *break a paragraph on a new thought-image, or action*. Thus I split the description of the confused gunfight in the desert into three parts. The first describes the death of the Brave Cowboy, the second the posse's confused reaction, and the third the gag's payoff as Dante has vanished in the dust and smoke. Reading this split-up version, we are onto the next thought-image almost before we have absorbed the previous one. We write to skip from image to image, from beat to beat like this to make the read faster. Now the same content feels more dynamic, and it draws our attention to the cinematic and dramatic meaning of each event, or beat within an event.

   Note also how sometimes I *isolate sentences for dramatic effect*:

   ```
   The POPULATION run, hide and take their own
   lives.
   ```

   Don't overdo this, because you will waste a lot of space over the course of an entire screenplay and the impact will be diminished through repetition, but sometimes it can make a dramatic moment really sing.

3. Furthermore, my version *moves through the story more efficiently*, while hopefully keeping and celebrating Nico's wry tone. Again, my intention as an editor was not to change his story, just to refine its delivery on the page. I am trying to *reveal the core language* that tells the story, making sure it isn't buried in redundant description. Screenplay style does not require you to write like a clone or an automaton. On the contrary, the trick is to find a way creatively to integrate your own voice into the format professionals use and expect to be used. I picked Nico's exercise as my case study for exactly that reason. Well, that and because it always makes me smile.

4. I am less concerned with writing action in complete sentences than I would be if I were writing a prose story. I deploy punctuation as a tool to reduce the number of words I need to use. For example, I *cut down personal pronouns* ("he") and often *make the phrasing terser and more compact.* I also use -- double hyphenation -- to link moments -- in action sequences -- a common screenwriting technique. Here's a brief example from the screenplay for *Green Lantern* (Revised 12/07/10 thru 01/16/11, Yellow Revisions, by Greg Berlanti & Michael Green & Mark Guggenheim and Michael Goldenberg):

```
As he plummets into the abyss he shuts his
eyes, braces for impact --

-- but it doesn't come. Instead he finds
himself suspended in mid-air -

-- in an enormous CAVERN . . .
```

   This is another way of accelerating the read through the sentence. Techniques like this may not be appropriate in every kind of story or situation, but in action sequences, or genre scripts of this type they work well. *If you were writing a conventional drama you would take fewer liberties with grammar and syntax, but you would still try and condense your descriptions and cut down the volume of text.*

5. I try to minimize itemizing who is looking at whom and when, unless it is vital to our understanding, or the look directly signifies an important story beat. Action is better signified by . . . action. In Nico's script, there are several examples of looks *as* actions, and a few where such wording is unnecessary. The following decisions will make the distinctions clear.

   So, for example, when Dante bursts out of the saloon and into the desert I cut the line:

```
Dante glances up at the Random Brave Cowboy.
```

   Can I imagine that, at this point in the story, Dante will be doing exactly that? Of course, and a halfway decent director will be right on it. However, on the page it felt kind of like a given, and it slowed down the moment. The information is incidental to the plotting and characterization and just takes up space. Remember, this scene is itching to turn from tense encounter to comedy bloodbath and it felt wrong to hold it back. On the other hand, I kept the line that has all the Cowboys looking at their friend killed by Dante's toothpick, because it sets up the gag to come.

I also kept the line at the end where Dante is gazing at the photograph of his beloved dog. This speaks to deep (oh so deep) motivation, and felt organic and necessary to the moment:

```
He gazes at it, lost in thought.
```

I changed the wording from "for a long time" to "lost in thought" to direct it as intention, not duration, however. Now it plays effectively as the desire beat for the quest story to come.

I kept the gag in which Dante sees the Cowboy reflected in the shards of glass that are stuck in his hand. That moment is all about style and operates the turn of the encounter. I also kept the gags when Dante breaks the mirror with his stare (although I cut the redundant words "looks up" from the description), and when he out-glares the snake. These are scene beats that speak to his character and mythic status. Besides they are just funny, and that earned them a reprieve.

Key stylistic and formatting mistakes to avoid when writing a screenplay

1. *Don't over-describe.* As we've just discussed, there is a limit to how much description we need to "get" a situation. This applies to character description also—Nico's revised description of Dante is perfect. A *stylish minimum* is your goal.
2. *Don't overtly direct your professional colleagues.* Minimize shot calling, minimize literal signposting of character emotion and motivation, minimize calling cuts or **transitions** and anything else that will annoy the directors, actors, cinematographers, editors and other professionals who will read and work with your script. They should know their jobs and won't appreciate being told how to do them. Your well-written dramatic scenes will direct them well enough.
3. *Don't put full actions in **parentheticals**.* The description of events should be formatted in general action. In the new spec format it is permissible to put brief actions in a parenthetical (in the middle of dialogue), but don't overdo it.
4. *Don't write internal dialogue.* We see what characters *do*. We can't see what they *think*, so don't tell us. Communicate feelings and intention through action, reaction, and interaction. Remember the line I changed to "lost in thought"? See how I didn't change it to: "He gazes at it, thinking of all the good times, frolicking amongst the cacti with his poor lost Fido and remembering the rasping slobber of her tiny pink tongue on his unshaven cheek"? Yeah? I thought so.
5. *Pick dramatic vocabulary to tell your dramatic story.* Note that I replaced a few words, changing out general language for more

dynamic examples. In the final scene, for example, Dante no longer `walks` towards the mountains, he `strides`. Similarly he doesn't just `see` his reflection in the barroom mirror, he `glares` at it. And finally:

6. *Don't obsess about format as you write your first draft.* Learn as you go by all means, but focus on pushing your story through, not on every minute question about proper form. The time for that comes when your first draft is done. Indeed, your next task after you finish your first draft might well be to take a pass through the script just to cut down description and check format. If you don't save yourself ten pages—and probably more—just from this technical exercise I'd be surprised. Remember, this is not about changing story, just cutting away the descriptive fat.

Lesson Break: Modes of Expression in Screenplay Writing

We are taught that screenplays are more **blueprint** than literature. Their primary function is to provide clear information to professional colleagues in a format that is easy to access. Thus, screenplays should be written succinctly and clearly and with as little editorializing as possible (indeed I am passing on some of that teaching in this book, although with important qualifications). One way of expressing this distinction is through a tension between *denotation* and *connotation* in the style of screenplays or (loosely) between facts and instructions on the one hand and more subjective or emotional expression on the other.

In screenwriting this is also reducible to the old exhortation to show rather than tell. However, while it is important to emphasize the specific communicative requirements and challenges of screenplay writing in a book like this, it would be wrong to imply that individual authorial style and expression have no place in screenwriting. On the contrary, many of the most successful and influential screenwriters bend "rules" and engage us dramatically with the individuality of their writing while they pay due diligence to the underlying techniques and forms of professional practice. More extreme examples such as Shane Black and Quentin Tarantino come easily to mind, but good writers of all kinds show their talent in merging their personal style with accepted forms as much as they do in the structure and premises of their stories.

However, no matter the writing style of its author, every screenplay is a site of the tension between connotation and denotation at the level of form and format that already speaks to the requirement to address different readership constituencies simultaneously. Any professional screenplay is always speaking both as a work of drama and as a set of guidelines or instructions for colleagues and this is clear in the way writers "juggle" different modes of expression as they write. From screenwriting studies Claudia Sternberg suggests that there are three key modes of expression in a screenplay:

1. *Description* – of the story world and its design.
2. *Report* – of action (what happens in a scene).
3. *Comment* – editorializing about events and characters.[25]

Of the three, it is *comment* that creates the clearest tension with the so-called rules of screenwriting. Typically, too much comment is discouraged by screenwriting teachers and manuals, but it turns up in different forms and in the work of the best writers. Either obliquely or directly, writers find ways to comment on the situations they are writing. The judgment comes in terms of degree and form.

Here's an example of a typical—and certainly stylistically extreme—*comment* from Shane Black's famously idiosyncratic script for *Lethal Weapon* (1987). Detective Riggs is in a firefight:

```
For your information, gentle reader: The Beretta
Belle. 9 millimeter handgun offers fifteen
bullets in its magazine, and one in its chamber.
For you math majors, that's sixteen.

[same scene, later]

Arm held rock steady, FIRING SHOT after SHOT, on
some of them he isn't even looking, and when the
coroner finally examines the sniper's body he
will discover a total of nine bullet wounds, all
of them fatal.

BAM. BAM. BAM. BAM. BAM. BAM. BAM.

Click.
```

---

[25] Claudia Sternberg, *Written for the Screen: The American Motion-Picture Screenplay as Text* (Tübingen: Stauffenberg, 1997).

FAIR WARNING: this is an example of a famous instance of personal style in screenplay writing offered to illustrate the farthest boundaries of comment as a mode of expression. Don't be tempted to copy Black's style of writing. For one thing, every aspiring thriller writer already did so in the early 1990s, to little effect. *Find your own style*, like our friend Nico Bellamy is beginning to do in the case study above. Let it speak your own talent, not somebody else's.

Writing in the *Journal of Screenwriting*, Ann Igelström offers a similar model, this time of three *narrational voices* that operate in a screenplay:

1. *Personal fictional voice* – the voice of a character, expressed through dialogue for example.
2. *Extrafictional voice* – writing that refers to the extrafictional world of production, the world of **slug lines** and professional format.
3. *Impersonal fictional voice* – the narrating voice that offers description and reports action.[26]

She makes an important distinction between the fictional and extrafictional contexts for which screenplays are both written and read. A typical screenplay switches back and forth between these voices as it addresses different readerships and works alternately within and outside its own narrative as it progresses.

It is important to note here that, although the lessons above have explored the format that is common to most broadly conventional screenplays, not all movies are written this way. Indeed, not all movies have scripts. Before we move on to our core case studies, all of which have screenplays that follow the principles outlined, we can take a few pages to introduce the model of story structure we will be following and to consider important complementary and alternative approaches.

Case Study: "Show Don't Tell" in *A Coffee in Berlin*

As I noted above, "show don't tell" is one of those maxims you will read and hear from just about every screenwriter you talk to and from every screenwriting industry source. What it means in practice is that, because

---

[26] Ann Igelström, "Communication and the Various Voices of the Screenplay Text", *Journal of Screenwriting* 4.1 (2013), 43–56.

movies are a visual medium, the more your writing *shows* us what you want us to pay attention to and the less it *tells* us about it literally, the better you are serving the visual potential of your chosen medium. There are many ways of "showing," but they are all encapsulated by this generalization: tell your stories through images more than words, through action rather than just dialogue. Here action doesn't mean only battles and car chases, but simply having characters do things rather than talk about them.

Here's a simple example of how to work with showing rather than telling from the opening of the recent German indie movie *A Coffee in Berlin* (2012, scr. Jan Ole Gerster, original title *Oh Boy*). At the start of the film, twenty-something law school dropout Nico Fischer is trying to leave his girlfriend's apartment without waking her. He fails and they have an awkward conversation in which she wants him to stay (and be a proper boyfriend) and he obviously wants to be out of there. The scene ends as she realizes how badly Nico doesn't want to stay. Her expression hardens and she walks out of the bedroom.

We cut to the next scene as Nico arrives home, carrying a cardboard box. He places it on top of a pile of similar boxes—he hasn't moved into his apartment, just like he hasn't really moved into his adult life. Nico takes a small box out of the larger one and opens it, to reveal photographs of himself and the young woman we recognize from the previous scene. He looks at them wistfully. Obviously we are meant to deduce that, in the space between her look and his, they have broken up. We learn a lot about Nico from this brief, expositional sequence but, more importantly for our present purposes, we are spared the breakup conversation that would simply confirm what we have intuited about him from his actions. Nico's actions, and his girlfriend's response, establish his opening emotional position. The story of *A Coffee in Berlin* is about what Nico does next, when the continuation of his easy slacker lifestyle is threatened and he is called out for his disengaged attitude to life and relationships. The screenwriter opens the story using eloquent visual cues (and narrative economy) to set things up and to move forward quickly.

Modeling movie structure: The W model of story structure

In the words of Balzac: "first act, clear; third act, short; interest, everywhere."
Francis Ford Coppola

I first introduced my W Model in *Write What You Don't Know* as a flexible way of thinking about conventional and mainstream-alternative story structure. We will be using it again here in *The Pleasures of Structure* as our key explanatory framework. The W is informed both by industry practice and by my long experience of teaching students who are stepping up to the challenge of long form cinematic storytelling. One of the key lessons I have learned in my career as an educator is that most students do not want a template to copy, but they welcome a "straw man" model to help keep them on track with the complexities of writing a screenplay. The W is flexible enough to fit a wide range of movie types and to serve as just this kind of helpmate for budding writers.

As we will see in the following section, however, for all its flexibility the W is not an exact fit for all movies in the American independent tradition, also much less works from the truly avant-garde and experimental end of the filmmaking spectrum.[27] For now, this section outlines in brief the model we will be working with in detail through the core case studies that follow.

A basic binary structure

One of the lessons the W learns from ring compositions is that binary parallelism is a powerful starting point for storytelling. Many movie stories work in two halves, they build to a transformative Midpoint and then resolve that change in the second half. The same story may also be understood in terms of three acts (see below) but, in contemporary American screenwriting, the Midpoint turn is often as important in articulating structure as the work of those three acts. To this end, the W divides the second act into two angles hinged at the Midpoint and it interrogates the relationship between parallel beats in both halves of the story as a means of developing structure.

We will consider examples of the transformative power of this straightforward binary relationship between two halves of a story below. However, as an introductory shorthand for character-driven stories, the commitments required of protagonists at a movie's Midpoint are what turn them into heroines and heroes. They are still dealing with the same theme— the same internal story logic—that they were in the first half, only now their understanding of their motives and actions in so doing has matured or deepened, to say nothing of the increased personal risks they are now taking.

Three acts in four angles

The W also divides a feature story into four sections (we will call them *angles*), but three acts. The logic of this system of acts is that each act asks the writer

---

[27] For reasons of brevity and focus in this book I am also not addressing approaches to screenwriting developed and used in other national cinemas.

to undertake specific story work. In conventional screenplays these tasks should be completed in time so that the shift to the next act feels significant and confident on the screen. General audiences don't think in terms of the detail of acts and beats as they watch movies. However their experience of cinema has given them expectations of storytelling and they exercise judgment just the same. They respond to story development—they appreciate creative storytelling and notice poor structure just as you would and often as a kind of absence of pleasure.

In diagram form, the W looks like a letter… W—I know, who would have thought? The letter W has four angles: down, up, down, up—and these directions correspond to a kind of emotional shorthand for the typical tone of the section in question. In my model, the first down angle corresponds to the first act, the second and third (up and down) angles to the second act and the final up angle to the third.

So the first act and angle describes a negative move. In the first act of a screenplay we explore what is wrong in the world, or in the life of our protagonist, and establish an overall need for our story. In the most reductive terms, act one asks and answers *what is broken* and *what needs fixing*?

The third act and angle describes a positive move—this is the part of the story that resolves the problem, or fixes the world, or brings your protagonist to a new understanding of their life, their goals and/or their relationships. It may not offer a simplistic, successful resolution but, in thematic terms, any kind of resolution is in some sense a positive. Understanding may bring trauma of its own, but it has likely been hard won and thus worthy of acknowledgment.

The second act is more complicated—it is comprised of two angles after all. The basic movie model is for early progress (an up angle) to lead to resistance, necessitating a second and more fundamental commitment from your protagonist at the story's midpoint. After the midpoint things get much harder (a down angle), leading through some kind of personal crisis to a revelation about how to address the problem with the theme and the plot that drives the story.

The W gives you four angles through which to tell a three-act story:

Act One: we set up the world of the story, our protagonist and their social
   network, the thematic and plot terms of the story (what's at stake), how
   the oppositional, *antagonistic* force that stands in their way will be made
   manifest (through the actions of characters and in the story world) and
   we get our hero or heroine through their initial uncertainty about what
   to do about their problem or challenge.

Act Two: second acts are all about character change. At the end of act one our protagonist has decided to do ... something. But they are unprepared to resolve the story at this point. If they were ready it would be a short film, not a feature! Typically, the second act shows them trying, learning, resisting and developing in the face of increasing opposition, both internal (story) and external (plot).

At the end of the second act your protagonist has become the kind of person who has a fighting chance to succeed at resolving their story. That's why the W is still a three-act model of story structure, not a four act model. *The work of the second act takes both angles to complete.*

Act Three: now that your protagonist has grown and learned enough about themselves and the story world to have a chance to succeed, the third act follows their attempt to do so. They may succeed or fail in that attempt, but either way the theme of the story should be resolved through their actions in a satisfying way.

Half angles and story beats

In the W model we have different levels of magnification through which to examine and plan our stories. Specifically we can look at the action at the level of the whole story, the act, the angle, the half-angle (eight beat model) or the story beat (sixteen beat model). In your own writing, story beats will, in their turn, be divided into sequences and scenes—many with their own internal story beats—but in terms of understanding the basics of a movie's story structure we will focus on magnifications the size of story beats and above.

Here's a shorthand breakdown of the W in half angles and story beats. We will cover them in detail in the chapters that follow. (Those who are familiar with *Write What You Don't Know* will see that the beats have been renamed in this version, but their story functions have not changed at all.)

Act One: First down angle (recognition)

A. First half-angle: Primary exposition
Story beats: *Story world* and *desire*

B. Second half-angle: Debate
Story beats: *Hesitation* and *first commitment*

Act Two: First up angle (avoidance)

C. *First half-angle: Early progress*
Story beats: *B Story* and *progress*

D. *Second half-angle: Raising stakes*
Story beats: *Challenge* and *decision*

MIDPOINT: Second commitment

Act Two: Second down angle (commitment)

E. *First half-angle: Commitment*
Story beats: *Acceleration* and *assistance*

F. *Second half-angle: Crisis*
Story beats: *Crisis* and *revelation*

Act Three: Second up angle (resolution)

G. *First half-angle: Confrontation*
Story beats: *Plan* and *pushback*

H. *Second half-angle: resolution*
Story beats: *Resolution* and *resonance*

> NOTE: I have linked the story beats for each half-angle on a single line to indicate that there is often some flexibility in the order in which screenwriters deploy beats within a section. Typically all of the beats will be addressed, but sometimes one comes before the other or they happen in parallel rather than in strict sequence. We will see an example of this later in our case study of *Winter's Bone*. This does not affect the overall lessons we can learn from the W, but perhaps offers us a slightly more flexible development map.

Here is the W in its diagrammatic form. For clarity and simplicity I have put the beats in linear sequence here—indeed this is the usual order in which they are worked in the acts—but the above note still applies.

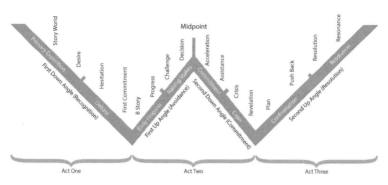

Figure 2 The W model of story structure, by Ken Cope

Alternative approaches to scripting

Of course not every movie follows the structural model we use in this book. The further away from the Hollywood mainstream you travel, the more likely it is that different principles and priorities will apply. The W is a model designed to help those of you who are trying to develop your screenwriting skills through writing more or less conventional narrative features. However, there are and have always been filmmakers whose creative practice lies elsewhere, or who adhere in part but also push boundaries and take chances in their storytelling. Here I'm not referring only to screenwriters who play clever games with narration or linear structure but still write broadly conventional stories, such as Christopher McQuarrie (*The Usual Suspects*), or Christopher Nolan (*Memento*). Their work, while interesting and sometimes brilliant in its way, is not really changing the paradigm, just pushing at the edges. We will work through some other examples of paradigm pushing in detail in our case studies.

While a full exploration of screenwriting and scripting at the wilder edges of filmmaking is beyond the scope of this book, it is worth acknowledging such important work to provide a little context for your own thinking and to help position the case studies that follow this chapter. Indeed, there are a number of good books available—some people call them "anti-manual manuals"—that deal exclusively with alternative or hybrid-mainstream narrative forms of one kind or another.[28]

As I have already noted, many of the higher budget American independent films that get multi-screen theatrical distribution do so under the auspices of "Indiewood." Typically these films are produced or distributed by companies that have been bought out by or merged with the majors, such as Miramax, or by the prestige arms or specialty divisions of those same studios, such as Fox Searchlight. Indiewood is a term used to describe the institutional context for much low to mid-budget independent filmmaking in the 1990s after Hollywood co-opted the boom in independent production. While the institutions that comprise Indiewood have contracted since the turn of the millennium, it is still the case that many so-called independent films are really low-budget studio movies in all but name. Certainly their relatively conventional story structure often reflects this.

During this period, American "indie" became something of an identifiable genre in itself. American Indiewood movies from the 1990s onwards developed into a marketable hybrid between the truly independent edges of the film culture and the Hollywood core. American indie and Indiewood movies tend to be character-driven, personal and often formally playful. Some, such as *Pulp Fiction* (1994, scr. Quentin Tarantino), overtly foreground that ludic quality in a kind of self-reflexive and nostalgic engagement with existing genres and styles of filmmaking.

Most Indiewood movies broadly follow the Hollywood model of story structure. Their alternative status is defined more by the package of hip attractions and stylistic quirks they build around it than by any ground-up reinvention of storytelling. For all the hype surrounding it, *Pulp Fiction* was basically a conventional hard-boiled genre story told out of sequence. Recent examples might include films such as *Little Miss Sunshine* (2006, scr. Michael Arndt) and *Juno* (2007, scr. Diablo Cody), both of which had crossover commercial success after their release by Fox Searchlight.[29] The films of Wes Anderson also fit into this quirky (twee) category for example. Indeed the trope "quirky" or, as Geoff King describes it, a film characterized by "small, slightly odd and sometimes comical departures from familiar/mainstream

---

[28] Among the most useful of the "anti-manual manuals" are: Linda Aronson, *Screenwriting Updated: New (And Conventional) Ways of Writing for the Screen* (London: Silman James Press, 2001) and Ken Dancyger and Jeff Rush, *Alternative Scriptwriting: Beyond the Hollywood Formula,* 5th edition (New York: Focal Press, 2013).

[29] Domestic grosses: *Little Miss Sunshine* $59 million off an $8 million budget. *Juno* $143 million off a $7.5 million budget (figures from http://boxofficemojo.com accessed May 29, 2014).

norms" is often viewed within independent filmmaking as something of a badge of Indiewood sell-out.[30]

Other writers and filmmakers, often working at even lower budget levels where experiment and innovation are less economically risky, position themselves within another loose tradition of American independent filmmaking by using different methods of coming to script. There are many approaches here but one of the most persistent involves placing a greater reliance on improvisation. In recent years this technique has been popular with several of the microbudget mumblecore filmmakers, for example.[31]

Lesson Break: Screenwriting and Improvisation

For decades, using improvisation has been one of the go-to tactics of independent filmmakers. Improvisation with actors on set has long been seen as a way of injecting authenticity, immediacy and realism into a film and there is certainly some truth in that, when the techniques are well-handled. It is also often viewed as a valid route towards circumventing what some filmmakers perceive as the tyranny of conventional screenplay form and to free narrative from the straightjacket of formula. Directors who have used improvisation are often lionized by filmmakers who aspire to a working practice that positions itself in some way against that of a meretricious Hollywood corporate mainstream.

For example, the American actor and independent filmmaker John Cassavetes is famous for having used improvisational techniques in the production of his films. His association with that technique has inspired subsequent generations of independent filmmakers and yet, as is often the case with legends, the myth has run ahead of the truth. Perhaps it doesn't help that Cassavetes himself often played fast and loose with the term. For example, both release versions of his first film, *Shadows* (1959), end with the statement: "The film you have just seen was an improvisation," and yet the film was the result of rigorous workshopping with actors in rehearsal and the second version was significantly re-shot and reconfigured, not devised spontaneously in front of the camera. Incidentally, Cassavetes himself went on to work with full scripts on his subsequent films, but

---

[30] Geoff King, *Indie 2.0: change and continuity in contemporary American indie film* (New York: Columbia University Press, 2014), 26.

[31] Further scholarly material on the recent history and current state of American independent cinema can be found in the following: Michael C. Newman, *Indie: An American Film Culture* (New York: Columbia University Press, 2011), and: Yannis Tzioumakis, *American Independent Cinema* (Edinburgh: Edinburgh University Press, 2006).

indicated that he was always open to change and further interpretive development through performance: "The lines were written down. The emotion was improvisation." His writing style, however, and the style of performance he elicited from his actors both evoked and maintained something of the "feel" of improvisation in his later films.

Of course many of the "master directors" of classical Hollywood also used improvisation in their working practice, Howard Hawks and especially Frank Capra notable amongst them. Very few contemporary writer-directors use a predominantly improvisational approach to their filmmaking, but a number are strongly influenced by it as a technique both for writing and directing. Mike Leigh (*Secrets and Lies*, 1996) uses a lengthy improvisation-based approach to developing character and story with his actors. The results are then distilled into script form. Theo Angelopoulos (*Ulysses' Gaze*, 1995) varies his use of improvisation from project to project. Ken Loach uses improvisation tactically, as in the critical discussion about collectivization and land reform between Spanish peasant farmers (played by non-professional local farmers) and members of the left-wing POUM militia in *Land and Freedom* (1995, scr. Jim Allen). For his part, Wong Kar-Wei (*Days of Being Wild*, 1990) uses improvisation based on a developed story **outline**: "I just wrote down the scenes, some essential details, and the dialogue. I gave the rhythm of the scenes to the actors and skip all these technical things."

Case Study: Improvisation in Microbudget and Mumblecore Movies

It is in the recent microbudget arena that many more filmmakers are experimenting with improvisation, approaching story through what I call the **transcended screenplay**. I discuss this phenomenon in more detail in the critical glossary, but a single example here might serve as illustration. Barret Hacia, producer on the recent microbudget feature *Falling Uphill* (2012, scr. Richard J. Bosner), describes their approach to script on that project:

> *Falling Uphill* had a script that the director and I spent several months developing. Going in, we knew it would be heavily improvised so the focus was to develop a solid story structure, where the foundation would be strong enough to allow leniency with dialogue. Performers were instructed to "address A & B to get to C" in a specific scene, and were "never married to the dialogue." As a result, the story was truly written during editing. With each

take being from slightly to dramatically different, the editor had the flexibility to deviate from the script. Though that may sound like a god-sent gift, it inevitably made the back end of the project extremely long ($). I believed the first time director was overwhelmed with the endless choices which resulted in "my indecision is final." It took nearly 6 months to get picture lock. As you are well aware, we did come across some structural issues in post, but spending that long to ruminate and edit is not the worst thing to do, *if* you can afford it.[32]

Barret describes a relatively common approach to using a creative and fluid combination of screenplay and improvisation. The challenges he outlines—challenges which prompted him to bring me in as a **story consultant** in post-production—are also pretty common when dealing with improvisation. Indeed, two other movies Barret produced—the feature, *Chemical Cut* (2015) and the short, *Stepsister* (2013) both used improvisation in different ways during their respective development and production. (My student Joey Izzo's terrific film *Stepsister,* a finalist for the Cannes Film Festival 2013 Cinéfondation Award, was a Cinema MFA thesis film at SFSU.)

Another example of improvisation-based scripting practice can be taken from the work of mumblecore director Joe Swanberg. Mumblecore is a term used to describe the work of a number of microbudget filmmakers in the last decade. Although many of their films share a very general set of concerns and stylistic approaches, the idea that mumblecore is/was a genuine movement is largely a construction imposed by canny film festival programmers (notably at South by Southwest) looking to distinguish their content. Notable filmmakers in the loose mumblecore association have included Andrew Bujalski (*Funny Ha Ha*, 2002), Lena Dunham (*Tiny Furniture*, 2010), Joe Swanberg (*Hannah Takes the Stairs*), The Duplass Brothers (*Baghead*, 2008) and Lynn Shelton (*Humpday*, 2009). What linked the mumblecore movies was their very low budgets, the use of digital video (with the exception of the work of Bujalski, who shot on 16mm), the casting of largely non-professional actors, an approach to story that was about professional and emotional stasis and drift amongst the current post-college twenty-something generation and, for some, an openness to improvisation.

Not all mumblecore filmmakers use improvisation to the same extent. However, for *Hannah Takes the Stairs* Joe Swanberg put all his actors up

---

[32] Barret Hacia, email to author, May 19, 2014.

in the same apartment in Chicago for a month and devised the story with their collaboration. He gave the key performers (including Greta Gerwig, Andrew Bujalski and Mark Duplass) shared writing credit on the film.

At the time of writing, several of the key mumblecore players are now working with higher budgets and in more conventional narrative frames. These include Lena Dunham (*Girls* on HBO), and Joe Swanberg (*Happy Christmas*, 2014) as well as Mark Duplass and Greta Gerwig who are gaining success as actors in more mainstream material. I mention this to reinforce the idea that success at the microbudget level can be a stepping stone to other opportunities. The issue of whether, and to what extent, the unconventional story choices of filmmakers like these will, can, or even should be sustained at higher budget levels is open.

Another way in which writers and filmmakers are pushing beyond the traditional conception of script and screenplay is through the use of visual elements in the pitching, development and writing process. This is happening in different ways both at the tentpole and microbudget levels of movie production. Visual materials are being used both as aids in selling and conceptualizing story.

Lesson Break: Visual Scripting

In recent years it has become increasingly common, in both the high- and low-budget arenas, to use visual materials as part both of the prototyping and scripting process of movie writing. In the avant-garde/experimental world this is not a new phenomenon and filmmakers have long been working with a wide range of visual scripting techniques. The following examples give a sense of some of the contexts in which this kind of work is happening now:

1. *Proof of concept visuals.* Screenwriters are using a wide range of visual resources to complement their spec screenplays in marketing original (and thus "risky") high-budget genre concepts. For example, Joseph Kosinski, the director of *Oblivion* (2013, scr. Karl Gajdusek and Michael Arndt (as Michael deBruyn)), produced a kind of graphic novel and a book of glossy images to help sell his story to Hollywood. This is not merely a contemporary phenomenon. Although the film itself was famously never made those who have seen the wonderful

documentary *Jodorowsky's Dune* (2013) will be familiar with the remarkable script books put together to raise budget for the director's proposed science fiction epic. These books contained integrated storyboards and other stunning design materials.

2. *Sizzle reels.* Sizzle reels are one particular manifestation of the proof of concept visual. Writers and filmmakers will shoot sample scenes or elements from the screenplay and screen them when meeting with other industry professionals. Screenwriter Michael Grais (*Poltergeist*, 1982) is not alone in reporting that, in his experience, the screening of sizzle reels is now very much an accepted part of the contemporary pitching process.

3. *CeltX and other software options.* CeltX is an open source screenwriting program that is commonly used by students and independent filmmakers who have no need of—or can't afford—industry standard screenplay formatting **software** such as Final Draft. One feature of CeltX that speaks both to the times and to the assumed working practices of its core user-generation is the option to integrate visual materials such as images, storyboards and even videos into CeltX projects. At the time of writing, most of my students use CeltX in preparing their microbudget productions and many of them are integrating visual materials through the program, both as scripting aids and as proof of concept for crowdsourcing and other fund-raising efforts.

4. *Avant-garde scripting.* Experimental and avant-garde filmmakers use all kinds of visual materials to contribute to, or even replace the conventional screenplay. These include individual images of every kind, designed text and video. For example, Steven Price notes that John Moritsugu's " 'plans' for *Der Elvis* (1987) combine drawing, newspaper cut-outs and handwritten text to produce a collage that gives a clear indication of some of Moritsugu's ideas for the film . . . without enabling any other reader to visualize the progression of the proposed film in a manner analogous to that of a conventional screenplay."[33]

Revision: What have we learned in this chapter?

- We have learned about the important connection between the kinds of stories we tell and our unique nature as human beings. Specifically we know that stories have always been used to help us in our ongoing quest both as individuals and as a species to survive and to thrive.

[33] Steven Price, *A History of the Screenplay* (Basingstoke: Palgrave Macmillan, 2013), 228.

In this way *stories perform significant evolutionary functions*. They bind us and teach us, warn us and encourage us and they give us selective advantage.

- We have learned that there are *underlying principles of storytelling* that emerge independently across human cultures, many of which are still fundamental to our storytelling today.

  These principles, with the idea of *parallelism* notable amongst them, speak to our species talents in pattern recognition and are fundamental to the pleasures we engage in through our encounters with narrative.

- We have learned about early story forms called *ring compositions*. Ring compositions teach us about the importance of parallelism—structures linking moments of foreshadowing and resolving in narratives.

  Ring compositions also teach us about the importance of establishing a *theme* or purpose for a story, of sticking with it, reinforcing it and resolving our story in relation to it.

  Ring compositions offer us a simple model in which *a successful story turns in the middle*. In this way stories can be considered as a partnership between establishing beats and resolving beats, articulated around a thematically relevant central event.

- We have learned that all stories play out as sequences of *cause and effect*.

- We have learned that there are other key elements to the *internal logic* of story structure that help to organize that causal chain of storytelling into a well-articulated structural skeleton.

- These elements include theme, which expresses the true meaning and unchanging purpose of your story.

- Linked to theme is your protagonist's *arc*, which tracks her progress and changing attitudes as she struggles to resolve her theme.

- We have learned that the events we see on screen are moments of *plot* and that these events have deeper meanings relevant to character and theme that speak to the underlying *story*.

- We have learned that *narration*, the process of storytelling, is bound into all of these ideas. One important aspect of narration is how you control knowledge and information and organize your plot and story revelations. As a screenwriter, mastering structure and narration is fundamental to the pleasure your audience gets from your stories.

- We have learned that, because movies have only a short duration, you need to make the most of every page of your script. This teaches us the importance of following the principle of *narrative economy* in your writing and of learning to support it with appropriate *screenplay format*.

- We have also learned through case study examples about specific techniques of screenplay writing that will help you keep control over your narrative economy and formatting.
- We have learned that the conventional format and style of screenplay writing is typically expressed through three modes of expression and in narrational voices that take on the denotative and connotative functions of communication necessary for the screenplay successfully to communicate to its various readerships.
- We have learned not to copy Shane Black but to develop our own style and voice as screenwriters!
- We have learned that improvisation is a flexible tool that has many applications and that individual filmmakers take different approaches to its use both in developing screenplays and in replacing more conventional forms of script.
- Finally, we have learned that in mumblecore—and in the microbudget sector more broadly—the conventional screenplay is often transcended by and combined with other documents and visual materials.

Section Two

Case Studies

The following short chapters are each dedicated to one of the key beats of the W model of movie structure. In each chapter we will explore the structural choices made by screenwriters and filmmakers through ongoing core case studies of recent movies as well as through a wider range of specific examples. Our three primary texts will offer variety in terms of genre and budgetary level. The central example we will analyse will be a well-crafted, animated adventure film: *How to Train Your Dragon* (2010, scr. William Davies and Dean DeBlois & Chris Sanders, adapted from the book by Cressida Cowell); a Swedish horror movie: *Låt den Rätte Komma In / Let the Right One In* (2008, scr. John Ajvide Lindqvist, adapted from his own novel) and a low-budget, character-driven independent drama: *Winter's Bone* (2010, scr. Debra Granik & Anne Rosellini, adapted from the novel by Daniel Woodrell). We will lead with *How to Train Your Dragon* as our default mainstream text and catch up with the other two stories at regular intervals and in the occasional lesson.

On the surface, these core case studies are very different in terms of their genres, styles, narrational strategies and intended audiences. Despite this, the three movies all adopt the same basic, underlying story structure, deploying their key beats in the same sequence. What makes for an interesting comparison is the way other screenwriting choices—and sometimes risky ones—show the range and depth of this basic structural model of movie storytelling. We will learn as much about what unites these movies as what obviously divides them. If story structure is all about exciting pleasure in your audience, then these three films are building very different kinds of pleasure (or perhaps, in the case of *Let the Right One In*, a kind of *unpleasure*) off the same model.

In each chapter—for each part of the story—we will also step back from the analysis of our core case studies to offer more general lessons and specific examples from a wide range of other movies. So, in the first chapter there is a general lesson about how to approach writing exposition. That lesson is followed by a short case study example that illustrates a particular technique of writing exposition. In turn that case study is followed by a series of short examples showing how opening beats are handled in other movies. In this way, each chapter gives both general guidance and specific examples to help you get to grips with the kinds of creative choices you may be working on at each stage of your own screenplays. This is important because, although the point of this book is to provide you with a general model of movie story structure, the breadth of example and advice is there to encourage you to see the enormous creative range and depth that model allows.

I have picked our core films for practical reasons as well as for the creative structural choices they present. Two of our examples test the model established through the W and *How to Train Your Dragon* almost to destruction. *Let the Right One In* undermines the status of the protagonist as the operating force in a screen story, for example and *Winter's Bone* pushes the power of the story world to block a protagonist's progress. Between them, however, they also embody great writing from the four-quadrant mainstream, through off-beat genre cinema to the low-budget independent sector.[34] All three movies have won multiple awards; and all three have been awarded specifically for the quality of their writing. For example, *How to Train Your Dragon* won an "Annie" in 2011 for "Best Writing in an Animated Feature Production." *Let the Right One In* won several national and festival awards for best adapted screenplay and *Winter's Bone* won the prestigious "Waldo Salt Screenwriting Award" at the 2010 Sundance Film Festival.

Act One: First down angle (recognition)

Typically, the first act and angle of a mainstream or mainstream-independent screenplay is all about your protagonist *recognizing* two linked truths:

1. She recognizes a problem or challenge that needs addressing. If she chooses not to address this challenge, either she will remain somehow unfulfilled and in personal or emotional stasis or bad things will happen (or continue to happen) to her or to those about whom she cares, depending on the kind of story you are telling.
2. She comes to accept—albeit often hesitantly and without fully understanding what acceptance means—that she is the only person that can do something about that problem and decides she will try.

This first section of the W is represented as a *down angle* because these revelations signal an immediate future for the protagonist filled with nothing but trouble and trouble feels like a downer.

---

[34] The industry term "four-quadrant" refers to a film that can be marketed at men and women of all ages—or, in other words, at everyone.

In a well-written screen story, the problem or challenge that your protagonist faces will manifest in both the story and the plot.

Remember:

- *Plot problems are external* to the protagonist but still affect them directly in some way. Forces in the world may threaten them or those they care about, for example.
- *Story problems are internal* but also manifest practically in the world. A character flaw or challenge is good story material when it affects not only the protagonist but also, by extension, those around them.

Remember that in my W model of story structure we can choose to break the angles down into ever-smaller elements to help us understand how they work and to plan our stories. As a first stage, we can split each angle into two *half angles*.

In the first act, each half-angle deals with at least one of the two truths we began with.

The first, *Primary Exposition*, is focused on recognizing the protagonist's opening problem. The second, *Debate*, follows her as she comes to terms with how she feels about it and what she is going to try and do.

In order to consider in more detail how each of these tasks is achieved, we can make a further split in each half-angle. In this way, the first half-angle is comprised of two beats. The first: *Story World*, introduces us to the lived context of the story and sets the protagonist and their problem within it. The second beat: *Desire*, sets up their desire for change. This half-angle also introduces us to the *theme* of the story. It will be developed further as things move along, but by the end of the second beat we should have a good sense of what is personally at stake for the protagonist. If she *desires* something important, that desire will speak to the theme of the story. It may not yet be directed towards the specific task that the story will assign, but we will know enough from this beat to intuit how our heroine's desire will be engaged when that plot direction is revealed.

We do the same thing with the second half-angle, which divides into its own two beats. *Hesitation* reflects initial resistance to dealing with the problem – change is hard! *First Commitment* brings us to the end of the act and angle as the protagonist recognizes they have to do something and takes a first step onto the path of change.

Let's work this through, using *How to Train Your Dragon* as our first example.

In *How to Train Your Dragon* the story beats of the first angle work like this:

A – Primary exposition

1. **Story World:** Hiccup is brave and intelligent, but also a weak and skinny little Viking boy. He is innovative and imaginative, but he lives in a world that praises physical strength and steadfast adherence to "the old ways."
2. **Desire:** Hiccup wants to be a dragon-slaying Viking hero, but he gets into trouble and proves a liability while trying to make his mark. Hiccup also has a crush on a Viking girl, Astrid, but we see that he will have to slay a whole lot of dragons—metaphorically at least—to have a chance with her.

B – Debate

3. **Hesitation:** The other Vikings are certain that Hiccup will never make it as a dragon slayer. What's more, when he finally has the chance to be a hero, he can't bring himself to kill a dragon.
4. **First Commitment:** Hiccup accepts his failure as a dragon slayer just when his father (Stoick, the village chief and the film's **antagonist**) finally relents and lets him train as one. He accepts the training with great reluctance as he knows now that it works directly against his nature. At the end of the act, Hiccup has been given the chance that he originally wanted. However, paradoxically, he feels lost. He needs to find new purpose after his dreams have been shattered.

Poor Hiccup has an internal story problem that adversely affects his relationship with his community and thus his future hopes for any kind of happiness and success. The first act and angle is all about helping both Hiccup and the audience to recognize the enormity of that problem and having Hiccup decide to do something about it.

The theme of *How to Train Your Dragon*

- The story of *How to Train Your Dragon* is all about *fitting in.*
- The manifestation of this in the story is *acceptance.*
- The manifestation of this in the plot is *accommodation.*
- In plot terms: *Hiccup can't slay dragons in a world where dragon slayers rule.* See his problem?

At the start of the movie the protagonist, Hiccup, is shown to be different from the rest of his tribe. In fact he's so different that the other Vikings are the collective antagonists of the story. Their antagonism is embodied primarily in the person of Hiccup's father, Stoick. Even though Stoick is the antagonist character, what Hiccup really has to overcome is the centuries of Viking "thinking" and tradition that Stoick stoically represents.

Hiccup knows that he's different and wishes desperately that he wasn't. As a result, he starts out dead set on finding a way to transform himself into the perfect dragon-killing Viking. As the story plays out he comes to understand that he is never going to fit in with his community as it stands. He ends up following his own path towards heroism in empathizing with, befriending, training, flying, and finally *understanding* a dragon, the mortal enemy of his people.

Eventually, Hiccup's path leads the rest of the Vikings back to him. He comes to understand himself and learns to find value (*acceptance*) in his difference. More than that, through his very difference Hiccup comes to understand that the Vikings have got everything wrong about dragons and his change serves as a catalyst for theirs. The other Vikings change when, finally, they are able to see the value in Hiccup's choices and in his unique brand of heroism. As a direct result, they find out how to live with (*accommodate*) their former enemies, the dragons. This is another kind of fitting in.

As a consequence both communities, Viking and Dragon, are strengthened. Hiccup is redeemed and accepted by his peers and he begins a romantic relationship with his worryingly skinny tomboy love object, Astrid. Story bends to theme and the world at the end is not the world of the beginning. As it should in all well-told tales, the story has changed the world. It has an *up ending* in this case, as Vikings and dragons now live in harmony. This is all a direct consequence of the struggle its protagonist undergoes with his theme.

A – Primary exposition

This half-angle establishes your protagonist as a desiring being in a coherent story world. By the end of the first two beats your audience should know enough about your protagonist to understand what she wants from life at the start of the story and why it will be a challenge for her to achieve those aims.

1. Story world

Typically the first beat of a movie sets up a context for external or plot motivation while the second focuses more on introducing internal or story motivation. This doesn't always hold true, in fact there is almost always some bleeding between the two if for no other reason than, in a well-written story, the one implies or requires the other. In the case of *How to Train Your Dragon*, these general truths hold.

First, remember that there is a big difference between the world as you experience it in your life and a story world in a screenplay—even if you are writing about your own experience and the world you live in every day. The former is objective reality, filtered by your own perception, in all its complexity and substance. The latter is an always subjective *distillation* of that reality, or an act of pure creative invention, that is designed to speak to the needs of a specific narrative. If you are creating an imaginary world it should also operate by its own internal logic, as the prolific science fiction author Alan Dean Foster explains:

> Nothing breaks a reader's immersion in a story faster than an obvious error in world building. This holds true across all genres but is especially true for science fiction. You can insert anything you please into your imaginary world as long as you maintain the internal logic. The more realistic your invented world appears and the more consistent it becomes, the more the reader [and viewer] will recognize it as a reality, albeit an alternate one.[35]

In a movie you show us *only what we need to see* of your story world to *understand* your story.

One of the hardest tasks any screenwriter faces is writing exposition. Introducing your story world, its protagonist and key story challenge both elegantly and efficiently is not an easy task. The idea is to avoid your audience feeling like they have been the victims of a nasty case of info-bombing. *How to Train Your Dragon* manages it with style and dash, so I am going to go into extra detail with the first act and angle of that movie, in order to help us understand how it works. (We will catch up with our secondary case studies of *Let the Right One In* and *Winter's Bone* in detail after we have worked through the structure of act one.)

Before we go too far, I think a few quick revision notes on exposition might be in order . . .

---

[35] Alan Dean Foster interviewed by Janice Gable Bashman.

Lesson Break: Exposition

One of the first questions I am often asked early on in my screenwriting classes and workshops is: "How do you write exposition?" The questions always comes out early because my students—and many of the writers I meet professionally for that matter—quickly come to understand, from their own experience, how hard it is to write with elegance and efficiency.

Exposition is the process of informing the audience of everything they need to know to follow the story.

That means exposition may be about getting us up to speed with character introductions, significant prior events, historical context, story world training ("A long time ago in a galaxy far, far away..."), ongoing revelations and new information as the story unfolds and more.

Exposition is difficult to write well because it feels like you are always trying to cram too much information into too small a narrative space. It feels especially counter-intuitive in screenwriting because the admonition to show, not tell, is always already in your mind. But remember, we don't need to know everything at once. We just need to know enough to be going on with.

Typical movie stories are front-loaded with exposition—we need to catch up to the issues fast but, once again, catching up does not mean drowning in facts and information. Providing information does not stop with act one, however. Central to the pleasures of structure is the way you control plot and story revelations throughout your screenplay through the process of narration—the process of story*telling*. We should be learning new things and be surprised, delighted, amused, terrified and generally engaged by different kinds of exposition all the way.

Sometimes, on the other hand, especially in mystery, thriller or puzzle plots (*Memento, Three Days of the Condor*), the pleasures of structure decree that the audience should start off gloriously in the dark. Often in these kinds of movies we share our position of comparative ignorance with the story's protagonist and our acquisition of knowledge mirrors theirs exactly.

Good exposition uses a combination of techniques variously to announce and disguise itself. These range from written or spoken (voice-over) narration and subtle dialogue through simple visual display and the use of more complex motif, metaphor and metonymy to work on the audience.

The most important technique is to write exposition through character action. It is not their words, but what characters do that tells us the most about them and how they relate to their world. Characters are more than just action in your mind, but it is through their actions that your audience learns the most about them. Talk, in this sense, is cheap.

Importantly, the more techniques—and variants on techniques—you use to achieve your exposition, the less you rely on one "delivery mechanism," the less awkward and forced it will feel. Try to reinforce your exposition by giving us different perspectives on similar information. Use different techniques to address the same issue—dialogue, character behaviors, visual motifs, the use of props or what have you.

Good exposition involves a process of condensation and paring down on the part of the writer. Ask yourself: "What is the minimum my audience needs to know at this point to understand and accept what is happening and to keep things moving?" Aim for that, but make the resulting base of your story sauce as rich and thick as possible without curdling it. When you have worked out a version of this minimum then by all means ask yourself: "What else would be fun to give them at this point?" "Do I have time and space to do it?" "If not, can I afford to make time and space?" Be aware that the answer to these questions may (should) often be: *no*.

Case Study: Masking Exposition With E.Buzz

As the opening credits roll for the classic supernatural horror movie, *Poltergeist* (1982, scr. Steven Spielberg & Michael Grais & Mark Victor), the American national anthem plays over distorted television images. When this movie was made television broadcasting stopped late at night so, after the anthem ends, the TV goes to static. We pull out to reveal a man asleep in his chair in front of the TV. Right then, the family dog, "E.Buzz" appears and scarfs some potato chip fragments from the man's plate, conveniently left on the floor.

E.Buzz heads upstairs and we catch up with him in the master bedroom. The mother of the house is asleep in bed as E.Buzz searches the room in vain for more snacks. Next he noses open the door to the older daughter's room, snuffling her sleeping face and causing her to turn her head, revealing a bag of potato chips—success! E.Buzz scarfs some chips then continues his quest for food into the bedroom shared by the family's two younger kids, revealing in turn a boy and a younger girl. He snuffles around but finds nothing edible.

However E.Buzz seems to have woken the little girl, Carol Anne, and so—tag, you're it—we lose E.Buzz and begin to follow her own night-time journey, back along the now familiar path to the family television and a strange encounter that sets up the supernatural plot to come . . .

This is a technique called *masking exposition* and E.Buzz has earned his paycheck. While we are enjoying watching the greedy dog hunt for tasty treats we learn about the layout of the house that will play a central role in the scary events to come. We also learn about each member of the family and see them all at rest in their personal spaces. Our little journey with E. Buzz lulls us into a false sense of peace and security as he pads through the rooms of sleeping kids. Nothing bad could happen in this house, with this friendly dog on patrol—could it? Watching E.Buzz masks the expositional info-dump. We are focusing on his quest for food and learning important information about the story world as we go. There are many ways of doing this and it is a very useful trick to have up your writer's sleeve.

> NOTE: For a longer case study outlining the techniques of writing exposition, see my account of the opening sequences of *The Ipcress File* in *Write What You Don't Know* pp.140–147.

Now we can travel back to the opening of our story world of Vikings and dragons: We open flying towards a village of wooden huts perched on a rugged island called "Berk," rising out of frigid, choppy seas. Right away, Hiccup's bone-dry voice-over narration gives us the movie's first important expositional technique. Subjective, cynical and dryly humorous he tells us: "it's twelve days north of hopeless and a few degrees south of freezing to death. It's located solidly on the meridian of misery." Or, if we speak the subtext: "that's how I feel, so that's how I see my world." We don't even know his name, but we're a few seconds into the movie and already we kind of know who he is. In fact he's us. . . only maybe more nasal.

Immediately we see that the village is under attack from all sorts of sheep-stealing dragons. Now we know that the *plot* involves an ongoing battle to be at the top of the food chain. Starting your genre story in the middle of a battle is smart writing, because it is fun for your audience. As we have seen, action of any kind can be a great mask for efficient exposition—and, in contemporary Hollywood genre screenwriting, the pressure to open on action (and on more dramatic action than following poor old E.Buzz around) is increasingly prevalent.

As an aside, recently *Poltergeist*'s screenwriter, Michael Grais, impressed upon me this pressure to accelerate storytelling. Michael reflected that although he opens the movie with a teasing first encounter between Carol Anne and the "TV People" to set the tone and create anticipation in the audience he played the first act slowly after that. He built character and context using light comedy, so that we would really care about the Freeling family by the time the ectoplasm began to hit the fan. You couldn't write that way today, he noted: "No longer can you spend the first act building character in a genre film like that, or [a] thriller or action adventure... the action has to be almost immediate as the audience's minds are tuned to video games and such and don't have patience."[36]

We already have a sense of what dragons are about from every other story about dragons, but we get an efficient introduction to the movie's human culture with one line of narration accompanied by a single encapsulating image. "Most people would leave," Hiccup's narration suggests, "not us, we're Vikings and we have stubbornness issues." As if on cue—because it is on cue: set-up leads to payoff and plays to the ever-present driver of narrative economy—a hairy Viking leaps into the air to grab a sheep dangling from a flying dragon.

Now we meet Hiccup in the flesh. He's the skinny kid getting in the way as usual. He ignores the warriors telling him to get inside. Enter Hiccup's dad, the village chief, Stoick the Vast (who is well named). He grabs Hiccup and literally chucks him out of the way. Animation is always dealing in visual hyperbole and this example is also efficient exposition.

With Hiccup dumped, Stoick asks for a situation report and we get a fast sequence introducing us to the various dragon types in action. The etymology and proper classification of cartoon dragons will play a role in what is to come and having a quick visual lesson narrated via a report to the chief works the idea into the story world pretty fluently.

This is the first of a number of taxonomies of dragonkind we are offered in the movie. This part of the movie's ongoing exposition is planned as a series of visual lessons, each a little more complex than the last. It's a smart teaching tool (see the lesson on complexity later for more on this) and the style of presentation and the social and emotional context in which it is delivered changes each time, keeping the lesson fresh.

By now a depressed Hiccup has reached the village forge and we discover he is the apprentice to the one-legged blacksmith, Gobber the Belch. In

---

[36] Michael Grais, email to author, February 1, 2014.

passing we are also introduced to the other village teenagers who are busy doing their bit and fighting fires. We learn that Hiccup fancies Astrid because, as the screenplay puts it:

```
A SLOW-MOTION explosion erupts behind her, framing
her in a sexy ball of fire.
```

And with that moment of animated lustful teenage yearning we slip seamlessly into the second story beat: Desire.

Before we move on to consider what happens next, however, let's have a quick reminder of how structure is all about pleasure in this beat. We enjoy the process of primary exposition in *How to Train Your Dragon* thanks to all the different techniques the writers deploy in its service:

- *Subjective narration* – how I see my world tells you how I see myself.
- *Visual reinforcement* – grab hold of that sheep: stubborn, see?
- *Repetition with variation* – Hiccup gets no respect from *anyone*.
- *Character is action* – Stoick chucks Hiccup, the disposable boy, out of the way.
- *Story world briefings* – masked as situation reports.
- *A spoonful of comedy* – helps the exposition go down.

Case Study: Story World Beats

Mr. Blandings Builds His Dream House – **a story world from (white middle-class) hell**

Mr. Blandings Builds His Dream House (1948, scr. Norman Panama and Melvin Frank) is a comedy about a couple who decide to move from "cliff living" in a tiny Manhattan apartment to a spacious country house, designed to their specifications. As you might imagine from the movie's premise, they find things don't go as easily as they had imagined. *Mr. Blandings...* opens with a long sequence highlighting the cramped conditions for a well-to-do family living in a New York apartment in the late 1940s.

The movie allows itself almost fifteen minutes to show us a typical morning in the life of the family. There is little dialogue, but much family ritual expressed as physical comedy as the members of the Blandings family work around each other in small spaces and wrangle the contents of groaning closets to get ready for their day. The film allows itself all this time—all this repetition of the trope of cramped living—because it must establish their heartfelt need to get out of their little box of an apartment and have room to breathe. Everything is going to go so very wrong as soon as they embark on the project of the new house that we need to be kept reminded what the alternative was. On the scale of white people problems, almost anything, we are going to be reminded again and again, is better than where they used to live.

Although a contemporary comedy film would accelerate the process, sometimes we simply need to spend time in a story world to truly understand it. One joke about small apartments, or better two or three, would set up the situation but it is only by sharing the full ritual of the morning that we bond our own experience with the family's on screen. When we finally get to leave the apartment, following Mr. Blandings to his job in advertising, it is with a feeling of some relief. It is that very feeling which sustains the entire comedy plot to come.

Capote – clashing story worlds

Where *Mr. Blandings Builds His Dream House* introduces its story world through a single location, *Capote* (2005, scr. Dan Futterman) does so by showing us two very different worlds which are about to collide. We open in the flat bleak Kansas plain. Terrible crimes have been committed in a lonely house and we are witnesses to their discovery. Abruptly, we cut from Kansas to a Manhattan party at which the writer, Truman Capote, is being feted by crowds of young admirers. Capote plays up to his flamboyant image and projects his urbane wit and wry cynicism to the full. When he's alone the next morning, however, we see a more serious man with a need to find a new writing project worthy of his attention.

These two worlds, hardscrabble rural Kansas and trendy, sexually liberated New York, will encounter one another as Capote decides to write the story of the murders for the book *In Cold Blood*. The movie follows him as he travels to Kansas to document the trial and the events around it, accompanied by his friend and assistant Nelle Harper Lee. The opening sequence is providing its audience with a specific foreshadowing of future events of course but, more than that, the two distinct locations play as a kind of discordant thematic tone poem. Capote and Lee will have a hard task ahead of them in accommodating one world with the other.

Dredd – action movie exposition

By contrast, the opening of the hugely underrated science fiction action movie *Dredd* (2012, scr. Alex Garland, based on characters created by John Wagner and Carlos Ezquerra), follows a simple, but well-trodden path to introducing its story world: 1. Show the world in its uniqueness; 2. Speak *words of import* in voice-over setting up its story context; 3. Prove your action hero has genre chops.

We fly over a barren landscape towards an immense, walled city as the voice-over reveals expositional context: "America is an irradiated wasteland. Within it lies a city. Outside the boundary walls a desert, the Cursed Earth. Inside the walls a cursed city, stretching from Boston to Washington DC. An unbroken concrete landscape, 800 million people living in the ruin of the old world and the mega-structures of the new one. Mega-blocks, mega-highways – Mega City One. Convulsing, choking, breaking under its own weight. Citizens in fear of the street, the gun, the gang . . ."

Now we see images of poverty and news reports of violence intercut with a man putting on a leather uniform and helmet. This is Judge Dredd, future lawman and the anti-hero of the story. We fly round the dark, imposing edifice of the Hall of Justice: "Only one thing fighting for order in the chaos, the men and women of the Hall of Justice. Juries. Executioners. Judges." The man turns round, his helmeted head threatening and shadowed and we cut to the movie's title.

The next sequence follows Judge Dredd on motorbike (Lawmaster) patrol as he demonstrates his action hero bona fides by defeating a gang of criminals with professionalism and utter ruthlessness. This establishes not only his own character but also his expectations of the others who wear the uniform. This will be important later as he assesses whether the rookie Anderson is worthy of the title Judge. The opening of *Dredd* doesn't play cute. Garland knows he's writing a piece of mythic high-genre fun and he plays that identity to the hilt.

Of course there are many more ways of introducing a story world than these three examples. However, although the tactics filmmakers use in terms of establishing the initial relationships between genre, location, characters and theme vary tremendously, all movies need to make those links and all do so efficiently according to their own lights. The corpus of genre movies simultaneously buys you shortcuts (*Dredd*) and allows you to linger. *Mr. Blandings. . .* plays its opening slow, for reasons of comedy; but then so does *Blade Runner*, for reasons of science fiction.

```
                        IMPLIED YOU
            So, I'm putting you on the spot now.
            Tell me what I need to do to set up
            my story in Temptation?

Friendly Me stares blankly.
```

IMPLIED YOU (CONT'D)
My romantic comedy screenplay. Green
eyes, remember?

FRIENDLY ME
Oh, right.

IMPLIED YOU
How would you start? If you were
story consulting, I mean.

FRIENDLY ME
Well, we'd begin casually. We'd just
talk through your idea and explore
it. We might even run it through the
W beats as an exercise and think
about how the internal structure of
the story might develop. The plan is
always to help you understand your
story well enough that you can begin
writing your first draft. But getting
there takes a lot more than a single
conversation.

IMPLIED YOU
Nice. I could use a number two brain
to bounce off. I guess yours would
do in a pinch – kidding! Come on.
Jokes.

FRIENDLY ME
That's some top grade funny stuff
you're working there. Clearly your
screenplay is going to write itself.

IMPLIED YOU
Oh lighten up, sourpuss. I'd
appreciate your help. Really. I
would. I'll even buy the coffee.
How's that for a sweet deal? It must

be like double your usual rate for
story consulting, right? BOOM!

Beat.

                    FRIENDLY ME
Make it a large and you've got a
deal . . .

                    IMPLIED YOU
Excited. Soon to be caffeinated. So
how do we start?

                    FRIENDLY ME
Ok, we'll throw out ideas and work
them, as much to reject what we
don't like as to confirm what we do.
There's only one rule for this
kind of first conversation: no
idea is off limits, no matter how
dumb or cheesy you think it is.
Better to get everything out there.
First task: show us your heroine in
her world.

                    IMPLIED YOU
Ok, wait up, I'm going to take some
notes. Let me just open my Moleskine
here . . .

                    FRIENDLY ME
(Cough) Poser.

                    IMPLIED YOU
Huh?

                    FRIENDLY ME
Ready? Show her world. . . And use
her world to tell us what we need to
know to get us into her story.

```
             IMPLIED YOU
Like her friends, her family. Where
she works?


             FRIENDLY ME
Sure. But your story is about love
and trust, right?


             IMPLIED YOU
Right.


             FRIENDLY ME
So to be useful, what you show us
needs to illustrate her attitude to
love and relationships. Show us how
her friends read her as a romantic
being. And then there's trust. Do
her friends rely on her for everyday
stuff, or for important things? She
might be a complete flake, but they
know she'll come through when it
counts, for example.


             IMPLIED YOU
Gotcha.
```

2. Desire

Desire is the yearning beat. This is where we establish what's at stake for our protagonist in both plot and story.

This story is about a teenage boy so there's going to be a lot of messy yearning. In *How to Train Your Dragon* this yearning is for everything Hiccup hopes to be, but it turns on sexual desire. Hiccup's attraction to Astrid slides us directly into the Desire beat and motivates his immediate action.

Emboldened by the sight of Astrid, Hiccup immediately pleads with Gobber: "Ah come on, let me out please. I need to make my mark." Sometimes being on the nose is fine as long as you pick your moments wisely. Here, the vision of Astrid has grabbed Hiccup and he suddenly finds that his hormones are giving him no time for clever dialogue.

Right now Hiccup's goals are simple: I'll kill a dragon. My life will get infinitely better. I might even get a date. We'll come back to them in more detail in the lesson break directly below. Although his future experiences are going to change his attitude to dragons and dragon killing as the story develops, his need for a date is pretty constant.

It is hardly an earth-shattering revelation that teenage boys are horny. However, this is also the constant that grounds Hiccup. It keeps any thoughts of total heroic altruism in appropriate check and reminds us that, no matter how much he changes, he's still a normal kid. In short we are going to root for Hiccup because of his underdog bravery and his empathy for dragons, but also because at heart he's just a boy with boy appetites and we can relate.

And now we are given the crux of Hiccup's problem. It's not just that he sucks at one aspect of "Vikingness"; he sucks in every way imaginable to them. It begins with Gobber telling him that he can't make his mark because he's weak as a kitten. Hiccup doesn't disagree, but he counters by bringing his home-made bolus catapult forward: "OK fine, but this will throw it for me." And of course it does so immediately and by accident, stunning a passing Viking.

The catapult revelation is an important piece of exposition disguised as slapstick. It is preparation for the moment, later in the beat, when Hiccup actually does something right, but it also establishes another important context of Hiccup's difference: he's a science geek in a world of jocks. The movie keeps reminding us that Hiccup thinks differently from his peers. In many cases that's because they seem to be a long way from embracing complex thought in any form. Indeed the average Viking seems most at home when he is acting on instinct or cultural memory alone.

The catapult introduces the idea that part of Hiccup's opening skillset is mechanical engineering. The movie will test that skillset properly in the next angle. Engineering skill will help Hiccup train his dragon. What he does after that (after the midpoint) is more about heroism than mechanical engineering but, in a practical plot-driven sense, engineering gets him to the point where he *can* be a hero. For now the gag is just foreshadowing. It plants the idea: *Hiccup = good at making stuff* into the back of our minds. This is another good example of narrative economy. For now the accident brings on a moment of deeper character reinforcement. In exposition, action earns clarity and Gobber tells it like it is:

```
                    GOBBER
         Hiccup. If you ever want to get out
         there to fight dragons, you need to
         stop all . . .

Gobber gestures in Hiccup's general direction.
```

```
                  GOBER (CONT'D)
    . . . this.


                  HICCUP
    (astonished)
    But. . . you just pointed to all of
    me.


                  GOBBER
    Yes! That's it! Stop being all of
    you.
```

This won't be the only time we get to hear this kind of assessment from the Vikings. It will eventually be transformed into a compliment in the final Resonance beat. *Repetition = reinforcement*, at least until it transforms into its second form of = *boring*. Once again, Hiccup makes his own Desire clear: "One day I'll get out there because killing a dragon is everything round here."

> By this point in the movie, the plot challenge of *How to Train Your Dragon* reads like this: *Hiccup wants to be a dragon slayer in a world where dragon slayers rule.*

We can tell that this challenge needs more development because it sounds like an opportunity more than a problem. Hiccup has a lack, but there's no great internal story blockage to get past—he *wants* to kill dragons at this point, after all. Of course he'll get a block before long. The down angle has to work on him some more for his simple problem of a lack of opportunity to mature into his worst nightmare.

Lesson Break: "Wants" and "Needs" in the Desire Beat

One common model screenwriters use to understand and organize character motivation in their screenplays is to ascribe "wants" and "needs" to them in relation to their theme. Indeed, you will find many variants of these terms in other screenwriting manuals.

In screenwriting language, *wants* are usually material or practical things the character desires in the story world. They are prompted by the impetus of the theme but are not it. Wants are objectives to be striven for and achieved in the plot.

Needs are internal story drivers which come closer to or actually embody the theme.

A well-rounded movie character will have linked wants and needs. Plot goals will imply subtextual story goals and underlying story goals will be reflected back in more transparent plot goals. Every action a well-written character takes will feel organic because clever exposition will have introduced their wants and needs to the audience. We follow a character's progress through the movie by checking in on where they stand in relation to their wants and needs.

In this expositional beat of How *to Train Your Dragon*, Hiccup just laid out his opening *want line*:

In the plot, Hiccup *wants* to kill a dragon ➜ get a girlfriend.

Over in the story, Hiccup just *needs* to be accepted: his theme.

Right now he's buying into the prime directive of his culture and, given his lack of experience with alternatives, he assumes that he wants what they want = Desire. He will end up with some of the same goals of course; it is his means to an end that will have changed. When a good screen story is doing its job it will test the protagonist's opening position to destruction if necessary. This will begin in earnest in the next beat, but for now Hiccup is all about dragon slaying.

Now, in the Desire beat, exposition is still taking place. It is *masked* by the newly revealed imperatives of the protagonist's wants and needs however. Hiccup takes us through another illustration of the hierarchy of dragons, this time in terms of how famous (how *accepted*) killing one would make him (*repetition with variation* once again): "The ultimate prize is the dragon no one's ever seen. We call it the Night Fury." As if on cue—because it is on cue—a half-seen shape destroys a big Viking catapult. "No one has ever killed a Night Fury. That's why I'm gonna be the first." There's the Desire beat again.

As if on cue—because it is also on cue (narrative economy again)— Gobber leaves Hiccup in charge of the smithy and goes off to fight. Immediately (he's a potential hero, remember: not short on courage, just short on thinking some things through) Hiccup acts on his Desire and pushes his catapult out the door. He sets it up, aims and shoots at the Night Fury:

```
KERTHUNK! The flexed arms SNAP forward, springing
the weapon off the ground. The bola disappears
into the sky, followed by a WHACK and a SCREECH.
```

Hiccup actually hit it! Our appreciation of his unique engineering skills is reinforced as the dragon goes down injured in the dark distance. This plot event emerges directly from the Desire beat and serves as the *inciting incident* of the story.

Lesson Break: The Inciting Incident

In conventional screenwriting we describe the event that gets the story moving as the inciting incident. It prompts the protagonist into action, "breaks" the story world or otherwise initiates the main action.

As we have seen, in *How to Train Your Dragon* the inciting incident is the moment in Desire when Hiccup shoots the Night Fury with his catapult. This action is prompted by his need to prove himself a proper Viking. It starts him on the path to transforming himself and his story world in ways he never imagined at the time.

The inciting incident establishes a clear moment of anticipated parallelism in your story. If the world is now broken, it must be fixed. If the bad guy has triumphed, he must be defeated. If romance is desired it must be achieved. When you write your inciting incident you set up in the mind of your reader an anticipated future moment when this need for restoration or resolution or revenge or romance is fulfilled. We do not yet know how it will occur, but we feel that it must. That gives you a job to do.

As I have discussed previously, screenwriters sometimes call this anticipated but as-yet-unknown future story event the *obligatory moment* or obligatory scene. Remember that anticipation is central to the enjoyment we get from stories. Once you create it you better pay it off!

For a moment, Hiccup is full of the joys of success. Things are about to go very wrong, but let's reflect for a moment on Hiccup the hero. *It is only the second story beat of the movie and already Hiccup has done something no other Viking ever has.* What's more, he has accomplished the feat through the exercise of one of his unique skills. In the future, these skills will give him hope of finding an alternative route to resolving his theme of *fitting in*. Of course, at this point Hiccup's problem is as much one of reputation as it is talent. We see his potential, but we also see the mountain he has to climb to get anyone to pay attention.

This is still the Desire beat so of course nobody sees his victory. Instead, Hiccup gets into a dicey spot with a big fiery dragon and needs rescuing. In the process he becomes the cause of a lot of very public destruction. A furious Stoick drags him through the village as the Vikings (including Astrid) watch.

Stoick tells him: "You're many things Hiccup, but a dragon killer is not one of them." This is largely true (foreshadowing again), but Hiccup is not ready to hear it. He needs the lesson of experience and that will come in the next story beat.

As Stoick's damning declaration demonstrates, in *How to Train Your Dragon* the Desire beat proceeds through a process of piling negative reinforcement on top of Hiccup's determination to be what he isn't. It accelerates the down angle onto a steeper decline. We learn that his determination transcends all opposition thus far—this is one of the things that will make him a genuine hero and will see him through his adventures—but for now it only gets him into trouble.

Back in the smithy at dawn, Hiccup laments his fate. As soon as Gobber goes out again, however, he's off out the back door to search for the dragon he hit. Now we're done with Desire and into the next half-angle and the story beat of Hesitation.

Case Study: Desire Beats

The World's End – the desire beat in a flash

In *The World's End* (2013, scr. Simon Pegg & Edgar Wright) when somebody asks middle-aged loser Gary King whether he is disappointed that he never completed The Golden Mile pub crawl with his old school friends we can see his insane desire to complete it written all over his face. *The desire beat happens as fast as that look.* Gary is still a child, trapped at the moment of his greatest happiness (and, subsequently, his greatest regret) on the night his life stopped moving forward. The movie will follow Gary's manic scheme to persuade his old school friends to try the pub crawl again after all these years. The story will turn into a weird science fiction adventure but at the heart it is about a sad guy trying to recapture his lost youth.

American Beauty – the desire beat in a fantasy sequence

In *American Beauty* (1999, scr. Alan Ball), unhappy middle-aged family man Lester Burnham introduces us to his family through subjective voice-over narration. He tells us explicitly that his wife and daughter both see him as a loser. He reflects that they are right: "I have lost something. I'm not exactly sure what it is but, I know I didn't always feel this sedated. But you know what? It's never too late to get it back." In Lester's case you might call this the "desire to Desire" beat, but it is really part of the Story World exposition. Lester is looking for something—anything—and he finds it first in an infatuation with his daughter's attractive, cheerleading school friend Angela. As Lester watches from the stand, he constructs a fantasy cheer in which Angela dances for him and strips. Rose petals (like the ones his wife grows) flood out of her. Lester will begin to reinvent himself and the Desire to do so is first focused here. This is a much longer version of Desire than the quick flash of need we are given in *The World's End*.

The Perks of Being A Wallflower – narrating the desire beat

In *The Perks of Being A Wallflower* (2012, scr. Stephen Chbosky from his book), introverted Charlie speaks his opening voice-over narration in the form of a letter to an unknown recipient. He has just started high school, his old friends ignore him, his sister won't even have lunch with him and he doesn't want to stand out and be picked on. About eight minutes into the film, as he comes home after a depressing first day, he finishes his letter: "If my aunt Helen were still here I could talk to her and I know she would understand how I'm both happy and sad and I'm still trying to figure out how that could be. I just hope I make a friend soon." His Desire will be achieved as he makes some very special friends who will transform his life and help him resolve the trauma of his past for good measure.

In these three examples, the Desire beat sets up the plot of the movie and begins to uncover the story that lies beneath. We know what each character *wants* now—to finish the pub crawl, to be desirable again, to find a friend. What each of them *needs* is wrapped up in those goals. A fuller understanding will take time, but now the audience have enough information to be going along with as we figure that out.

```
                IMPLIED YOU
     So, in Temptation, this is where
     I show the audience what my heroine
     wants from love?


                FRIENDLY ME
     Yes. But as it plays to the idea of
     trust. The film is going to turn on
     her lies and stupidity, so we need
     to set up her opening position. At
     the start of the story love, or
     romance, or even lust, is more
     important to her than trust.
     Something like that?
```

IMPLIED YOU
Getting romance is more important
than keeping it. Yeah, that's the
idea.

FRIENDLY ME
That's why she will deceive him
about the green eyes and other
things. She's all about finding the
romantic moment in the now and
reveling in it?

IMPLIED YOU
He's more serious because of his
past and he misreads who she is and
gets in too deep. But he brings her
with him and that's where the
trouble starts. But the theme is
love, not trust. It's a romantic
comedy, remember?

FRIENDLY ME
But when you pitched the concept to
me it turned on deceit. That makes
your story about trust. I mean it's
still a love story, just love is
serving as the context for a story
about trust in relationships.

IMPLIED YOU
I'm thinking about her romantic
goals.

FRIENDLY ME
But her goals change through the
story as she does smart and dumb
things. She experiences their
consequences and she decides what to
do about them. Then she gets into a
real relationship. Suddenly trust is
a big issue.

                    IMPLIED YOU
You mean she still wants love, but
by the end she has learned more
about what it takes – what it
costs – better?

                    FRIENDLY ME
Exactly – if that's what you
want her to learn. It's your story
and you need to be clear what
you want to say about your themes.
Here, however, you can pay off
the Desire beat with her meeting
the guy. That's an obvious option
for your inciting incident, by
the way. Or you can use this beat
just to make the terms of her
desire crystal clear. That way, when
she does meet him, we know that he
could be the perfect fit, and we see
just how far she has to travel to
make it work. You have set it up and
now your payoff is fun for the
audience.

                    IMPLIED YOU
They're going to meet early. I want
the Halloween night to take a big
chunk of the first act.

                    FRIENDLY ME
Remember to set up story and
plot here. Will he fit into her
world as easily as he fits into her
heart?

                    IMPLIED YOU
Ooh, that's almost slick enough
to go on the poster. So this
beat continues all the Story World
stuff?

                    FRIENDLY ME
Exposition is ongoing, remember?
Maybe you could have fun if he's
a hard sell for her friends. He
could be a fish out of water in her
everyday world. He's Hugh Grant on
the Jersey Shore.

                    IMPLIED YOU
Or Rosie Perez most places. Ok, I
get it. What if he's too adorable?
All her friends are into him —
jealousy problems?

                    FRIENDLY ME
Right. Or they empathize strongly
with his trauma over his dead
wife and that will put them on
his side over the whole trust
issue. You need so much more than
green eyes as a plot problem, by
the way.

                    IMPLIED YOU
Yeah, yeah. We'll get to it.

                    FRIENDLY ME
Having said that, remember to set up
her eye color and the contacts. What
costume was she wearing?

                    IMPLIED YOU
I haven't decided. Something classy
but kind of sexy. I want her to look
good. I want her to be confident. The
costume should reflect her smarts and
sense of humor as well.

                    FRIENDLY ME
And the contacts need to be integral
to the gag somehow.

```
            IMPLIED YOU
    Like if she was going as "Jealousy"
    she'd have green eyes. But that
    wouldn't work of course . . .

            FRIENDLY ME
    Unless you change the eye color.
    Does it have to be green eyes?

            IMPLIED YOU
    I liked green. It's kind of
    mysterious. Also they are rarer than
    blue or brown. How hard would it be
    to avoid all those brown-eyed girls?
    I'll think about it though.
```

B – Debate

This half-angle moves your protagonist from wanting and needing something to taking action. They may be reluctant, quite possibly ignorant—or at least lacking in self-awareness, and generally unprepared, but at least they are moving forward.

3. Hesitation

Hesitation beats give protagonists pause before they embark on their quests to address their story's theme. Hesitation is where the enormity of the challenge is made apparent.

In *How to Train Your Dragon*, the Hesitation beat is going to come under dual ownership. Part one will be all about reinforcing Hiccup's failures by proxy as well as finding a mechanism to get his dad out of the way for a while. Part two will bring Hiccup up against his own nature and test the strength of his determination and his opening *want* position. Can he really be a dragon killer?

We left Hiccup trudging away through the forests and hills to find the dragon he shot down the night before. Instead of following him immediately, however, the story takes a break from his quest to catch up with some important plot issues affecting the village as a whole. Cut to a crisis meeting—raising the stakes—in the village hall. In the aftermath of last night's raid, Stoick is trying to persuade his fellow Vikings to accompany him on a dragon hunt: "either we finish them or they finish us."

His fellow villagers are less than enthusiastic however because long experience has taught them that dragon hunts always fail and those who embark on them tend to end up dead. Stoick realizes he is losing the crowd and threatens them with dire consequences if they don't go: "those who stay will look after Hiccup." Suddenly Viking hands shoot up all around the hall. More comic hyperbole: they would rather face death than deal with Hiccup's accident-prone chaos.

For all their individual courage and fighting abilities, this scene proves that this is a story about a culture in stagnation. Locked into a pattern of heroic failure it is unable effectively to overcome its challenges. This endemic failure actually provides Hiccup with an opportunity to enact change, but he is not yet prepared to do so.

Stoick asks Gobber to stay behind and train the new dragon slayer recruits, but what to do about Hiccup? "Put him in training," says Gobber. "You can't stop him, Stoick; you can only prepare him."

This is Hesitation by proxy. Even though Hiccup doesn't witness the moment, *we* know that the whole community has written him off as a complete liability. Even Gobber's suggestion to put him in training speaks of resignation in the face of a bleak inevitability.

Even though we cut away from our protagonist, he is still in the game. The writers take care to work the larger global plot crisis back to comment on the personal story crisis that we care most about. In one sense, this isn't strictly necessary. After the blockbuster opening battle we would have no problem justifying the Vikings going off hunting dragons without reference to Hiccup. The fact that the scene does turn on the problem of Hiccup even in his absence is an example of sound structural writing.

Cut to Hesitation part two. Oblivious to the events we have just witnessed, Hiccup is searching methodically for the dragon. Just when he thinks he'll never find it he comes across the trail of destruction where the dragon crashed to earth. This trail leads him to a small, black Night Fury, all bound up in the bola from Hiccup's catapult and completely helpless. Hiccup has both a knife and the perfect opportunity to slay the creature: "I did it! This fixes everything! I'm going to kill you dragon. I'm going to cut out your heart and take it to my father. I'm a Viking. . . I'm a Viking!"

And yet he can't do it. It's much easier to fire a non-lethal catapult at a half-seen shape in the night than it is to walk up to a living creature and coldly stick your knife somewhere intimate and impolite. This is where the *empathic transfer* between Hiccup and the audience is completed (see next Lesson Break). We felt for Hiccup, now he feels for the dragon. We are bound to him all the more tightly because our identification and investment has paid off directly and in kind. We identify his good emotion as a natural extension of our own.

"I did this," he reminds himself, before taking the much braver decision to *undo* it. As he cuts through its bonds, the dragon pounces on him and pins him to the ground. Something passes between them now, a sort of understanding perhaps? The dragon takes off, only it can't fly properly on account of its injured tail. It ends up getting itself stuck in a steep sided hollow.

Lesson Break: Empathic Transfer – Sympathy and Admiration

The immediate effects of the collective rejection the Vikings give the absent Hiccup are, first, that we are now bound more tightly to him by empathy. Secondly, when we do catch back up with him in the woods, his hopes and dreams now appear even less realistic to us than they had before. The stakes seem higher for him now even though he doesn't know it. Indeed, his very ignorance makes us even more sympathetic and his decision to free the dragon more potentially heroic.

This is all part of the ongoing process of allying audience with protagonist. Empathic transfer is an elegant and simple means of achieving it. That's why we see it in some form in just about every Hollywood and indie movie. Some people refer to it as a process of making the audience "root" for the hero.

Of course this process of empathic transfer has been building all the way through the story and will continue to do so. It works in two ways. First by eliciting *sympathy* on behalf of the protagonist and secondly by eliciting *admiration* for their actions and heroic potential.

A well-written Hollywood protagonist needs to engage with the audience in both ways. Too much sympathy and not enough admiration means we will soon dismiss them as a whiny loser. Too much admiration and not enough sympathy means they are probably just an asshole.

Of course sometimes being an asshole—as long as you are *our* asshole—has been enough to sustain a protagonist (John McClane in *Die Hard*, for example). That doesn't mean you should be content to settle for "just enough" in your character development. Even action heroes deserve some depth to their personalities and McClane's marital problems give him just—just—enough depth to be going on with.

A protagonist can start with a surfeit of one or the other. Hiccup overloads our sympathy response at the start of the story, for example. In a case like his, he had better start showing some more admirable gumption soon, however, or we will come to despise him pretty quick (see *Youth in Revolt*). Once again, in Hiccup's case his story problem crystallizes out of his own empathy—he can't kill the dragon. That's a very neat way of embedding our empathic transfer with his.

Case Study: Examples of Empathic Transfer

In *Let the Right One In* the audience identifies with Oskar the bullied schoolboy from the start. He is an outcast and a loner and we hope that things will turn out well for him. That nice "girl," Eli, who moved in next door would be a good friend for him—but why is she out in the snow in bare feet? She's a bit strange, but then that might make them a good fit for one another. Let's see how things develop… Oskar is the underdog and who can resist a sympathetic underdog? We admire him when he tries to be friendly to Eli and starts to transform himself following her advice and encouragement. However, we are also concerned for him as we begin to understand the truth about her own nature and her needs.

In *Winter's Bone* the audience bonds with Ree from the opening moments of the movie. We feel for her struggles as she takes responsibility for her younger siblings, making breakfast, walking them to school, helping them with lessons and generally being *in loco parentis* because her damaged mother is no help. Ree's poverty is evident, her spirit more so. By the time the law turns up to tell her about her father potentially jumping bail we are on her side and looking to her to find a solution and save her home and family. We sympathize with her situation and admire her determination.

Even action movies like *Conan the Barbarian* (1982, scr. John Milius and Oliver Stone) make sure to set up empathic transfer between their protagonist and their audience. At the start of the movie we watch with the young Conan as his family is slaughtered and he is taken as a slave. We watch the trials of his adolescence as he grows strong on the wheel and under the lash. By the time the story of Conan's adult adventures begins we are sympathetic and we hope he gets revenge on those who wronged him in the past. Once again, we sympathize with Conan's past and admire his determination in the present.

So now the movie's *plot* problem has properly matured:

Hiccup can't kill dragons in a world where dragon killers rule.

The writers have used the best part of an act of their screenplay to get Hiccup to this point. This is time well spent because, in witnessing and sharing our new friend Hiccup's descent, we can really appreciate the struggle he will have to make to rise up again.

Hiccup thought he had a problem before, but now he understands that he will never be a true Viking if that means killing in cold blood. His first close encounter outside his culture has taught him: *empathy trumps duty*. What the story will go on to teach him is that in fact *empathy transforms duty*, but that's for later. For now he is very much at the mercy of Hesitation and this determines his actions in the next story beat, First Commitment.

Case Study: Hesitation Beats

Star Wars Episode IV: A New Hope – **mundane refusal of the quest**

This one you know. In the first act of *Star Wars Episode IV: A New Hope* (1977, scr. George Lucas), old Ben Kenobi offers Luke Skywalker the opportunity to go on an adventure to deliver Princess Leia's message to the Rebel Alliance. At first he refuses, having too much moisture to farm and too much blue milk to drink at Uncle Owen's place on Tatooine. It is only when he discovers that his family has been killed that he agrees to go—that will be his First Commitment. This is a typical Hesitation beat in heroic adventure movies. The hero has business in the mundane world which initially seems more important that some silly quest.

Divergent – story world-driven hesitation

The Hesitation beat of the dystopian science fiction movie *Divergent* (2014, scr. Evan Daugherty and Vanessa Taylor) is played around the choice sixteen-year-old Tris has to make at her upcoming Choosing Ceremony whether to stay in her birth faction (Abnegation) or elect to change (to Dauntless). We see her temptation (Desire) to follow the adventurous and brave Dauntless route, but she knows there are risks and we see evidence of her uncertainty played out in interactions with family members before the ceremony. When Tris does choose Dauntless this is her First Commitment to a new life but an uncertain future. The Hesitation beat shows the importance and danger of that choice so we admire it (empathic transfer) more when Tris makes it.

IMPLIED YOU
So, in Temptation. . .

FRIENDLY ME
Green eyes. Drum-roll please!

IMPLIED YOU
Right. He tells the story about his
late wife and she freaks out inside.

FRIENDLY ME
Ok, Hollywood moment alert: she has
an accident with a contact lens
here. It's awkward that she has to
fish around in her eye, but even more
because of what we just heard.
What's her name by the way? We need
to call her something and we need a
name for "hot guy" also.

IMPLIED YOU
Yeah. Her name's Lucy and he's Bryce.

FRIENDLY ME
Bryce? Seriously? Don't tell me he's
a hipster?

IMPLIED YOU
More like he's trying too hard to fit
in. He's a country boy. Drinks
country beer. So some of that comes
off as "authentic". On a hipster it
would just be a pose. I guess he's
hipster adjacent. . .

FRIENDLY ME
And we're meant to feel sympathy for
him?

IMPLIED YOU
Hey. Hipsters are people.

Beat.

FRIENDLY ME
Let's just move on. What does Lucy
do?

IMPLIED YOU
I figured she was a couple years out
of college and she's locked into a

```
                series of internships. She's just
                hoping that something will take.

                     FRIENDLY ME
                Your audience will identify I'm
                sure. What does she want to be?

                     IMPLIED YOU
                I don't think she knows. But
                something that's creative, something
                interesting.

                     FRIENDLY ME
                She changed majors twice in college.

                     IMPLIED YOU
                Ha. Yeah, could be.

                     FRIENDLY ME
                She's a Greta Gerwig character. So
                this story will also help her find
                the answer?

                     IMPLIED YOU
                Could be. I don't want it all pat
                and tied up though. But Bryce will
                be a lens for her to see the future
                more clearly.
```

4. First commitment

Hiccup is back home now and trying to avoid Stoick. However, now the time has come for an awkward father–son chat before the chief leaves on his dragon hunt. The comedy in this scene comes out of the uncomfortable reversal each of the participants has undergone to get them here. Hiccup's change of heart about wanting to be a dragon killer wouldn't be such fun unless his father had finally been persuaded to give him a chance to be one. This comedy pays off the Hesitation by proxy beat in full.

So Hiccup tries to tell Stoick that he can't kill dragons, but Stoick is too absorbed in trying to be supportive for once to listen. In a final comic irony he lays out his very Viking vision of acceptance for Hiccup right at the moment that Hiccup has realized achieving that vision is impossible for him:

"It's time, Hiccup. When you carry this axe, you carry all of us with you. Which means you walk like us. You talk like us. You think like us. No more of this. . ." He indicates everything about Hiccup (*repetition as reinforcement* again). "Deal?" Hiccup, resigned, unable to make himself heard: "Deal. . ." In other words: First Commitment.

How to Train Your Dragon flips the usual story function of First Commitment. Usually by this point our protagonist has accepted they have a role in sorting out the story problem. First Commitment is usually a partial, provisional or generally contingent acceptance but an acceptance nonetheless. In this case, Hiccup has agreed to try and transform himself—so far a typical first act conclusion—but he already knows that what his father wants of him is impossible. He agrees because he realizes that he has no alternative. That means he is starting the second act and angle on what he already knows is a road to certain failure, rather than unlikely success. Despite this emotional twist the underlying W structure still holds, however.

Remember that, in emotional terms, the first act is a *down* angle. Hiccup's journey has certainly been downward from initial hope, via the promise of great success, to resigned despair. He begins act two with a plot task with which to move forward, but further from resolving the story theme of fitting in than ever before.

It's a great place to hang his story at its first major transition though. When you are so far down in the dumps the only way is up. The trick is to find the ladder and that requires a change of world view. Luckily for Hiccup that's exactly what second acts are all about.

That's the end of the first angle and it went by quickly. In fact the whole act only lasts around seventeen minutes on the screen—although it takes twenty-one pages in the shooting script, mainly due to the complex action sequence at the start. Now I'm not one of those bean counters who tell you that if on the sixth line of page seven your hero isn't spanking his first Nazi (or whatever) your screenplay sucks, but that timescale reminds us the writing has been taut and lean and yet also full of emotion, incident and excitement.

Another way of describing this kind of writing is: *professional*. And don't think for a moment that you can easily dismiss that as a synonym for bland or merely formulaic writing. Structure is pleasure; fun transcends formula. That's a hard thing to do well and the writers of *How to Train Your Dragon* do it very well indeed. This is clever professional writing and its intelligence comes through at every story beat and plot turn.

On screen, the maneuvering of story and plot to get us to the final scene of the angle with Hiccup and Stoick reversing their *wants* (but not their *needs*) seems natural and effortless. In the end we can tell that the writers have done their job well because we care about poor Hiccup. They have helped us see his potential, even if nobody else can. In the movie it's time for Hiccup to train as a dragon slayer, but we have one further vital question to ask of the writers before we start discussing act two:

Did you spank your hero/ine today?

At the end of our discussion of each angle we ask ourselves this question to make sure we are putting the right kind of pressure on our story and characters. In other words: *are the stakes high enough for Hiccup?* Well, the poor boy is a bad joke in his own community and has just discovered that the one way he hoped to "fix" himself is closed off to him by his own empathy. What to do now?

Lesson Break: Antagonists and Dramatic Conflict

This is also the first major scene between protagonist and antagonist in *How to Train Your Dragon*. As is only natural at this point in the story the antagonist wins, even though he doesn't fully understand or even intend his victory. Indeed, we know that he thinks he is making a major—and probably unwise—concession. This is how you want to play your antagonists. Whatever they do—and whether they know it or not at the time—they are always making the holes in the road ahead of your protagonist wider and deeper.

In a story with a self-doubting hero, like Hiccup, this means there are now two forces widening those holes: the protagonist and the antagonist. This can only be good for your plotting. It also makes for great comedy for that matter.

There is an old maxim that *drama is conflict*. This comes down to us, refracted somewhat, from classical Greek theater and is as true today as it was then. The ancient Greek word for a struggle or contest is *agon*, from which we derive the modern word "agony." This is a strong clue towards identifying the level of conflict a good genre story needs. Somewhere there will need to be drama sustained at the level of agony, not mild discomfort. Conflict is a two way proposition, however. That means you need to pay close attention to your antagonist, because they should be responsible for half your drama.

A well-written antagonist either causes your protagonist's problem directly or at least opposes its resolution in the plot. A good antagonist pushes back against every forward step your protagonist makes. More than this, a good antagonist does their best to deny your protagonist the chance of ever taking those steps. An antagonist is not pulling their weight unless they make the chance of your protagonist ever resolving their theme almost impossible.

Typically you need to establish the protagonist/antagonist relationship early in your first act. If you want your story to be dramatic, you have to show us the conflict early on. The origin of your story's conflict should be your theme.

In *How to Train Your Dragon* the conflict emerges from Hiccup's need to convince Stoick, the gatekeeper of true Vikinghood, that he has what it takes. Stoick will take a whole lot of convincing. That means Hiccup has a whole lot of work to do...

Work = action.

Action versus antagonist = conflict.

Conflict = drama.

Drama = the point.

Sometimes the true nature or identity of the antagonist may be disguised and only revealed later in your story. Examples here would be *Identity* (2003, scr. Michael Cooney), or *Secret Window* (2004, scr. David Koepp), in which we come to learn that other characters in the story are merely personalities contained in the mind of one man. Even so, the story problem the antagonist embodies needs to be clear from near the start. How else can we judge the nature and severity of your protagonist's situation and evaluate their success or failure in facing up to it?

Case Study: First Commitment Beats

Bridesmaids – needy but unprepared

At the end of the first act of the comedy *Bridesmaids* (2011, scr. Kristen Wiig & Annie Mumolo), Lillian asks her unhappy and unlucky best friend, Annie, to be her maid of honor. Having accepted the role, Annie will be brought into competition with the more glamorous (and competent) Helen and will have to face up to her own very evident failings as a functioning adult. The disastrous sequence of events that follow Annie's First Commitment accelerate her through increasing self-awareness and finally into recovering control over her life, redeeming her friendship with Lillian and even finding love. In other words, although Annie's First Commitment leads to hilarious disaster in the short term, it leads to success in the end.

Harold and Maude – an unlikely emotional breakthrough

In the wonderful comedy *Harold and Maude* (1971, scr. Colin Higgins), free spirit septuagenarian Maude has stolen young, death obsessed Harold's car (a hearse). She offers him a lift home and, when he tells her it's his car, she replies that he can give her a lift home from the funeral they were both attending. By the time they arrive at Maude's they are in full conversation and, although Harold has to leave for a session with his therapist, he promises to return. Maude has clearly made an impression on him so, when the therapist asks him if he has any friends he answers: "Maybe one." Now we know he means Maude. This First Commitment to a relationship built on genuine affection and a real human connection will blossom into an unlikely love.

                    IMPLIED YOU
          So, in this beat I need to get Lucy
          back onboard the Bryce train.

                    FRIENDLY ME
          It sounds so attractive when you put
          it like that.

                    IMPLIED YOU
          You know what I mean. I was thinking
          she would be on the verge of ducking
          out and then he says that one thing.
          You know what I mean? He says that
          one perfect thing: BOOM! Smitten
          kitten. She's in love. Or at least
          she thinks she is.

                    FRIENDLY ME
          That could be a cheesy,
          unbelievable, perfectly Hollywood
          moment. What does he say?

                    IMPLIED YOU
          No idea. Any thoughts?

                    FRIENDLY ME
          Well I don't have a line off the top
          of my head, but it's time to pay off

your exposition. What does love mean
to her? He basically says that. Or
he uses an example that speaks to
her emotions in a way that resonates
with what we already know about her.
The key is to link us to her by
prior knowledge so we share her
"Wow!" moment.

                IMPLIED YOU
That's empathic transfer.

                FRIENDLY ME
Yes. This is a romantic comedy, so
you want your audience – and your
readers for that matter – to invest
in your fantasy of romance. Whether
you intend to play the love story to
the hilt, or to undercut that
unrealistic romantic fantasy
somehow, the initial connection is
still very important. But there are
other ways of playing the sequence.

                IMPLIED YOU
You mean avoiding "the one thing?"

                FRIENDLY ME
What if that big Halloween night is
not about whether she stays after
the green eyes story? I know, I
suggested it just now. But now the
beat is about flaky Lucy realizing
that being with Bryce would be real
somehow. He has already taught her a
lesson in love. His example is
pushing against all her instincts.
She may lust after him, but the
Hesitation is really Lucy thinking:
"Am I ready for what this could be?"

```
                    IMPLIED YOU
          How about, at the start of the
          movie, we see her ending a
          relationship because the guy was
          getting too serious? I could open
          with that.

                    FRIENDLY ME
          Good. Then you reveal Bryce's eyes
          story after Lucy has decided she
          really wants to go for it. That
          plays the reveal forward more
          strongly into act two: "What do I do
          now?"
```

Act One of *Let the Right One In*

As we have just seen, *How to Train Your Dragon* is a story about an outsider looking in. Hiccup wants to be liked and accepted by his community—and especially by Astrid. The story is all about how he makes that possible by changing his culture to meet his unique understanding of his world. So, leaving aside all the specific components of the *story world* (Vikings and dragons and so forth), it would be logical to suggest that any story with the same, or at least a very similar theme would progress in the same, or at least a very similar way, right?

There is some truth behind that assumption. If you buy into the idea that there is a basic underlying structural model that serves most genre movies (call it my W, or use another similar model) then you could find familiar patterns in a wide range of outsider stories. What you would also find is a remarkable amount of variation and creative freedom as to how those patterns are used. Because a model, in the sense I am using the term, is not a formula to be repeated blandly, but a series of organizational elements which may be arranged in a familiar sequence, but which still offer the possibility of vastly different storytelling in detail.

I want to use this next case study to explore exactly this distinction. I think it is time to find some evidence to reassure ourselves that we screenwriters are not just searching for the holy grail of creativity purging. After all I have called my book *The Pleasures of Structure*, but where's the pleasure in knocking out endless arid story clones? As any real genre fan knows, there is pleasure to be had from thematic repetition but only because there is also a corresponding pleasure to be found in creative difference.

Let's look at what is, on the surface, a very different kind of movie. From Hollywood and animated family adventure, we move to Sweden and dark, cynical horror with a splash of perverse romance. *Låt den Rätte Komma In* is a vampire movie that is also a kind of outsider love story. Released in the USA in 2008, it is also another personal favorite. Those of us who love a good vampire story will forever be grateful to the filmmakers for providing us with an alternative to *Twilight* just when we needed it most.[37]

For ease of typing, from now on I will refer to the film by its English title: *Let the Right One In.* (It should not be confused with the American remake, *Let Me In* from 2010, a wholly unnecessary movie that nevertheless had some good qualities, including a fine performance from Chloe Moretz.) For those of you who haven't yet seen it—and you should remedy that omission as soon as possible—*Let the Right One In* is a reasonably faithful adaptation of a terrific horror novel by the Swedish author John Ajvide Lindqvist who also wrote the movie's screenplay.

I am not going to focus in detail on issues of adaptation in this case study. As with all the other studies in this book, my intention is to concentrate on the structure of the movie's story. We will catch up with *Let the Right One In* (and *Winter's Bone*) after every angle of *How to Train Your Dragon* to offer an exploration of each section and to offer correctives for standard structure as necessary as we go.

Theme of *Let the Right One In*

Let the Right One In will make a very interesting comparison study for *How to Train Your Dragon* because it shares a theme but addresses it very differently. On the surface, this will look very familiar:

- The story of *Let the Right One In* is all about *fitting in.*
- The manifestation of this in the story is *acceptance.*
- The manifestation of this in the plot is *accommodation.*
- In plot terms: *Oskar needs to be accepted into a world where Vampires need servants.* See his problem? Good, because he doesn't.

---

[37] I know I wrote that I'm not focusing on screenwriting traditions in other national cinemas, however my choice to work with *Let the Right One In* was due to the clarity with which it develops its challenge to our model. A quick admission before we get going. I don't speak Swedish, so my references will be based on the translated screenplay in the archive at the Margaret Herrick Library of the Academy of Motion Picture Arts and Sciences as well as subtitle translations from the movie itself. I will discuss its narrative structure, not its linguistic or literary qualities. Incidentally, the Herrick collection is the source of many of my script examples and is a wonderful resource for screenwriting research.

We've been here before—sort of. Like Hiccup, twelve-year-old Oskar, the protagonist of *Let the Right One In*, is an outsider. Unlike Hiccup, Oskar's problem is that he is already alienated from his community. He understands he is different and he is not really trying very hard to fit in with them. What he needs is an alternative, and he finds it in Eli, the vampire with her own, very particular needs.[38] Being with Eli will require a significant accommodation with the new reality of the world Oskar has uncovered and has to choose whether or not to accept.

This movie has a similar theme for its protagonist but the story will play out very differently because Oskar's opening attitude to his theme is the opposite of Hiccup's. He is also searching for acceptance, however he begins in a very different story position to Hiccup. At the start of the movie, Oskar has already been rejected by his peers at school. He is damaged and resentful. Oskar isn't looking for a way to be accepted by them. On the contrary, he is looking for revenge and for an alternative to his everyday world in which to find love and to be wanted.

Eli's introduction to Oskar comes as he stabs at a tree with his pocket knife, crying: "Squeal!," a reference to how he was himself bullied that day in school. We also see that he collects newspaper accounts of violent crime. To Eli, Oskar presents as an angry kid who wants to get back at a world he rejects and that rejects him. She can use someone like that. Who knows, she might also like him.

So, like Hiccup, Oskar's theme is also about acceptance but he starts from a very different emotional place. His arc goes on to address the theme through change and ultimate sacrifice in the usual way, only the key positions are reversed. Oskar wants very little from the mundane world, then opens himself to a new relationship—wanting to be accepted and needed by Eli. Finally he sacrifices his connection to the normal world to be with her:

Oskar's arc is reject ➔ *accept* ➔ *sacrifice.*

The thing I find most interesting about the structure of *Let the Right One In* is how it reveals the deeply ambivalent nature of the relationship between Oskar and Eli. Although the film establishes Oskar as a protagonist at the start of the first act (the first down angle), it repeatedly undermines his status by refusing to allow him control of his own story at critical moments. Oskar may be at the center of the movie, but his ability to take charge of his own destiny is often in question.

---

[38] I'm using the feminine pronoun for convenience as Eli presents as a girl. Of course the movie reveals his castration scar later and the novel makes Eli's masculinity clear.

Given how we have just been emphasizing the importance of characters taking charge of their destinies, you might suggest that this is an error on the part of the writer. After all, what kind of a story disenfranchises its hero that way? Well, a horror story for one. Horror stories offer some very particular and different kinds of pleasures to their fans. Many horror fans are happiest when we—and the story's characters—are *un*certain, displaced and vulnerable. A good horror film undermines our ability to feel secure in what we know and about what might happen, even when the story plays to a broadly conventional structural model.

I often refer to this kind of unsettling experience as *unpleasure*.[39] Unpleasure is one of those linguistically impossible words, like *undead*. It is a "both/and" construction, an attempt to reconcile opposites or fantastic non sequiturs through the power of language. For now, think about how words like *unpleasure* and *undead* break boundaries by combining ideas that we don't normally associate with one another. They are words teetering on the very edge of meaning and they illuminate the world in a different, stranger light.

Watching a great horror movie is simultaneously enjoyable and yet kind of… not. We are excited, yet also scared; we are thrilled, yet also disgusted. But that terror and disgust is also an important kind of pleasure. The critic Isabel Christina Pinedo talks about it in terms of bounded or "recreational terror."[40] For example, one of the most powerful experiences we get from a good horror film, along with its characters, is of a profound loss of control. This can feel strangely liberating, almost delirious even when it causes very bad things to happen to our proxies on screen. It is no accident, then, that a horror film might displace its protagonist from control of her story at times.

Lesson Break: Who Owns the Beats?

One way of thinking about how to make who controls your story clear and concrete in your mind—and in the minds of your audience—is to assign ownership of each significant story beat to a character or group. If you lay things out, as in the example below, you can clearly map the flow of power through your story. When you see it laid out like this it can be easier to make decisions and changes based on how you want the relationships in your story to manifest and develop.

---

[39] I am using the term here divorced from its stricter definition in psychoanalysis in relation to the pleasure principle.

[40] Isabel Christina Pinedo, *Recreational Terror: Women and the Pleasures of Horror Film Viewing* (New York: SUNY Press, 1997).

We can compare our first two case studies in terms of who does the work of advancing the story. Following the W model, I have assigned each of the sixteen key story beats (along with the midpoint) to the character whose actions *turn* it and move the story on. (In each case the name of the story's protagonist is italicized for clarity. In addition, when a character other than the protagonist owns a beat in *Let the Right One In* that was owned by Hiccup in *How to Train Your Dragon* I have indicated it in bold.)

How to Train Your Dragon	*Let the Right One In*
First Down Angle	
1. *Hiccup*	Oskar
2. *Hiccup*	Oskar
3. Stoick/*Hiccup* split	Eli
4. Stoick	Eli
First Up Angle	
5. Astrid	Eli
6. *Hiccup*	Oskar
7. *Hiccup*	Oskar
8. *Hiccup*	**Eli**
MID: *Hiccup*	**Eli**
Second Down Angle	
9. *Hiccup*	Oskar
10. *Hiccup*	Oskar
11. Stoick	Oskar
12. Astrid	Lacke
Second Up Angle	
13. *Hiccup*	**Bullies**
14. *Hiccup*	**Bullies**
15. *Hiccup*	**Eli**
16. *Hiccup*	Eli/*Oskar* split

You could argue the toss with a couple in either film, but note that in *How to Train Your Dragon*, the protagonist owns at least 11 beats, maybe 12 to 13 if you count the midpoint. That's most of them. This kind of protagonist-led storytelling is what we have come to expect from mainstream movies. On the other hand in *Let the Right One In*, the protagonist clearly owns only seven beats, less than half the story. Not only does this signal a very different story role for Oskar, but it shows us right off the bat how the same story structure, working through a very similar theme can accommodate enormous variation.

We will go on to discuss the beats in detail as we move forward with the case study. However, the problem of Oskar's status as protagonist, exposed by the beat comparison above, demands further discussion up front. Let's start by picking out a few notable differences in *Let the Right One In*.

1. *Oskar gives up ownership of his key decision beats in act one.*
2. *Eli controls the midpoint.*
3. *Oskar is never in control in the third act* (we can argue about the ending).

What this suggests is that Eli is at least as important as Oskar in terms of moving the story forward. It also begs questions as to the motivation behind their relationship. *We will see that Eli's actions in developing her friendship with Oskar often arise directly out of moments in which her own status and future are called into question.* Typically, the audience is privileged to observe these motivating events, while Oskar is not. In this way, our judgment is engaged vis-à-vis Eli's intentions in a way that his is not—at least not for a time.

Most reviewers talk about the delightfully strange friendship or romance at the heart of this movie. I think the structure is telling us the truth is much darker and more cynical. Eli the vampire needs a new human daywalker and Oskar is little more than the perfect mark. Indeed, an analysis of the late-draft script held in the Herrick archive shows that the tone of the relationship between Eli and Oskar changed significantly between this draft and the finished film. In the screen description in the screenplay, their encounters are played much more clearly on the track of love, or at least affection. In the finished film, however, the tone is more ambivalent and potentially cynical.

                    IMPLIED YOU
        But if she's the active one, Eli's
        the protagonist, right?

                    FRIENDLY ME
        That's a very good question. The
        short answer is no, because the film

takes care to establish Oskar in
that role from the start.

                    IMPLIED YOU
How come?

                    FRIENDLY ME
Lots of reasons, remember that
structure is about control. The
audience wants to feel that control
through the arc of the protagonist.
But sometimes that feeling can come
from appreciating a controlled loss
of control.

                    IMPLIED YOU
Oy. . .

                    FRIENDLY ME
Oh, I didn't write you as Jewish.

                    IMPLIED YOU
Hey, I live in the world.

                    FRIENDLY ME
Not really - but let's move past
it. We still need to identify
with a protagonist in the first place
for that to work. Start with this
open question: which is more fun, in
an unpleasure sort of way, to
identify with the cynical
manipulator or to gradually realize
you are taking the part of the one
being manipulated?

                    IMPLIED YOU
They could both be fun, or "unfun,"
I guess you could say.

> FRIENDLY ME
> But in very different movies. The
> same structure, different ownership.

> IMPLIED YOU
> So the movie asks us to identify
> with Oskar just so it can undermine
> our expectations of him?

> FRIENDLY ME
> Yup, and that's enjoyably unfun.

Now let's see how all this plays out as we work through the first act and angle of *Let the Right One In*.

Act One: First down angle in *Let the Right One In*

The story beats of the first angle of *Let the Right One In* work like this:

A – *Primary exposition*

1. **Story World:** Oskar is an uncomfortable, alienated, twelve-year-old outsider. Full of pent-up violence and rage and completely lost, he gets an interesting new neighbor who seems to be a girl of about his own age.
2. **Desire:** Oskar looks up at Eli's boarded up window—if only my interesting new neighbor were my friend...

B – *Debate*

3. **Hesitation:** Eli tells Oskar she can't be his friend. She's telling the truth (see previous discussion)—and through the rest of the story it will always be part of the truth—but Oskar doesn't realize this. Meanwhile, unknown to Oskar, Eli's daywalker (Håkan) kills a boy but fails to bring his blood home for Eli, who is furious with him.
4. **First Commitment:** Eli is intrigued by Oskar's Rubik's cube puzzle and it breaks some ice between them. Oskar doesn't know that somewhere behind this hesitant connection lies the troubles Eli has been having with Håkan and her blood supply.

Note that in the Debate sequence it is Eli who sets the terms of the budding friendship with Oskar. Oskar wants to be friends and it is up to Eli to Hesitate and make First Commitment based at least in part on the Håkan subplot.

Lesson Break: Subplots and Narration

The subplot that follows Håkan's attempts to service Eli's need for blood has exactly the same story functions as the subplot about the Vikings' fruitless search for the dragons' lair in *How to Train Your Dragon*. It lets the writers do two things simultaneously:

1. We get to cut away from our protagonist. This is, in part, a Hesitation beat by proxy again. Simple, but important because we can sometimes use a break from them. Don't scoff too quickly at the obviousness and simplicity of this statement: *perspective*—and when to change it—is an important consideration for a screenwriter. Remember that it is asking a great deal of writers, actors and audience to stay with the perspective of a single character, however engaging, all the way through a movie. It can work wonderfully of course, but it can also feel limiting. Sometimes you want that closeness, that almost oppressive connection, but it can be an unnecessary burden to impose on your storytelling.
2. In each case the subplot in question allows us to see what the protagonist's developing theme actually *means* for them. In *How to Train Your Dragon* the search subplot shows us the level of disregard the community has for Hiccup and how far he will have to go to gain acceptance. It also shows us how flawed the Vikings' world view is, as we learn more about dragons through Hiccup's adventures. In *Let the Right One In*, the Håkan subplot shows the grim reality of the life Oskar is beginning to desire. It shows us what waits for him in the future if his relationship with Eli develops. In both cases the subplot exposes to the audience an important truth about the protagonist's want and need lines directly after they have been established in the Desire beat.

In both these examples, subplots which follow other characters and have no immediate interaction with the protagonist are still fundamentally bound up with their story. After all, if a subplot *doesn't* have a direct thematic connection with your protagonist, you should be asking yourself: "why am I writing this?" Either turn it creatively to have such relevance or drop it, because right now it is only hurting your storytelling.

Act One of *Winter's Bone*

Winter's Bone provides us with an interesting comparison to the other two stories for two principal reasons. First, it offers its protagonist a different kind of challenge than either *How To Train Your Dragon* or *Let The Right One In*. The story tests its protagonist's will, but does not ask them to change their world view in a straightforward kind of way. Ree knows enough about her culture (her story world) at the start of the movie and her culture performs according to her expectations of it. Subsequently, she learns important plot information, but her fundamental understanding of her goal and her place in the story world is not at stake. Like Hiccup and Oskar, Ree needs to offer herself up as a kind of sacrifice to succeed in addressing her theme. However, this does not occur after a process of second guessing or changing her attitudes (accept, reject, sacrifice), rather it is a final demonstration of her always implacable drive to find her father and take care of her family.

Second, *Winter's Bone* pits Ree against her culture. The closed, dangerous, clannish, criminal culture of poor, white, rural Missouri is the antagonist. In setting up this structural opposition the writers, Granik and Rosellini, take risks with their storytelling because there are times when the culture simply shuts Ree out and denies her progress. In other words there are times when the plot just stops. Ree has to rely on friends and relatives and other contacts to get her unstuck. In this way *Winter's Bone* also takes important story beats out of the immediate control of its protagonist, but for very different reasons than we have seen in *Let the Right One In*.

Specifically, at three points in the story: the Progress beat in the first up angle; the Revelation beat at the end of act two; and the Plan beat immediately following at the opening of act three, other characters "rescue" Ree from moments of stasis. Some critics and figures from the screenwriting industry have suggested that this is a flaw in the movie's structure. For example, William M. Akers (author of *Your Screenplay Sucks*) blogged that "...it's a MOVIE, not real life. They should have figured out a way for her to *help herself* out of the hole she's in, in a way that we would believe." (Italics in original.) I disagree, and we will consider the cases as they come up.

Winter's Bone uses the same underlying story structure as our other key case studies, but it treats its protagonist's journey in a very different way. Also it "breaks the rules," according to a narrow definition of "the rules." It certainly pushes at the boundaries of our W model of story structure, but let's see how that works out in practice.

Theme of *Winter's Bone*

- The story of *Winter's Bone* is all about *responsibility*.
- The manifestation of this in the story is *determination*.
- The manifestation of this in the plot is *dedication*.

- In plot terms: *Ree needs to find her father in a world where helping is snitching.* See her problem?

As the de facto head of her household, Ree needs to take the *responsibility* to find her father. If she can't find him her family will lose their house and their land. She is already used to being the responsible one—as Primary Exposition makes abundantly clear. She may have fantasies of escaping to the army but, here and now, she is on the spot. What will be tested is her commitment to her responsibilities. The story tests her emotional and psychological *determination*—her stoicism and implacability in the face of increasing danger—and it tests her *dedication*—her intellectual commitment to solving the problem. What the story tests, therefore, is the depth to which Ree accepts her responsibility—and it tests her to breaking point.

Act One: First down angle in *Winter's Bone*

The story beats of the first angle of *Winter's Bone* work like this:

A – *Primary exposition*

1. **Story World:** Ree Dolly is a teenage girl growing up dirt poor in the Missouri Ozarks. Her mother is mentally unstable and so, in her father's absence, it is Ree who has to be the adult and take responsibility for the household—such as it is—and for her younger siblings. *This beat establishes responsibility as the theme of the movie.*
2. **Desire:** Ree wants a future, but the future her school sees for her is a choice between motherhood and the military. At school she signs up for an interview to join the US Army. Back at home, the local sheriff turns up looking for Ree's father. He is due in court (for cooking meth) and has put up the family home and its adjacent woodland as bond. This is the inciting incident, because now Ree needs to find her father and get him to court in order to keep a roof over their heads.

B – *Debate*

3. **Hesitation:** Ree goes to see a school friend, Gail, who is now married with a baby. She wants a lift south, where she heard her father might be. Her friend's husband refuses to let them use his truck and Ree guilts her friend for being weakened by marriage. The Hesitation comes from the world and specifically from Gail (who will become the focus of the B Story later on), not from Ree.

4. **First Commitment:** Out of other options, Ree visits a succession of relatives and connections in the area, each one more dangerous than the last. This is her First Commitment. She begins with her scary uncle Teardrop and then, despite his warnings not to, tries unsuccessfully to get information from her father's criminal associate, Little Arthur, and the local criminal clan leader, Thump Milton. Ree lives in a scary world and nobody will help her. (For more on this, see the plot paralysis case study.)

Case Study: Plot "Paralysis" in *Winter's Bone*

At the end of the first act and angle of *Winter's Bone*, Ree has already taken significant risks in trying to find her father, Jessup. However now the story world has temporarily shut her investigation down. Nobody will talk to her. Nobody will help her—neither her friends, nor her kin—other than to offer her a drink and maybe a joint "for your walk." She has done all she can and, unless something—or someone—relents, she can do no more.

In conventional screenwriting terms, this is a risky move because it takes control of the story away from its protagonist. However, we have already learned from our analysis of *Let the Right One In* that sometimes loss of control can be a good thing in storytelling. Here the pleasures of structure are not engaged by evoking the unpleasure of a horror film experience, however, but rather by the sense that this is a story world that works according to its own logic and its own pacing. It doesn't obey the rules of strict narrative economy, but it does respond to stimulus in its own good time and Ree has already given it plenty of stimulus.

At the break into act two Ree's story world slow cooks the results of her determination and serves up a suitably guilted B Story best friend who has found the courage to take her husband's truck without permission. Now the story can move on. Remember though, this wouldn't have happened if Ree hadn't berated her friend for a coward. The result just happened down the road a ways. In the interim, we have seen Ree's frustration and shared her sense of impotence in the face of a seemingly uncaring world—and we will do so again as the world repeatedly shuts her out.

Next time it will be uncle Teardrop who comes to help. The final time we will see the world in full tilt as those responsible for Jessup's death decide helping Ree is now safer than leaving her to make even more waves. Each time there is a gap between Ree kicking against the constraints of her culture and the culture inching in her direction. To my mind, this is a powerful expression of the strength of the antagonistic force she faces. It is also a structural choice that speaks to a kind of realism that William Akers doesn't approve of. To my mind it is strong writing, not weak, because it positions us firmly with Ree. We feel like very small beans in a nasty world. The uniqueness of *Winter's Bone* lies, in part, in its evocation of such an inimical story world. Its very immovability plays directly to the character of our protagonist and the nature both of her quest and her theme.

As a general rule in conventional screenwriting Akers has a point. You should be careful about following the model of recurring plot paralysis in *Winter's Bone* as if it would fit any story and any story world. I picked the movie as a case study because it takes risks in its storytelling however. *Winter's Bone* shows you the license a fully developed story world buys you in terms of pushing the paradigm. Just remember you have to pay for that license each time.

Questions to ask *yourself* as you write act one

Story world

Q: Is my story world both essential and detailed?

Q: Am I using it to illustrate (show, don't tell) or reflect, in different ways, the theme and story of the film?

Q: Is my story world the perfect place in which protagonist(s) must live and struggle?

Desire

Q: Have I written about what my protagonist lacks, wants and needs?

Q: Do those desires link to my theme?

Q: Are the desires of my protagonist(s) clearly illustrated by the first crisis of the *inciting incident*?

Hesitation

Q: Is the challenge of my story important enough that it gives my protagonist(s) pause before taking action?

Q: Have I shown how other significant characters view my protagonist?

Q: Does the supporting cast believe my protagonist can succeed?

Q: How do I show their positions and how does this set up their story roles?

First commitment

Q: Is my protagonist's first commitment realistic or unrealistic and how do I show how far they will have to journey or develop?

Q: Upon what kind of self-knowledge or understanding of the story world is their first, contingent decision to accept the challenge of the story based?

Q: How am I planning that this will change as the story progresses?

Questions to ask *your first draft* of act one

After you have finished a first draft of your screenplay, re-read your first act and ask the following questions:

Story world

Q: Have I shown my story world in enough detail for eloquent exposition?

Q: Have I overloaded the start of my film with unnecessary expositional detail?

Q: What expositional or narrational techniques have I used in introducing my story world and its protagonist(s)?

Q: Is there any way I can use more techniques and examples to say what I now say through fewer techniques (more show, less tell)?

Q: Does the opening parallel between the Story World beat at the start and the Resonance beat at the end offer satisfactory resolution in terms of illustrating the effects of the change my story has brought about?

Q: How can I write all of this just as effectively with fewer words and in fewer pages?

Desire

Q: Is it clear what my protagonist's attitude is to my theme?

Q: Does the parallel between the Desire and Resolution beats satisfactorily resolve my protagonist's story arc and theme?

Q: How can I write all of this just as effectively with fewer words and in fewer pages?

Hesitation

Q: Have I set up the potential of the opposition—the antagonistic force—in my story effectively and does it play clearly to theme?

Q: Does the parallel between the Hesitation and Pushback beats express the enormity of the challenge of the story?

Q: How can I write all of this just as effectively with fewer words and in fewer pages?

First commitment

Q: Does my protagonist's first commitment seem brave enough, or foolhardy enough, or ignorantly optimistic enough—or just plain *big enough* in story terms?

Q: Does the parallel between the First Commitment and Plan beats express just how far my protagonist had to struggle or develop to get to the point where they could see their way clear to resolving their challenge and their theme?

Q: How can I write all of this just as effectively with fewer words and in fewer pages?

Act Two: From avoidance to commitment

Second acts are about character change and we can see that change working through two angles.

The tone of the *first up angle* in a conventional screenplay is usually relatively positive. It charts the protagonist doing the best she can to address her problem without making a major, irreversible commitment to the resolution of her story. For all its progress, therefore, for your character and story the up angle to the midpoint is actually all about *avoidance*. Typically, your protagonist is avoiding making a life or death, all or nothing commitment to change and just trying to "do it on the cheap." This angle also represents the antagonistic force pushing back against the progress your protagonist has begun to make, so that a committed character has to take bigger risks. This is the case with *Winter's Bone*, in which it is the story world doing its own avoidance of Ree and her inconvenient need to find her father, Jessup. All Ree is personally avoiding is the final step of going and forcing Thump Milton's hand.

In the W, the *midpoint* is the fulcrum of the whole story. It is the moment after which nothing will or can be the same again. That's because the pressures of the previous angle have pushed your protagonist to the point where she can't just skate by on her initial skillset anymore. Something happens which forces a second decision, a second and deeper commitment. The midpoint is where your protagonist jumps into real danger. Of course that danger may well be emotional rather than physical.

After the midpoint, movies are typically organized so that their protagonists can't climb back to where they were before they "jumped." They can only try and move forward toward a resolution. Think of the second half of the act as being like diving into a fast flowing river. Events and revelations flow down this angle faster and faster towards and then through crisis. Think rapids before a waterfall. All the while your protagonist is trying desperately to keep her head above water. Without a total effort—emotional, physical, moral, intellectual, spiritual, in whatever combination is appropriate to your story—she will metaphorically sink and drown. So where the first half of the act was about avoidance, the *second down angle* of the W is all about increasing *commitment.* Your key task when writing second acts is to design and deliver the plot and story mechanisms to enable that move from avoidance to commitment in your protagonist.

As a shorthand rule, in mainstream and mainstream-indie movies the move from avoidance through commitment in the second act takes the protagonist from being (kind of) willing but completely unable to resolve their story to being more self-aware and determined and potentially capable of doing so. Their experiences in the act have changed them. At the very least, in the case of your basic square-jawed lunk of an action hero, the act has helped them to develop new skills, allies and information without which the pesky aliens, terrorists, drug pushers or zombies would win the day. At the end of act two they should still face a hard struggle— otherwise there's not much point in having an act three. Other constructions that track act two progress, depending on genre and story type might include: from *ignorance* to *knowledge,* from *incompetence* to *competence* or from *unprepared* to *prepared.* Some emphasize plot, others story, but they are all about change. Even so, we should be able to see a chink of light at the end of the tunnel.

For now let's focus on the first half of the act, the first up angle. Once again, we will focus on *How to Train Your Dragon*, bringing in supporting case study examples along the way. We will catch up with both *Let the Right One In* and *Winter's Bone* after we reach the midpoint.

Act Two: First up angle (avoidance)

At the start of this angle in *How to Train Your Dragon*, Hiccup is certainly willing to *fit in* with the rest of the Vikings. He still sees Viking cultural norms as something he should aspire to. This act will see him *learn from experience* (remember: show, don't tell) to question those norms from the ground up, but he's not there yet. He still craves *acceptance*, but he has just learned that the one sure-fire way of getting it—killing dragons—is closed off to him. That means he is at an impasse. His *want* line (dragon killing and dates) has been knocked off track and his *need* line (acceptance) is looking nervously over its shoulder as the wreckage recedes into the middle distance. Throughout the angle, Hiccup will be avoiding the chance to kill dragons while his burgeoning knowledge of them brings him inexorably closer to having to do so in front of the whole village.

You remember his want line: *kill a dragon* ➔ *get a girlfriend*? Now that the first step can't happen, all the other steps seem impossible. Whenever all seems lost a good writer digs back into what makes her protagonist unique to find the solution. Remember that in so many ways *character is structure* so, when a character is in trouble in your story, structure must come to the rescue.

Here, then is the professional screenwriters' solution to Hiccup's predicament: *If Hiccup is denied his want line by his difference, he must use that difference to find a new path.* This is a simple and elegant solution. Difference haunts Hiccup but it is his very uniqueness that will lead to his ultimate redemption.

This is a classic Hollywood story move. Like all the other classic Hollywood story moves we know and love it feels comfortingly familiar yet still charming, apposite and poignant in the hands of good writers. It doesn't just apply to Hollywood movies however. After all, whatever kind of movie you are writing, why are we interested in your protagonist if she isn't somehow unique and different?

The story beats of the *first up angle* work like this:

C – Early progress

5. **B Story:** Initially, Hiccup fails both at dragon training and at making friends with Astrid. Meanwhile, Astrid subtly announces her own uniqueness. She is the focus of the B Story. She and Hiccup will need each other before the end of the act but right now they couldn't be further apart. This initial distance makes the arc of their relationship *fun*.

6. **Progress:** Hiccup's burgeoning friendship with the Night Fury teaches him new truths. He uses this knowledge to find a new route to success in

the dragon training arena. He also shows his engineering skills as he develops a prosthetic tail and a riding harness for the Night Fury. Hiccup learns to train his dragon and in so doing is himself trained into new ways of thinking. Astrid isn't liking him any better, but at least she's curious about him now and, in terms of the B Story, that's a move in the right direction. Just.

D – Raising stakes

7. **Challenge:** Hiccup finds he needs to take greater risks to finish his harness and help his new dragon friend. This brings his heretical actions closer to exposure. Astrid's suspicions mount.
8. **Decision:** Hiccup wins the dragon training. That success earns him the right to kill a dragon in public, which we know he can't do. He decides to leave before all is revealed, but Astrid's B Story brings things to a head just in time for the Midpoint. . .

How to Train Your Dragon promises us adventure. Specifically it promises us a relationship between a boy and a dragon. We have been sold a structural premise by trailers and ads and now we want the pleasure of seeing that concept in action. We have had to wait through the first act, but now it is time for Hiccup to do what the title of the movie promised and to *train his dragon.* The first angle of act two is where that marketing debt is paid in full by story structure and it starts right away. This is what Blake Snyder called "the promise of the premise" in his entertaining screenwriting manual *Save The Cat!*[41]

Well, the portcullis on the training arena is already being raised, so let's see how it all comes together.

C – Early progress

This half-angle shows how your protagonist can take encouraging first steps in the direction of resolving their story and theme. They haven't moved far along the arc of change that will make resolution possible, but they will likely do enough to encourage themselves to keep going when things get tougher.

5. *B Story*

Cut—we are in the arena: "Welcome to dragon training!" It's a lovely, economical curtain-raiser into the new act and angle that gets right to the

---

[41] Blake Snyder, *Save The Cat! The Last Book on Screenwriting You'll Ever Need* (Studio City CA: Michael Wise Productions, 2005).

heart of Hiccup's challenge. Astrid leads the teenage wannabe dragon trainers inside. They are all pumped up and keen, apart from Hiccup of course. There's lots of bravado to go round, but Astrid shows her difference from the rest of the teenage Viking pack here, saying to herself: "Take a deep breath. No turning back." Again this is good economical writing. We know she is going to be important because we get early access to her more complex feelings. Already, in the first few seconds of the angle, she has begun to carve out her own uniqueness. She is gung-ho about the dragon training but, unlike the other kids she is also serious and self-aware. Dragon training is not a game for Astrid. It's about duty to your people, not about being tough-for-tough's-sake.

We like her for her introspection and for covering up her nerves. We appreciate her seriousness. We mark her as mature, a cut above the other Viking teenagers, including Hiccup in many ways. After all, Astrid already has higher ideals. At this point, all Hiccup wants is to fit in and get a little romance. We begin to see why Hiccup likes her, even though we don't yet know how they will get together. More to the point we can't see how it could ever happen, although somewhere in the back of our minds we are already humming: "Matchmaker, Matchmaker, make me a match..."

Back in the arena, Gobber tells the young Vikings that whoever does best in training wins the chance to kill their first dragon in the arena in front of the entire village. Then he releases a small grumpy dragon: "I believe in learning on the job." Chaos ensues and Astrid is the only one who is fully focused and who has the talent to see the challenge through. The others fail because they bicker, try to hit on Astrid or rely on theoretical, book-learned knowledge while losing track of the practical test at hand.

We are given a typically Hollywood B Story-beat moment during this combat, when Hiccup and Astrid are the last two Vikings standing. Hiccup turns to her and says, lamely: "Now I guess it's just you and me, huh?" Astrid, who has been focusing on the dragon, darts away just in time to avoid it, saying: "Nope, just you."

This dialogue formally opens the movie's B Story account. The lines are on the nose—they *speak the beat*—but, once again, the moment is full of action and humor so we go along with it. They may not realize it yet, but by the end of the act Hiccup and Astrid will have become a "you and me." Right now all we see is the gap.

At the end of this short beat we have also had our plot lesson of the previous angle confirmed through action. Hiccup has no hope of passing dragon training the conventional way. What he can do we begin to discover in the next beat. We get there off Gobber's line: "Remember, a dragon will always... always go for the kill."

Lesson Break: B Story as Story Beat and as Subplot

The second act of a conventional screenplay is typically bounded by the establishment and transformational resolution of the B Story. Setting up a B Story (a romance, friendship, mentoring relationship or similar) is not merely a convention or a convenience. It isn't simply a love-interest disconnected from the rest of the movie, for example. A well-written B Story should enable the resolution of the entire story. That moment of vital intersection usually happens later, at the end of act two. Although the relationship itself may continue to the end of the movie, the end of act two is typically where it plays its most important story role.

We will expect our investment in the B Story relationship to pay off. If it doesn't carry adequate story weight we will be disappointed and feel something was amiss. Sometimes more than one subplot share B Story functions, as with Gail and Teardrop in *Winter's Bone* (see later). But even here, the set-up and payoff still occur at the appropriate moments in the story. In between the importance of one character wanes as that of the other waxes.

Each story beat in your screenplay should have its corresponding beat—remember the ring and parallelism? Sometimes their correspondence will be obvious and up front. Other times it may be more subtle in the way it signifies character or story development. The one constant is that parallelism sets down markers for change. Thinking about a screenplay as an exercise in planned parallelism helps you to embed character change—the transformational arc if you will—in every part of your story.

In movies like *How to Train Your Dragon* we understand we are being fed a familiar story formula. Our pleasure is engaged by how imaginatively that formula will be worked—because formulas can be fun, remember? This is especially true at moments when we are willing a very unlikely story event to happen. Story challenges like this make us even more deeply invested in the writers' problem solving skills. Of course the collision of unlikely partners, whether in the A Story or the B Story, is familiar territory from romantic and other comedies (think of *When Harry Met Sally* or *Knocked Up*) and many other movie relationships, not least Hiccup and Astrid.

Goals of the B Story beat

The B Story beat typically has two goals, although they are not always played as being of equal importance:

1. First we need to start testing our protagonist's resolve as well as their opening skillset. This is part of the incremental function of the beat within an *angle-long* arc leading up to a second commitment at the Midpoint.
2. Secondly we establish a relationship in the B Story which will offer essential support for our protagonist's *act-long* transformational arc. It will finally pay off in the Revelation beat at the end of act two.

Once again, therefore, when we look at the way a B Story works in a conventional screenplay we are thinking about corresponding beats connected by overlapping or parallel arcs. Incidents can have multiple meanings and stories can do more than one thing at a time after all. Here are those mini arcs as an example. Note that 1 is followed by 2 but that 3 encompasses both 1 and 2:

EITHER:

1. First testing arc: beats 5 through 8. Pushes the protagonist to a deeper commitment at the Midpoint.
2. Second testing arc: beats 9 through 12. Tests this deeper commitment to the utmost, stripping away the last vestiges of the old protagonist and revealing (or at least equipping) protagonist 2.0.

OR:

3. Act Two transformational arc: beats 5 through 12. Transforms the protagonist into a tool for story resolution, supported and bookended by events in the B Story.

B STORY – *first testing arc* – **MIDPOINT** – *second testing arc* **–REVELATION**
---------*act two transformational arc*---------

In *How to Train Your Dragon* the first testing arc plays through a different kind of parallelism. We have two tracks: that of Hiccup's progress in the official Viking dragon training; and a parallel track following his personal investigation into the true nature of dragons. The lessons learned in the second track enable him to succeed in the first, by unconventional means. However, success also brings him towards an inevitable collision with his culture.

Viking dragon training ➜

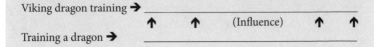

Training a dragon ➜

This is manifest, in the first instance, in Astrid. Their B Story relationship measures Hiccup's progress through Astrid's increased attention to him up to the Midpoint and in her friendship and increasing commitment to him after it. The emotional arc that bends her towards him plays through dismissal, to anger and frustration and finally towards assistance and the transformation of their relationship into a budding romance.

Case Study: B Story Beats

Easy A – perfect bad timing for the B Story

In *Easy A* (2010, scr. Bert V. Royal), thanks to a lie she told to get out of a camping trip, virginal high school girl Olive is reputed to have had sex with a college guy. Now her gay friend wants her to pretend to have sex with him at a party to "out" him as straight and help him back off the homophobic school bullies. Olive agrees (First Commitment) and, right after the pretend—but very public—encounter, she runs into her old crush Todd at the same party. Not the best circumstances in which to rekindle an old flame, but the perfect context in which to set up the movie's B Story.

Oblivion – the B Story arrives with a shock

In the post-apocalyptic science fiction movie *Oblivion* (2013, scr. Karl Gajdusek and Michael Arndt (as Michael deBruyn)), Tech 49 Jack Harper has been having visions of a strange, yet somehow familiar woman. When he investigates the wreckage of a spacecraft and finds intact stasis chambers he is shocked to discover that one of them contains a woman, Julia, who is the match for his visions. This discovery initiates the B Story as Jack begins to question his past, his identity and the truth about the story world. As a consequence he learns that he is a clone, employed by an alien race to protect its assets as it scavenges the Earth. Without this encounter with Julia he would not have been pushed into investigation and would not have learned the truth. Nor would he have been in a position to do something about it and save what remains of the Earth.

Note that the important subplot relationship between Jack and the head of the old-Earther resistance (the "Scavs"), Malcolm Beech, is not the B Story, even though it embodies important persuasive and explanatory functions. Indeed Beech takes on many of the conventional functions of the B Story in the second half of the movie. But his character is introduced almost an hour into the film in order to precipitate the Midpoint. His purpose is entirely part of the resolution: they have a nuke and the drone to carry it but they need Jack to program the drone to destroy the alien base-ship. Julia, on the other hand, is linked to Jack's emotional journey from the start and from the B Story beat in particular. In the end, Jack sacrifices himself for the greater good, but also for the chance to save her and somehow to continue their relationship "after death" through another of his clones.

                    IMPLIED YOU
          At the start of act two of
          Temptation, Lucy is in love, with a
          big problem. Act one story tasks:
          check.

                    FRIENDLY ME
          You know what I think about the
          scale of her problem though?

                    IMPLIED YOU
          Yeah. But now she goes to her best
          friend, Katya: "I just met this guy,
          but. . ."

                    FRIENDLY ME
          Good. B Story is on. What's Katya's
          attitude to relationships?

                    IMPLIED YOU
          I don't know. She's for them, let's
          say?

                    FRIENDLY ME
          You need to know this. Katya –
          and everyone else in your story
          world for that matter – isn't
          just a sounding board. She needs
          attitudes and those attitudes need
          to pay off in terms of both story
          and plot.

                    IMPLIED YOU
Right. I'll work on it. Making a
note.

                    FRIENDLY ME
Remember, if she's a conventional B
Story character, Katya is going to
be a catalyst for resolving the A
Story. Her arc is to help Lucy get
her act together, so she needs to be
a well-developed character in her
own right.

                    IMPLIED YOU
What you're saying is: if I don't
know what her first reaction will be
to the deceit, then I don't know
what I'm doing here.

                    FRIENDLY ME
Look, maybe she tells Lucy: "Don't
tell him. Go for it anyway. Love will
find a way." On the other hand, maybe
she says: "Tell him right now. Either
it will be over before you get hurt
or it'll work out." Both speak her
attitude to trust and romance. There
are lots of options, but they direct
your relationships in different ways.
They all speak to the opinions your
characters have about love and
especially to your theme of trust.
Together they build a kind of network
of thematic meaning.

                    IMPLIED YOU
Yeah. Trust. I get it.

                    FRIENDLY ME
By the way, I'm not sure Temptation
is the right title for this story.

```
                    IMPLIED YOU
          She's tempted by love to deceive
          him. It speaks to trust.

                    FRIENDLY ME
          If you didn't know that, is that
          what the title would mean to you? To
          me it sounds more like a dodgy
          erotic thriller about infidelity and
          murder.

                    IMPLIED YOU
          You have a B Movie mind.

                    FRIENDLY ME
          Titles can be key. First impressions
          do count. Ask your friends - you do
          have friends? Just asking. Ask them
          what they think a movie with that
          title is about.

                    IMPLIED YOU
          Ok, ok, I'll think about the title.
```

6. Progress

This is by far the longest beat in *How to Train Your Dragon*. The writers take their time drawing threads together and developing the relationship between Hiccup and the dragon promised in the trailer. Once again they use a parallel narrative structure to do this, working between dragon training and training a dragon. This allows the long beat to flow through multiple channels, using different kinds of dynamic action.

Although this beat runs long in terms of pages and minutes, it still feels tight and controlled. That is because the story is always being driven by the twin emotional and intellectual drivers emerging from the relationship between Hiccup and his dragon, "Toothless." Emotionally, Hiccup is changing and growing and filling with joy as his friendship with Toothless develops. Intellectually, he is learning the truth of the world and bending his mind towards harnessing that truth—both literally and metaphorically.

The beat begins as Hiccup replies to Gobber's assertion that dragons always go for the kill with a question of his own: "So why didn't you?" But he's not talking to Gobber now. The cut from beats 5 to 6 (B Story to Progress) has taken him straight to the forest, where he is observing the trapped Night Fury and reflecting. Hiccup has realized for the first time that what he is being taught at home doesn't match up to his experience of a wild dragon. This is the start of Hiccup's move in this angle from conventional failure to unconventional success and it begins with a simple but revealing question. Indeed, one of the most eloquent markers of his difference is that *Hiccup is the Viking who asks questions.*

There will be many more questions to follow, but he is already uncertain about the received wisdom of his culture. Without this he would never be able to find his own path. This is the core of the message the film is offering to its audience members. The movie's theme is not just about *fitting in*, it is about fitting in on your own terms. We are being persuaded that *accommodation* does not require simple conformity or acquiescence. On the contrary, it can be a much more radical proposition: transforming the culture to meet your vision of a better world. If you need to transform your culture, questioning orthodoxies is a good place to start. Of course Hiccup doesn't understand where this is going yet, but he'll catch up to the full significance of his story soon enough.

Hiccup watches the dragon trying to fly out of the hollow. He is taking notes (there's his difference again) and realizes that it has an injured tail. Hiccup and Toothless share a look.

The Progress beat is all about our protagonist showing potential. Hiccup understands the dragon's problem; now what is he going to do about it?

Back in the village, Gobber gives the trainees a copy of the *Dragon Manual* to study. The trainees all blow off the reading, apart from Astrid and Fishlegs. They have already read it (of course) and Hiccup is left alone with the book by the cool kids (and one other trainee, Fishlegs). He starts to read.

As he studies, we are given another catalogue of the dangers of dragonkind. This is a Viking book, so it addresses Viking concerns. Thus it documents dragon types only according to their supposed propensity for extreme violence. When Hiccup reaches the section on Night Furies he finds it empty apart from a predictably dire warning: "Never engage this dragon. Your only chance, hide and pray it does not find you."

Hiccup already knows better than this and he shows both his audacity and his intent by drawing an accurate picture of the Night Fury on the empty page in the Dragon Manual. This is where the narrative thread about Hiccup retraining his own people begins. The movie's title may be *How to Train Your Dragon*, but in the process it spends a lot of time showing us how to train your Hiccup.

Cut—and we segue briefly to check in with Stoick and the rest on their dragon hunt. The longships enter the fog banks at Hellheim's Gate. This is the dragons' home territory. We are given this scene just in case we had forgotten what the other Vikings were up to and so that we will recognize the location (foreshadowing) when Hiccup goes there himself, later in the story. It will also resonate in the next scene when Astrid reveals her motivation to succeed in dragon training.

Cut—and we're back with Hiccup in dragon training. He messes up by asking Gobber about Night Furies when he should have been watching out for today's dragon. Astrid beats the dragon and turns on Hiccup. This is where she tells us why she is taking things so seriously: "Is this some kind of a joke to you? Our parents' war is about to become ours. Figure out which side you're on."

Thus the B Story checks in with the A Story and reminds us where things stand between them right now. We are going to get further B Story updates in every beat of the act. This is because we learn about how our characters feel at any given point through their interactions with other characters.

In plots change is manifested through action, but in stories change is manifest through relationships.

This particular update shows us that Hiccup and Astrid are just as far apart as ever. At least now we know what Hiccup will have to do to get her on side. Astrid takes duty seriously so Hiccup will have to transform her understanding of her duty—for which read the nature of dragons—to win her over. Once again, this is progress in B Story terms because Astrid is actually engaging with Hiccup, albeit negatively, and she is doing so in relation to the B Story's theme.

Let's play it out briefly: if Astrid were the movie's protagonist her theme would be duty. *As she is a supporting character, her engagement with the movie's theme of acceptance emerges from her sense of duty.* To be accepted as a Viking you do your duty as a Viking. Thus, she will support Hiccup—she will *accept* him—if she can be brought to understand how her sense of duty aligns with his new vision of their world. This is another example of the same kind of logical and elegant story construction we saw with Hiccup's difference becoming his strength.

Now this long beat really takes off. We cut back and forth between Hiccup and the Night Fury and the Viking training as Hiccup's experiences in one arena help him succeed in the other. To start with, Hiccup feeds his new friend. They bond over shared fish, and play together. Finally Toothless lets Hiccup touch his face. All the while Hiccup has been designing a prosthetic tail to help the dragon fly again.

Back in the village, Gobber tells war stories round the fire: "If it can't fly, it can't get away. A downed dragon is a dead dragon." Pressure to help the Night Fury escape grows and Hiccup sneaks away, lost in thought. Astrid makes to follow—who is this guy? But in the end she returns to the confederacy of idiots. She couldn't tell you why she is intrigued yet, but she just made the first teeny tiny move towards Hiccup in the B Story.

Hiccup designs and builds the prosthetic tail—remember, engineering is part of his starting skillset. In fact he's making Progress. He fixes the new tail to the Night Fury and gets an impromptu free flight. It ends badly and they crash because the dragon can't control the device. What if Hiccup makes a harness and flies it himself?

The rest of the beat sees Hiccup refining and flight testing his harness designs while using the dragon lore he is learning from being around the Night Fury to win in the arena. He discovers that dragons are scared of eels and uses that to his advantage. Likewise he finds they love a certain type of grass and pacifies a dragon with a handful. With each victory more and more people come to watch the dragon training—Progress. In the B Story, as Hiccup is becoming famous Astrid is becoming furious, but her focus is directed at him.

Things are going to get harder in the next beat, but we have now spent a good part of the first up angle witnessing and enjoying the heroic potential of the kid we all but wrote off only a couple of story beats back.

Lesson Break: Complexity Through Multiple Perspectives

This lesson is about the importance of complexity in any kind of storytelling. Note that complexity does not necessarily equate to wordiness, long windedness, or general pretentiousness. Indeed we have already praised *How to Train Your Dragon* for marrying complexity with admirable narrative economy.

On the contrary, complexity in screenwriting often means allowing us to engage with a narrative proposition from many angles or perspectives. You will remember that our earlier case study of *The King's Speech* spoke directly to this. We are going to encounter an idea a number of times in a script anyway (parallelism), so use each instance to deepen and broaden its significance to your characters and story world. In other words: don't repeat, develop. We see this at work in *How to Train You Dragon* with the little lessons on the nature of dragons.

These lessons allow the filmmakers to establish and reinforce Viking culture in the minds of the audience. They build our knowledge of the different types of dragon *from one perspective*. They also establish the importance of education within the story. The lessons have their own educational arc, their story function moving from simplicity to complexity, from pedagogy to andragogy, from the informational to the discursive.

In the beginning, the lessons are part of a simple job of primary exposition: look, different types of dragon. By this point in the story the point is less about the dragons and more about the inadequacy of the lesson itself. This duplicates in miniature the larger lesson we are learning with Hiccup about the failings of his culture. Think of a movie story a little like a matryoshka—one of those Russian nesting dolls. A well-written screenplay will work in the same way and to the same ends at different levels of magnification. Part of the fun of writing—one of the pleasures of structure—is to add richness and complexity in this way.

Remember, *How to Train Your Dragon* may be an animated family adventure movie. It may be about a misfit kid trying to fit in with his friends. It is also about a budding public intellectual reimagining and rewriting his own culture. Most importantly, it is all that and fun too.

Case Study: Progress Beats

Whip It – progress in sport is progress in life (and maybe love)

The Progress beat in *Whip It* (2009, scr. Shauna Cross, from her novel *Derby Girl*) sees oddball teenager Bliss play in her first Roller Derby match. Bliss has joined the team partly as an act of resistance against her mother, an ex-beauty queen who is pushing Bliss to enter pageants. Before the game, her teammates give her a gift of a mouth guard, a sign of acceptance (Progress). Her coach puts Bliss in for the first time at the end of the match, but she scores and shakes off the pain of a nasty check to do so (Progress). At the party after the match Bliss gets some interest from the cool local rock singer (Progress) before her best friend's drunkenness derails her thoughts of amorous adventures for that night at least. Things are going to get a lot tougher, both emotionally and physically, but for now she's making Progress in this exciting new aspect of her young life.

Safety Not Guaranteed – contradictory progress through deceit and affection

Darius, a disillusioned magazine intern, is investigating Kenneth, a man who claims he can travel through time in the indie movie *Safety Not*

Guaranteed (2012, scr. Derek Connolly). Darius poses as a potential travel companion to win his trust. In the Progress beat she undergoes a range of training exercises (Progress) with Kenneth, to get an angle for the story she and her colleagues are working on. The exercises are Kenneth's way of building trust. He is impressed with her performance (Progress) and it looks increasingly likely that he will take her on as a traveling companion. Darius has already made Progress in getting close to the paranoid guy, but now she starts to like him also. This is another kind of Progress that complicates things in the short term. Of course, although she is playing it straight at this point, Darius assumes that Kenneth is just a harmless crackpot. However, the Progress she makes in this beat ends up guaranteeing her a most *un*safe, but incredibly exciting exit from the present tense of the story at the end of the movie.

                    IMPLIED YOU
          Progress in Temptation is all about
          Lucy and Bryce getting closer, right?

                    FRIENDLY ME
          But don't forget your plotting in
          the story world. What else is going
          on in Lucy's life? How does it
          interface with the love story? What
          else is Lucy doing to make progress
          in her life? In what ways is that
          progress contingent on the success
          of her relationship with Bryce? In
          what other ways can you play to your
          theme of trust? And so on.

                    IMPLIED YOU
          Maybe Lucy's boss meets Bryce. She
          is so impressed that now she thinks
          better of flaky Lucy. Now Lucy seems
          - aha: trustworthy. Now she's up for
          a big promotion?

                    FRIENDLY ME
          Yes, this could be a Sandra Bullock
          movie. . .

                    IMPLIED YOU
Yeah, I know. I was thinking she
just became Darrin in <u>Bewitched</u>. But
that's the kind of thing you mean?

                    FRIENDLY ME
In general terms. But think about
her family. Think about her personal
and even her professional goals more
deeply. How is Bryce supporting her
progress as a whole person? How can
you set up this relationship being
the solution to the problem of Lucy?
Ouch. I really just suggested that.

                    IMPLIED YOU
Yeah. Sexist much!

                    FRIENDLY ME
Ah, but listen. Yes, cliché option
one is the dodgy "you complete me"
take, but cliché option two is her
learning not to invest in her
relationships that way. So you set
her up for the fall and she grows
from the experience. I know that
also sounds reductive, but that's
where your good writing comes in.

                    IMPLIED YOU
That could be the indie take: Men
bad. Irony good. Me find manic-pixie-
dream-boy. Me quirky. Me have quirky
hair. Me have quirky shirt. Him
shirt match him wallpaper.

                    FRIENDLY ME
Alright, alright. Look, I'm just
spit-balling illustrations of how
life and love can intersect in the
storytelling. Great dramatic

> relationships affect their lovers'
> story worlds as well. Romeo's and
> Juliet's romance impacts the world
> of the Montagues and Capulets,
> right? Discover a nuanced solution,
> but link your story and your plot as
> you do it.

D – Raising stakes

This half-angle pushes your protagonist out of their comfort zone and forces them to make a more meaningful Second Commitment to change and action at the Midpoint. Your task here is to help the audience understand that things got more serious for them and their choices not only have greater consequence in their story world but also demonstrate personal development. One way of thinking about the story weight of the Second Commitment is that it turns a protagonist into a heroine or hero.

7. Challenge

The previous beat took a big chunk out of the angle's running time so now we start to accelerate towards the midpoint decision in this shorter half-angle. The Challenge beat is signaled by the antagonistic forces in the story world coming closer to collision. The Challenge is to keep them apart, despite their proximity.

We see this in two ways. First, Hiccup has to bring Toothless to the Viking village in order finish his harness at the smithy. The chances of being caught just increased on the beat. So far Hiccup has done well on his opening skillset but already he is beginning to realize that he will need increased resources. Things will get much more fraught and complicated soon, but this increase in risk signals the way they will be going.

Of course by now Astrid is actively looking out for Hiccup and she comes over: "I normally don't care what people do, but you're acting weird. Well weirder." Yes he is, but somehow Astrid manages to miss the large dragon hiding nearby. The close call brings us back down to earth after the idyllic bonding and flying sequences. Hiccup's fellow Vikings will want Toothless dead and, sooner rather than later, he will have to deal with the ramifications of that fact in terms of his own future plans. We are not quite there yet, but pressure has begun to ramp up.

Secondly, the narrative pressure chamber gets a further injection when Stoick and the dragon hunters return, predictably battered and unsuccessful. The antagonist is close by again. Stoick is amazed and delighted to learn of

Hiccup's remarkable progress in dragon training. He is very proud and does his best to show it by giving his son a horned helmet, made from one of Hiccup's mother's breastplate cups. This is the only mention we get of his mother. It is strongly implied that she is dead, but we are never told the circumstances. (Of course in the sequel it turns out she is still alive, but that revelation must await the events of the rest of this movie.) Again, the writing lesson here is that happiness and pride can be just as ominous as anger and disdain when so handled.

Before that deeply uncomfortable exchange, Hiccup tests his newly revised flying harness. Finally it really works, although the test flight is not without its moments of terror—or, in the context of this beat, we might better call them moments of Challenge. Part of the learning process is for Hiccup to forget his list of instructions and to learn to fly on instinct. This is a big moment for him. Not only has he designed and made the mechanism but he has finally found a way of letting go and trusting himself. He allows himself to rise to the Challenge of being good at something outside of his comfort zone.

Hiccup and Toothless rest on a cliff ledge after their exertions. A group of tiny little dragons approach, hoping to share their fish. Toothless plays with them charmingly and, when Hiccup feeds one, the tiny dragon immediately becomes friendly.

>   HICCUP
> "Everything we know about you guys
> is wrong."

That's a great catalyst for internal moral pressure. If everything the Vikings know about dragons is wrong, then the logical conclusion for Hiccup must be that it is no longer enough for him not to kill dragons. He should look to the Challenge of changing the minds of the other Vikings as well. Whether he has the will and the bravery to attempt that is another matter entirely. We will find out in the next beat.

Although the pressure on Hiccup in Challenge is nothing compared to what will come later, we can see another kind of move from simplicity and towards complexity here. We have had our fun and now things begin to get more serious. In *How to Train Your Dragon*, Hiccup is outrunning his ability to be self-reliant while staying on his thematic track and that inevitable process is what the first up angle of conventional movies is really about. Soon he will have to make a choice either to quit while he's ahead or risk everything to change the world.

Much of the pressure that has built and will continue to build through the rest of the story is external and obvious. It comes from threats and obstacles in the story world and plays through events in the plot.

There is another kind of pressure, however, and that is the kind any well-realized character puts *on themselves*. This kind of pressure may be emotional, moral, spiritual or a combination of these and more. *In story terms it is the kind of pressure that puts the theme at risk but without which the theme would remain unattainable.*

Remember, once you have decided on a theme, that choice determines every important decision point for your protagonist. If their key choices—the hard, painful moments that define them as real heroes or heroines—are not in some way related to their attitude towards the theme ask yourself whether they have any place in your story.

In *How to Train Your Dragon* the Decision Hiccup will have to make in the next story beat will speak directly to his attitude to theme. His Decision clarifies and confirms that attitude and sets the agenda for the rest of the story as we shall see very soon.

Case Study: Challenge Beats

Good Night and Good Luck – challenge as political pressure

In the Challenge beat of *Good Night and Good Luck* (2005, scr. George Clooney, Grant Heslov) crusading journalist Edward R. Murrow is given a package of evidence that suggests he was a communist sympathizer. This is a clear warning that he should desist from his critical reporting of Senator McCarthy. As such it is also a marker of the Progress his previous journalism has made. The documents cause tension between Murrow and his boss at the network and also exert potentially divisive pressure within Murrow's team as his journalists are asked to divulge any possible links to left-wing groups and similar conflicts of interest that could be used to undermine the credibility of their reporting. In structural terms, Progress leads to Challenge as the antagonistic force in the story responds to the threat posed by the protagonist.

Panic Room – challenge as siege

In *Panic Room* (2002, scr. David Koepp) the Challenge beat begins with the gang of burglars going onto offense against the mother and daughter who have taken refuge in their home's panic room. The gang realize they can't get into the armored room so their only option seems to be to force its occupants to come out. In this way the Challenge beat temporarily upends the power relationship between the groups within the building and initiates a series of increasingly tough tests for the trapped pair to overcome. To get things rolling the gang member, Burnham, connects a gas canister to the air conditioning and opens the valve. In the panic room Meg, the mother, defeats the gas by setting it alight and venting the explosion back into the room in which the burglars are located. Harder trials are to come, but for now the good guys have overcome a real Challenge.

> IMPLIED YOU
> I need to decide the first Challenge
> for Lucy and Bryce in <u>Temptation</u>. I
> was thinking maybe they have a week-
> end away. They move their
> relationship beyond dates.

> FRIENDLY ME
> They already slept together?

> IMPLIED YOU
> Yeah, because Bryce is totally easy.
> Seriously, this story isn't about
> the preciousness of sex. Maybe they
> even have sex that first Halloween
> night. Several times, alfresco, in
> gritty yet conveniently picturesque
> urban settings. This is a modern
> love story. Sex isn't the issue,
> trust is.

> FRIENDLY ME
> Good, I like it. It's moving towards
> indie territory despite all your
> best efforts.

> IMPLIED YOU
> That's indie?

> FRIENDLY ME
> There's no hot sex in Hollywood
> movies anymore. Hadn't you noticed?
> It doesn't play four-quadrant or on

planes. It kind of works against his
grief at the loss of his ex-wife
though.

                    IMPLIED YOU
The way I figure, he's vulnerable but
he's ready to move on as long as
he's not brought back into collision
with all that emotional stuff too
harshly.

                    FRIENDLY ME
I see. Yeah, a weekend away could
work. Challenge can be about helping
good things get better as well as
bad things getting worse. Quick
thought: what if, by chance, they
meet one of Lucy's old friends who
doesn't know the deal?

                    IMPLIED YOU
"Your eyes look totally different."
So where they go exposes Lucy to her
past in other ways? Maybe she takes
Bryce to see her childhood small-
town home. Yeah, yeah, that could be
a cliché also, but it's about
getting to know one another and
showing not telling. I mean people
do that kind of thing. I've done
that kind of thing. Also a road-trip
buys a cheesy progress-montage.

                    FRIENDLY ME
We'll take it better if there's a
good story world reason to get them
there. Now this is also a cliché –
romantic comedy, formula can be
fun – but they could be trying to
get somewhere and have to stop over,
or detour to Lucy's home town. Bad

weather is the number one kill-me-
now convenient option of course.

                  IMPLIED YOU
The bridge is out, but there's this
nice bed and breakfast next to a mom
and pop diner run by Lucy's Auntie
Plot-Device.

                  FRIENDLY ME
Of the Connecticut Plot-Devices.

                  IMPLIED YOU
Yeah, and she's all: "Don't you kids
just look precious together and what
the heck happened to your eyes?"

                  FRIENDLY ME
Here's a problem with working out
story. It's easy for anything to
sound clichéd out of context and
before you have worked it and turned
it. Don't be put off. Try and think
about how you could turn that kind
of situation and make it fresh.

                  IMPLIED YOU
Auntie Plot-Device is actually Delia
the waitress. She's a girl who
bullied Lucy at school. Oh! Delia
called Lucy "poopy-peepers" because
of the color of her eyes. Crap. Now
everything sounds dumb. I guess it
takes a lot of spitballs to make a
screenplay page?

                  FRIENDLY ME
Well, yeah actually. The more you
spit out the closer you get to. . .
Something. . . Swallowing. Story.
Eh. . . I need a coffee.

```
              IMPLIED YOU
On point. Totally. Impressed even.


              FRIENDLY ME
The point is now you are doing the
right kind of story-thinking. What
you need to do is build more
deception on top of her initial
deception. That's why I'm telling
you the green eyes thing isn't
enough. They are the signal problem
that takes Lucy down a path which
forces her into making more and more
deceptive choices that cover up the
initial deception. It's comedy as a
kind of mendacious hyperbole. That
way, when the green-eyes-reveal
happens it exposes all the other
crap she's done to keep The One
Secret secret.


              IMPLIED YOU
Oh. Oh! Yeah, yeah. Totally makes
sense now.
```

8. Decision

Back in the arena it's time for the final test and a frustrated Astrid lays it on the line to Hiccup: "Stay out of my way, I'm winning this thing." Of course the dragon goes right for Hiccup and Astrid charges only to find it lying next to him, happily subdued. The crowd cheers. Astrid is livid. The village elder declares Hiccup the winner of dragon training (plot running counter to story) and he is carried out of the arena on the shoulders of the other Viking teens. Stoick's emotional track is also running counter to story: "That's my boy." He will renounce Hiccup as his son all too soon (this little parallel pays off in Crisis, later in the act), but for now it confirms that Hiccup has finally earned the acceptance for which he had been searching all along.

Of course by now this success doesn't make Hiccup happy. Victory means that he will have to kill a dragon in front of the whole village. His success has put him in an impossible position and that is exactly where he should be approaching the midpoint of his story.

Hiccup's immediate response—his instinctive Decision—is: "I am so leaving." On one level, that of basic human sympathy, who could blame him? On another, the higher level on which we have expectations of Hiccup as a budding hero, we are disappointed in him. Back at the Night Fury with his possessions on his back Hiccup says: "Looks like you and me are taking a little vacation forever." He looks up and there's our B Story sharpening her axe—busted!

Astrid wants answers and gets pushy, so Toothless threatens her. Hiccup calms the dragon but Astrid runs off, setting up Hiccup's midpoint decision.

Case Study: Decision Beats

Coraline – decision as temptation

In *Coraline* (2009, scr. Henry Selick, from the novel by Neil Gaiman), the Decision plays off the lure of the Other Mother who inhabits the Other World behind the walls of Coraline's family home. Young Coraline has been acting out, feeling neglected by her parents and unhappy at their move to a new place. In the strange Other World she has encountered a version of her mother with buttons for eyes who has nothing but time and care for Coraline. Coraline has been warned about the motivations of this seemingly perfect alternative to her flawed but very human mother and things come to a head when the Other Mother makes Coraline an offer. She tells Coraline she can stay forever in this seemingly perfect world if only she will consent to have buttons sewn in place of her own eyes. Surely that would be a small sacrifice to buy her eternal happiness? Coraline's refusal—her desire to return to her own world, with all its flaws—will set the rest of the story on a roll towards eventual resolution, but for now the Decision beat plays to temptation—to the choice of worlds before her and to the price of her choosing.

Captain Phillips – decision as turnabout

The Decision beat of *Captain Phillips* (2013, scr. Billy Ray, adapted from the book *A Captain's Duty: Somali Pirates, Navy SEALs, and Dangerous Days at Sea* by Richard Phillips and Stephan Talty) comes after the engine room crew have captured Muse, the leader of the Somali pirates who have taken control of the container ship MV *Maersk Alabama*. The ship's captain, Richard Phillips, breaks the standoff between the pirates and his crew by persuading the pirates to take the Decision to leave in a lifeboat with the money from the ship's safe. For his part, Muse takes his own Decision to force the captain to stay in the lifeboat when it launches. So, at the Midpoint, both the captain and the pirates are alone in the lifeboat for the rest of the story.

> IMPLIED YOU

So by now, in <u>Temptation</u>, Lucy and Bryce are kind of a thing.

> FRIENDLY ME

She got what she wanted, but she got it, in part, through deception.

> IMPLIED YOU

What to do?

> FRIENDLY ME

Hence the Decision beat. Her basic choice is still: tell him or fix him, right? Only now there's an emerging commitment between them to make that decision even tougher.

> IMPLIED YOU

Fix him?

> FRIENDLY ME

Well, she tells him and she takes the consequences, or she decides to help him deal with his trauma and move past it so the reveal will be easier for her to manage and easier for him to take. I mean it won't be easier, of course. It's a comedy; she's an idiot. But for now she can convince herself it will.

> IMPLIED YOU

She's already basically decided not to tell him.

> FRIENDLY ME

So Decision is about clarifying her intention to help him? The second commitment is to him as a person and as a partner, while also being naïve

```
                and self-serving of course. That's
                what the crisis will go on to
                expose.

                         IMPLIED YOU
                Because really Lucy's arc is about
                growing up?

                         FRIENDLY ME
                She learns that mature relationships
                are built on trust.

                         IMPLIED YOU
                So what I need here is a moment that
                brings her decision into focus.
                Bryce reveals the depth of his
                grief. Just when they are really
                making things work, something
                happens that exposes just how far
                they still have to go. . .

                         FRIENDLY ME
                Yeah. It isn't strong enough yet,
                but we'll keeping thinking.
```

Did you spank your hero/ine today?

I think it's safe to say Hiccup has been in the wars. After all despite, indeed because of all his successes, the angle has brought him to the brink of running away from his life, his love, and his people. That's very serious, very real. The revelations of the angle have allowed Hiccup to show real bravery, to develop his skills and to make a remarkable new friend. On the other hand these events have led him to a new understanding of how the world works which makes the resolution of his theme seem harder to reach than ever. So yes, he's been spanked by his writers.

Midpoint – Second commitment

The Midpoint is the culmination of the Decision beat, but I give it its own section because of its pivotal importance as a moment of storytelling in most movies. It is a key element of structure, if not exactly a beat in the sense of the others.

There's the choice. There's the precipice. Astrid is the one who brings Hiccup to the edge, which is as it often should be with a a B Story relationship. She is still at the end of his *want* list so who better to give him the final push. In structural terms we have now reached the Midpoint. Hiccup either runs or he jumps. If he runs, the story is over because he will have abandoned its theme. If he jumps—in other words if he takes a leap into a Second Commitment—there is no going back and things are only going to get harder.

Astrid is running through the forest when she is grabbed by a dragon and lifted into the sky. It's Hiccup and Toothless. Hiccup didn't run, he "jumped." Welcome to the Midpoint.

Lesson Break: Midpoint Options

This is another classic Hollywood story move. The first up angle is usually about one or both of the following: either it is all about slapping the pretense out of the protagonist to prepare them for a real commitment or it gives them what they began by wanting only to find that they no longer do. The Midpoint gives them the easy thing only to find they want the hard thing that was hiding underneath the easy thing this whole time.

In *How to Train Your Dragon* we get both options together.

1. Hiccup wins dragon training, which theoretically puts him right back on track with his 'want' line—ahead of the game in fact. He gets what he always wanted. Only now it has become an empty victory.
2. From his second angle successes Hiccup has learned that the Vikings are wrong to hate and fear dragons. Now his own need for acceptance has been eclipsed by the greater need of a whole species. That gives him a moral obligation to try and change things. But what can one kid do against an entire culture and centuries of tradition? It would take a much deeper commitment to his theme, indeed a more altruistic and potentially sacrificial commitment. In short he would need to be a hero.

You can see how neat this is. The decision Hiccup makes at the midpoint not to run transforms him from protagonist to hero. In screenwriting, "neat" may imply "simple" but should never mean "simplistic."

Case Study: Midpoint Beats

Transcendence – midpoint as unwise fulfillment

At the Midpoint of *Transcendence* (2014, scr. Jack Paglen), Evelyn Caster, the wife of deceased computer scientist Will Caster, connects his digitally uploaded mind to the World Wide Web. She does so against the advice of her friend Max Waters. The consequences, for all three characters and for the movie's story world, are literally world-changing. "Will" takes control over the network to the extent that only his elimination (in this case self-inflicted) and the consequent global destruction of modern computer culture and all that goes with it will restore the world. Now Evelyn and Max must struggle with their own moral and emotional attitudes to accept and then work the fix but, after this Midpoint nothing can ever be the same again—and, sadly, the script falls apart. But that's another story.

The Spectacular Now – midpoint as pact

At the Midpoint of a much better movie, *The Spectacular Now* (2013, scr. Scott Neustadter & Michael H. Weber), Aimee makes Sutter enter a pact with her that they will confront their mothers who, both teens feel, stand in the way of their respective futures. She does this after she has sex with Sutter for the first time and we feel she wouldn't have had the confidence to take the initiative before this. Aimee is deadly serious about their pledge and there is no going back for her. Sutter goes along in the way he always goes along, taking the path of least resistance. However, because he is with Aimee her determination will become his, for long enough to make him take that step at least. As a consequence, he learns much about himself and also the hard truth about his father and his family history. Sutter goes through pain. He experiences a real personal crisis, but he comes out better for it on the other side. None of this would have happened without Aimee making her pledge.

Despicable Me – midpoint as revelation

Reluctantly, at the Midpoint of *Despicable Me* (2010, scr. Cinco Paul & Ken Daurio), supervillain protagonist Gru has taken his adopted kids to the funfair. Seeing they have been cheated of a prize he destroys the booth with one of his amazing weapons and wins a fluffy unicorn for the youngest child. Their adulation and joy melts his heart and teaches him a lesson, finally setting him on the road to becoming a real father to three kids he adopted only as pawns in a nefarious scheme. Once Gru has opened up to love and parenthood there is no going back and his supervillany is now tempered by higher motivations.

Your Sister's Sister – the midpoint resets the agenda

At the Midpoint of *Your Sister's Sister* (2011, scr. Lynn Shelton) Iris admits to her sister, Hannah, that she is in love with her old friend Jack who is staying with them in their rural cabin. This further complicates an already complicated situation as Hannah (who is a lesbian but wants a baby) and Jack had drunken sex the night before Iris' unexpected arrival. To add fuel to the fire, Iris is the ex of Jack's dead brother and Hannah doctored the condom in the hope of being impregnated by Jack. All of these events might have passed off without recrimination had Iris not admitted to Hannah that she has feelings for Jack. Now there will be awkward revelation piled on awkward revelation and the relationship between all three people will be strained to the limit before, finally, they come to terms. After the Midpoint, therefore, there is no going back.

What these examples demonstrate is that a strong Midpoint changes the game for good. If it was easy to restore the story world to its status before the consequences of your protagonist's second commitment bite it wouldn't be such a brave undertaking. Most conventional movies use their Midpoint choices as a way of locking in the inevitability of change. There will be more personal development to come as the story moves through its crisis, but after the Midpoint there should be no going back. You can't untell someone you love them (falling out of love is a different matter). In a realistic world you can't un-kill an enemy—or even a friend. If you defy or renounce your boss, your government, your superior officer, your family, this may be repairable in time and through heroic action but your future relationship with them—for better or worse—will never be the same.

IMPLIED YOU
In Temptation, Lucy decides to fix
Bryce, not tell him.

FRIENDLY ME
Of course she does. I look forward
to reading how you make that moment
sing. But, for now, prepare to make
things get harder for her fast.

IMPLIED YOU
Yeah, I'm planning on punishing that
deceitful minx for all her deceitful
minxery. It's a word.

```
                    FRIENDLY ME
        It is now. It could also be the big
        "I love you" moment. We probably
        need one of those.
```

First up angle in *Let the Right One In*

This angle develops the relationship between Oskar and Eli from a hesitant friendship to the point at which they start to "go steady." In a similar fashion to *How to Train Your Dragon,* events progress along two main parallel tracks as well as through a largely independent B Story. In this case, one parallel is hidden from the protagonist rather than assisting him in his progress. Indeed, these "unseen" events expose the illusion of progress made in the relationship between Oskar and Eli, rather than reinforcing it. Once again we are privileged to witness this development in counterpoint with the implosion of Eli's partnership with Håkan, so we understand the darkness that lies in the future of Oskar's hopes.

Oskar and Eli make friends ➜ _____
                            ↑   (Influence)   ↑   ↑
Håkan's failure to provide ➜ _____

The B Story, in which Lacke seeks the murderer of his friend and fellow drunk Jocke, doesn't intersect with the A Story until near the end of the next angle. For now we see Lacke's pain, but he doesn't have enough information to make progress. The B Story in *Let the Right One In* is unusual in being so disconnected from the A Story, but it will resolve to generate an important plot move, forcing Eli to leave her home and initiating some of the events of the third act of the movie. This is not a conventional model of B Story writing but has precedent, notably in horror movies (see the next Lesson Break). It serves an important plot function in bringing on a *plot crisis,* when Lacke attacks Eli and is killed, but does not resolve the story. We will discuss this further in our account of the next angle.

The story beats of the second angle of *Let the Right One In* work like this:

C – *Early progress*

5. **B Story:** Needing to feed, but let down by her daywalker, Håkan, Eli kills the local drunk, Jocke. This initiates the intermittent—and largely independent—B Story detective plot as his friend, Lacke, tries to find out what happened to him and who is responsible. Again, the B Story is out of the hands of the protagonist.

6. **Progress:** Eli and Oskar's strange, but charming friendship develops. It seems that Eli has accepted him as a friend now, but not yet as a partner.

D – Raising stakes

7. **Challenge:** The school bullies make Oskar's life even more hellish and he is driven onto Eli's advice to fight back hard.
8. **Decision:** Håkan fails again and is arrested. He tries to kill himself with acid and ends up in the hospital. As a final sacrifice he lets Eli drink from him and falls from the high window. Eli needs a replacement and goes to find Oskar, who is asleep in bed.

MIDPOINT: Second commitment

Eli gets into bed with Oskar and agrees that they are now a kind of couple. Once again, it is Eli who controls the game and who sets the terms of *her* Second Commitment. Oskar gets his thematic wish—acceptance from Eli— but he has yet to understand the nature of that relationship—or indeed "her" nature as a vampire.

Lesson Break: Separated B Stories

Most movies link their B Stories directly to the progress of the protagonist's transformational arc. In some cases, however, movies keep their B Story subplots largely distinct. In *Let the Right One In* the loose thread of Lacke needing to find the killer of his friend is still a B Story—it provides the catalyst in the Crisis and Revelation beats to move the A Story towards final resolution—but it only connects occasionally with the activities in the main narrative. Indeed, when it does so it is through Eli's actions, not Oskar's. For example, Lacke sees Eli attack his girlfriend, Virginia, quite independently of Oskar's story.

This tactic is more common in some genres, notably horror films, than it is in others. In *Halloween* (1978, scr. John Carpenter, Debra Hill), for example, the B Story follows Dr. Loomis investigating Michael Myers' escape from the mental hospital. This subplot parallels the story of Laurie Strode and her impending encounter with Michael, but rarely intersects with it. Loomis' investigation pays off as he arrives just in time to shoot Michael at the end, but otherwise it is largely distinct. The inability of figures of authority to understand what is really going on, much less successfully intervene in many horror films sets up the tendency for this kind of disconnection. It is particularly common in Italian horror movies and *gialli*, for example.

First up angle in *Winter's Bone*

This angle provides the necessity for Ree to do the most dangerous thing she possibly can in her closed-off world: force Thump Milton's hand. She makes progress of a kind, notably in building up a small group of helpmates, including her uncle Teardrop. He is on the edges of her world right now, a little bit like Astrid is on the edges of Hiccup's world in this angle of *How to Train Your Dragon*, but we sense he's working his way towards helping.

However, in practical terms, at the Midpoint Ree is no closer to finding Jessup than she was at the start. She has deflected attempts to distract her from the truth and she is clearer about who was responsible for his disappearance. She is even coming to understand the likelihood that her father is dead, but that doesn't remove the threat of eviction from her family's future.

The story beats of the second angle of *Winter's Bone* work like this:

C – Early progress

5. **B Story (Progress):** Ree's neighbor, Ray, turns up. He is angry at her for making a nuisance of herself thus far. He takes her to see a blown-up meth lab and tells her that's where Jessup died. Ree realizes this is a lie, due to the height of the weeds growing inside the building. She calls Ray out for his attempt to deceive her. This is the first example of the clannish Ozarks meth-cooking culture actively trying to deflect her quest to find her father. It begins the long arc that will band their response towards her need for a solution. In that sense this apparent negative is actually a very important marker of Progress.

Unconventionally, the B Story *doesn't* engage in this beat. Ree's friend Gail initiates it in the next beat (see later) and Teardrop will turn up again later, in Challenge. Gradually he takes on the role of helpmate and protector for Ree. Right now, however, the act starts with Ree alone. Her friends and supporters will trickle in, but this is an A Story waiting for its B Story to happen. This follows the pattern in which Ree has to work hard for everything she achieves. Sometimes she is blocked and sometimes she is friendless. There will be a B Story but, like much in this movie, it will take its own sweet time to arrive. In fact the act begins with the Progress beat, built around negative reinforcement from Ray.

> NOTE ONE: It is not uncommon for close or adjacent beats to switch around in a movie. This is especially true of independent dramas like *Winter's Bone* and that is one of the reasons why I picked it as one of our

running case studies. We will get all of our B Story, Progress and Challenge beats from the W, just like in more conventional movies. The order in which they occur is mixed up, however, and some beats and characters (Teardrop and Gail) combine functions. The Challenge beat (see later) combines the functions of B Story—Teardrop comes to help—and Challenge—the news he brings raises the stakes for Ree. Arguably, the delay adds to our sense of Ree's isolation and of the enormity of her task. That's how I respond to the storytelling personally, but of course that's a subjective observation.

NOTE TWO: Ray coming to visit is an act two beat because it is a response to Ree's First Commitment. Ray's attempt to deflect Ree is part of the work of the second act because without Ree's commitment the antagonistic forces would have nothing to react to.

6. **Progress (B Story):** Ree's girlfriend, Gail, turns up with her husband's truck and they go to the state border. Ree's emotional and moral blackmail has paid off. They don't find her father, only ominous stories from Jessup's ex-girlfriend about the bad company he was keeping shortly before his disappearance.

NOTE: Unconventionally, Gail and Teardrop share some of the responsibility for the B Story. Their respective subplots are both supportive but, while Gail initiates the supportive subplot and is present for the crisis, Teardrop takes over the role of primary support and initiates the action at Revelation, resolving the B Story at least as a narrative of support, although not personified clearly in a single relationship. Teardrop's relationship with Ree is the most significant in the movie. In that sense he "earns the right" to be the B Story. It is Gail who gets things going however. Once again, even though in this indie movie the beats have shifted a little from the typical Hollywood structure, the structural development of the story proceeds conventionally through a process of alliance building and support. The B Story function is still set up and paid off in act two and initiates the resolution in act three.

D – Raising stakes

7. **Challenge:** Teardrop arrives and tells Ree he hasn't forgotten her, but Jessup missed his court date. More than this, her father's car has been found burned out. He wasn't in it, but Ree realizes this

likely means Jessup is dead. She's pretty much alone, she's going to lose her home and she doesn't have much time left to save it. That's a Challenge.

8. **Decision:** Ree is desperate and tells her mother: "I don't know what to do." Her mother is no help, of course, and Ree feels more alone than ever. Her desperation only needs one more incentive to make her take the ultimate risk.

MIDPOINT: Second commitment

A bail bondsman turns up at Ree's home, informing her that she has only a few days left before she loses the house and land that were part of Jessup's bond. The story's clock is ticking faster now and Ree has to do something. She goes to find Thump Milton at a cattle auction, breaking cultural taboos and sticking her neck very far out.

Questions to ask *yourself* as you write act two – first up angle

B Story

Q: Have I planned how to develop the B Story that I have established in this beat through the rest of the movie?

Q: Does the resolution I have planned for the B Story help resolve the protagonist's own arc at the end of act two?

Q: Does the B Story relationship have the potential to play out with pleasurable complexity—is it more than a "how is my protagonist feeling" info-dump?

Q: Is my B Story arc emotionally vital to the story and to my theme?

Progress

Q: Is it clear how this early progress is being made in terms of the theme and the arc of my protagonist?

Q: How do we see and understand the lack—the need for further change, understanding, development or progress—still evident in my protagonist through the very progress she is making?

Q: How is the progress leading us towards a second, Midpoint commitment?

NOTE: *Your protagonist may not realize this yet, but certainly you should and your audience may—either because they are just smart and cine-literate, or by your explicit design.*

Challenge

Q: Is it clear that things just got tougher?

Q: How does the Challenge beat also expose my protagonist's at least partial inadequacy in the face of the thematic and story challenge?

Q: How is my antagonistic force speaking to theme and goal as it ups the ante in this beat?

Decision

Q: By the end of this beat, is the need for my protagonist to make a second commitment clear and unavoidable?

Q: Upon what level of (likely still imperfect) self-knowledge or understanding of the story world is my protagonist's second, less contingent decision to accept the challenge of the story based?

Q: How am I planning that this will change as the story accelerates after the Midpoint?

Midpoint

Q: In story terms, can my protagonist "turn back" without disastrous consequences after their second commitment? NOTE: *If they can, fix it so they can't.*

Q: Is the Midpoint a clear progress beat—however fraught the notion of progress might be at this moment?

Questions to ask *your first draft* of act two – first up angle

After you have finished a first draft of your screenplay, re-read it and ask the following questions:

B Story

Q: Does the emergence or transformation of the B Story relationship at this point feel organic to the story or somehow "bolted on"?

Q: Does the establishment of my B Story impede the flow of the story at the start of act two?

Q: Does the parallel between the B Story and Revelation beats offer satisfactory resolution in terms of illustrating the effects of the change my story has brought about—has all my planning worked?

Q: How can I write all of this just as effectively with fewer words and in fewer pages?

Progress

Q: Does the parallel between the Progress and Crisis beats show how far my protagonist has come in learning / experiencing / coming to terms with themselves and their goals?

Q: How can I write all of this just as effectively with fewer words and in fewer pages?

Challenge

Q: Does the parallel between the Challenge and Assistance beats show how the allies and support gained with progress start to pay off as we move towards crisis?

Q: How can I write all of this just as effectively with fewer words and in fewer pages?

Decision

Q: Looking back, does my protagonist's first commitment at the end of act one now seem even more appropriately naïve or contingent?

Q: Does the parallel between the Decision and Acceleration beats set up and pay off the deep significance—often the peril—of the Midpoint decision and second commitment to come?

Q: How can I write all of this just as effectively with fewer words and in fewer pages?

Midpoint

Q: Does the Midpoint commitment potentially involve and/or affect the entire world of my story or is it a small thing, relevant only to my protagonist—is it a big enough deal?

Q: From the hindsight gained by having written the ending, does my Midpoint turn the story?

Q: How can I write all of this just as effectively with fewer words and in fewer pages?

Act Two: Second down angle (commitment)

This angle is all about making the resolution of your protagonist's story possible.

Something big just happened at the midpoint. As we have already established, in conventional screenplays midpoints are vital story moments after which *nothing can be the same again*. They are *not* the solution to your protagonist's story problem. They are *not* the moments of revelation which finally allow that protagonist to see their way towards solving that problem. No, midpoints are the moments where your protagonist makes a commitment that—should she survive the crisis that is about to engulf her—will allow her to reach those future goals.

Whether your midpoint has redirected your protagonist's *wants* or just forced them to finally take the plunge and give their all to get where they *need* to be, the rest of the second act should be an accelerating slide downhill through crisis. They have not yet been seriously tested. They may think they have been, but a narrow escape from a trash compactor will look like a walk in the park after battling Imperial stormtroopers and after having your Jedi mentor killed by Darth Vader.

We have already discussed the shift from *avoidance* to *commitment* as the watchwords for our protagonists at the fulcrum of act two. I won't repeat myself here other than to remind you of the importance of this change because it signals that our protagonist is getting serious about becoming a hero or heroine.

This is the angle where their commitment to the cause against all obstacles and all the odds makes your hero or heroine worthy of that appellation. Another way of thinking about it is this is the angle where their experiences finally force them to see themselves objectively. If you are doing your job, this angle will strip them bare emotionally and give them nowhere to hide from hard truths. In an action script it will take them through hell to get within sight of the prize. Only by doing so, Hollywood storytelling would have it, will they be able to see past themselves and understand the bigger picture. When they do this they will see their way to resolving their problem in the final act and angle.

```
            IMPLIED YOU
Haven't we already seen that with
Hiccup? I mean the whole village
thinks he's a doofus, right?

            FRIENDLY ME
Sure, but being the village doofus
is a whole lot easier to come back
from than being a traitor.

            IMPLIED YOU
That's the Crisis, right?

            FRIENDLY ME
Yes - and that's how far your second
act has to push your hero.
```

Of course proving your heroism in a story might be about learning to have the courage to become an activist, or start a new career in middle age, or come out of the closet, or commit to your boyfriend, or reconcile with your mother, or stand up to your bullying dad, or finally walk out on a toxic marriage. It does not have to involve swords and guns and dodging dragons or laser blasts. Unless your mother is actually a killbot in disguise of course. Hey, it's commoner than you might think.

In mainstream movies the *second down angle* is probably the most loosely structured of the four that make up your screenplay. Even in Hollywood movies the order in which things happen in the second down angle is less "set in stone" and that's a good thing for writers. On the other hand that doesn't mean it's easy to write.

Structurally, the angle is actually quite a straightforward set of accelerating and intensifying beats. Enemies or bad situations pile on top of one another until there's nowhere for your protagonist to hide, literally or emotionally. That simplicity enables a whole lot of raising of the stakes. Writing that intensification as satisfying drama rather than empty hyperbole is where the difficulty comes in.

The story beats of the second down angle of *How to Train Your Dragon* work like this:

E – Commitment

9. **Acceleration:** In this beat, Hiccup earns a promising new friend and ally in Astrid. He also learns about the "big bad," an enormous queen

dragon who is behind the dragon raids. The plot accelerates, bringing the inevitable future confrontation with this monstrous opponent into focus.

10. **Assistance:** Hiccup tries to teach the Vikings the truth about dragons but everything goes wrong. Help comes from Astrid and Toothless, but Stoick and the Vikings capture the Night Fury and ignore Hiccup's lesson.

F – Crisis

11. **Crisis:** Stoick renounces Hiccup and brands him a traitor. Hiccup reveals that the Night Fury took him to the dragons' lair. Stoick sets off with the Vikings to raid their enemy's home, with a trussed up Toothless as his compass. Despite Hiccup's attempt to warn them, they have no idea what they will be facing when they get there.
12. **Revelation:** The B Story resolves as Astrid kicks Hiccup's butt and makes him finally embrace his role in all this, as well as his potential. Suddenly energized he rushes off, determined to save the day.

The first task of this angle is to think in terms of *parallelism* and pay off the Midpoint crisis immediately. The Midpoint commitment is only worth its story weight if your protagonist knows that their decision will lead to even more danger (Decision). That's what makes it a heroic choice. This payoff begins in a beat called Acceleration . . .

E – Commitment

This half-angle begins the acceleration to an inevitable Crisis that was brought on by your protagonist's Second Commitment at the story's Midpoint. There should be no turning back now and each challenge becomes harder than the last.

9. Acceleration

Acceleration pays off the Midpoint by showing the value of the protagonist's Second Commitment. Things get harder fast.

In *How to Train Your Dragon* this down angle is short and simply plotted. It earns the luxury of simple plotting because everything that comes before it is handled so professionally by the writers. We have reveled in the set-up, now all that has to happen is the payoff into crisis and that's already waving from the wings.

Job one for Hiccup is to get Astrid and Toothless to play nice. And yes, Astrid is the first danger, the first accelerated plot challenge to overcome.

There's also the whole unlikely-teen-romance plot bubbling underneath of course. Hiccup has decided not to run, so that means now he has to bring the Vikings on side. The process starts with Astrid because she already knows about Toothless. Without Astrid as a friend, Hiccup can't choose when and how to break the news to the village. He won't be able to do it on his own terms. Of course it will all go horribly wrong anyway, but that's what tends to happen after the Midpoint.

Right now there is no time to think (again, welcome to the *second down angle*), he just has to act. His first act is to swing Astrid onto Toothless' back. The dragon is not happy about this, having an understandable aversion to warrior girls who swing sharp axes at its head. He tries to shake Astrid off.

> HICCUP
> Toothless, what are you doing?! We
> need her to like us!

Lots of mid-air spinning and tumbling follows until Astrid apologizes. The Night Fury relaxes.

Now that Astrid has also relaxed a little she opens up to the wonder of the moment. Although by the final movie some details have been added, like Astrid touching a cloud, here's the screenplay description. It's a perfect example of show, don't tell, as Astrid is sold the joy of dragon—and even Hiccup—friendship:

> They emerge from a blanket of clouds under the
> dancing Northern Lights, shimmering in ribbons
> across the vast sky.
>
> Below them, Berk's torches flicker in the inky
> darkness. The new perspective is breathtaking.
>
> Astrid tucks her arms into Hiccup's vest, burying
> her chin into his shoulder. The moment is not lost
> on either of them. Hiccup smiles nervously.

Unsurprisingly, Astrid admits the experience is "...amazing." This signals that Hiccup's first post-midpoint task has been completed, the first danger averted . . .

                  IMPLIED YOU
So, Astrid is like the guy with the
knife who attacks Brendan after the
midpoint in <u>Brick</u>?

                  FRIENDLY ME
Wow - you remember that from the
case study in <u>Write What You Don't
Know?</u>

                  IMPLIED YOU
Huh? Oh no, I didn't read it. I just
watched the movie the other day.

                  FRIENDLY ME
Because I screened it in class.

                  IMPLIED YOU
I've read Robert McKee. I worked it
out, natch.

                  FRIENDLY ME
Yeah. . . I talked about that moment.

                  IMPLIED YOU
Wasn't listening.

                  FRIENDLY ME
Are you just trying to piss me off
now?

                  IMPLIED YOU
How's that working out for you?

Beat.

                  FRIENDLY ME
Oh, I get it. We are after the
midpoint so you are trying to raise
the stakes between us. Actually
that's kind of sweet.

Implied You golf-claps patronizingly.

> IMPLIED YOU
> And you worked it out. Well done
> you. Now move on. I have some well-
> earned basking in the glow of my own
> meta to do.

> FRIENDLY ME
> Well, I will. Because right now in
> the plot a much bigger and much
> nastier danger is about to
> emerge . . .

The magical moment between Hiccup and Astrid is broken as Toothless suddenly veers off and joins a great stream of dragons of all types heading for the fog. All the other dragons are carrying food, hauling in the kill. Hiccup and Astrid are carried along into an opening in a huge volcano. They hide inside the caldera and observe the other dragons dropping their food offerings into the steamy opening in the middle of the cavern.

> HICCUP
> "What my dad wouldn't give to find
> this."

Now we learn the big secret of dragon ecology when an enormous, bloated monster rises up suddenly through the clouds of steam to swallow a sluggish hunter in a single bite. The beast smells them and they just make it out safely. They land on a nearby beach and Astrid lays it out for us: "It's like a giant beehive. They're the workers... and that's their queen. It controls them." Although she is never given a name in the movie, in the screenplay the queen dragon is named the "Red Death," so we'll call her that from now on. Moreover, now we have seen the big bad we realize (foreshadowing) that maybe Hiccup will have to kill a dragon after all. And what a dragon . . .

This is an excellent example of how story world exposition continues through your story. In one sense storytelling is all about the control and timing of revelations.

This revelation is bigger than both of them. First order of business is for Hiccup to persuade Astrid not to tell everyone about the dragon lair right away. He asks for one day to try and sort things out and she agrees. This pays off the beat, showing Hiccup has earned her trust. Whack! She punches him on the arm: "That's for kidnapping me." She kisses him: "That's for everything else." Hiccup just got a great big step closer to the happy end of his *want* line of course. Given what we already know about Hiccup's world, however, that's got to mean things are going to fall apart really fast.

When they do, he will need more than a little Assistance . . .

Lesson Break: Plot Acceleration and Act Length

I have already mentioned that the second down angle is quite short in *How to Train Your Dragon*. This is not uncommon in Hollywood movies, but by no means required. I suppose an obvious, if imperfect rule of thumb would be that plot accelerates faster in action genres and broad comedies than it does in dramas. Even so, after the midpoint we should always be feeling that events, fate, circumstances are beginning to push harder and faster.

As always, parallelism can be your friend here. Remember that all of your set-up work in the first half of the movie should now be paying off. One benefit of that is that your audience's expectations allow a kind of narrative shorthand if you handle them well. If we are expecting a series of micro-resolutions to previous story beats—and, as experienced pattern recognizers, we will be—you have the luxury of not having to explain yourself over and over again. If you have done your job to this point, the connections between first and second half events and actions should be pretty clear.

Once again, clarity does not mean going for bland transparency or dumbing your story down. Clarity implies structural eloquence. For example, mysteries and puzzle films organize their revelations very carefully and clarity here can mean simply that we understand what we don't yet understand! We can enjoy cleverness, complexity and the pleasure of working to find the clarity your clues will reveal. The point is to free us to appreciate the pleasure of progression.

Another rule of thumb is to think about the length of acts in a screenplay as a ratio of 1:2:1. The second act is usually at least as long as acts one and three combined. In the late-draft screenplay for *How to Train Your Dragon* the page counts are approximately as follows:

Act one (first down angle): 21 pages
Act two (first up angle): 43 pages
Act two (second down angle): 18 pages
(Act two (entire): 59 pages)
Act three (second up angle): 24 pages

Note that this is a rough example as, although the screenplay drafts I have read were clearly developed further, they were pretty much shooting scripts. However, given also the pre-planning of visual sequences required in animated features, the distinction between development draft and shooting script is perhaps looser than in live-action screenwriting.)

As you can see, acts one and three are a similar length in terms of pages. Act two is more than twice as long as both of them combined. Admittedly, in terms of balance, the first up angle is rather long and the second down angle is on the short side in this film, but the general model holds for most screenplays.

Note that act three is longer than act one in page terms, which is somewhat unusual. Normally a third act is the shortest, but in this particular case there's not that much in it. I did a rough timing of the angles for comparison. This is how they play out:

Act one (first down angle): 17 minutes
Act two (first up angle): 36 minutes
Act two (second down angle): 17 minutes
(Act two (entire): 52 minutes)
Act three (second up angle): 19 minutes

Note also how closely the page numbers equate with the running time of these angles. Admittedly the angles are shorter on screen than they are on the page. This is especially true of the second and fourth and is mainly because these angles have more action. Complex action increases the page space required for a scene.

The full screenplay ends on page 106. The film (minus credits) is around ninety minutes. That's not an unusual equation for a late-draft/shooting script. As we know, the rule of thumb is that one page of script equates to a minute of screen time, but the actual equation varies somewhat depending on the ratio of action to dialogue.

Case Study: Acceleration Beats

The Town – acceleration by proxy

In the Acceleration beat of *The Town* (2010, scr. Peter Craig and Ben Affleck & Aaron Stockard) FBI Special Agent Frawley interrogates former bank manager Claire Keesey. Frawley informs her that Doug MacRay, the man she is seeing, was a member of the gang that assaulted her during a robbery. He threatens Claire with prosecution as an accomplice and pressures her towards cooperating with the authorities. This takes place after Frawley fails to get MacRay or any of his associates to confess to a recent robbery. Later, Claire will break up with Doug. Frawley raises the stakes—and gets more success—by coming at MacRay through his emotional life, finding ways of putting on pressure that the career criminal is less prepared to handle.

Captain Phillips – acceleration through scale

We know we have passed the Midpoint in *Captain Phillips* because the plot Accelerates as we cut to the US Navy Arleigh Burke-class guided missile destroyer *USS Bainbridge* on anti-piracy duty. The captain is briefed on the *Maersk Alabama* incident and he tasks his ship to intercept the lifeboat. On the cut back from the powerful warship to the tiny lifeboat we can appreciate the increase in danger its approach represents for the pirates and their hostage onboard.

Note that, unlike in *How to Train Your Dragon*, both these examples play Acceleration by proxy. I picked them as examples for that reason, to show that there are many beats than can still be effective if played away from the protagonist. This works as long as the impact on their ongoing story is clear or at least provocative.

                    IMPLIED YOU
        Acceleration can be funny, right?

                    FRIENDLY ME
        Sure. You're writing a comedy.

                    IMPLIED YOU
        I was planning out all of these
        eye-related gags. Not just for this
        beat, but in general for the movie.

                    FRIENDLY ME
     Great idea. You need the jokes to
     come both from the characters and
     their situation.

                    IMPLIED YOU
     So, I have it that Lucy doesn't wear
     contacts. The Halloween ones are
     just cosmetic.

                    FRIENDLY ME
     So her poor eyes will really be
     going through it. Maybe she doesn't
     know how to take care of contacts
     properly . . .

                    IMPLIED YOU
     They will get so uncomfortable she
     has to keep giving her eyes a rest.
     She always wears shades; inside and
     out, good weather and bad. Or she
     loses one contact and she goes around
     squinting and not looking Bryce in
     the eye. That sort of thing.

                    FRIENDLY ME
     Maybe she pretends she is having
     LASIK surgery and she wears a
     bandage over her eyes just so she
     can rest them. Only the most
     tasteful fake-blindness gags follow.

                    IMPLIED YOU
     Now I'm imagining an eye patch
     sequence! Maybe she keeps switching
     eyes to give each a rest in
     turn. . . Well maybe not.

                    FRIENDLY ME
     It depends how zany your comedy is
     going to be. But that kind of

physical work is a gift to a great
comedy actress.

                IMPLIED YOU
Do you have ideas about who could
play her? You didn't like Sandra
Bullock.

                FRIENDLY ME
No, I like Sandra Bullock. I was
just being sniffy about some of her
movies. My advice would be, unless
you have an "in," don't write too
overtly for one star because that
can also turn off any reader who
doesn't have a relationship with
her. It's like hanging a big sign on
your script reading: "Not for you."
Try and thread a needle in your
writing between "perfect for" and
"exclusively for."

                IMPLIED YOU
Also, if this story is moving to
indie as you said, then that's
another reason not to think about
specific casting?

                FRIENDLY ME
Well it can help to have actors in
mind, even if, strictly speaking,
you aren't writing for them. I mean,
if you play Lucy younger, someone
like Jane Levy or Greta Gerwig could
be great in the role. If you write
her somewhat older than a recent
college grad, then Kristen Wiig. I
mean the list goes on. You don't
write for them exactly, you just
keep them or someone similar in
mind. Someone who has range and

> plays both straight and goofy. Lots
> of writers work like that. Thinking
> about a star's talent also reminds
> you to write characters with breadth
> and depth, to make full use of it!

>   IMPLIED YOU
> I loved that in <u>Bridesmaids</u> the
> comedy came from so many sources. I
> mean it was character-driven, but
> also situational and physical.

>   FRIENDLY ME
> And that's what you are starting to
> do with <u>Temptation</u>. Of course Lucy
> will drive it as a fully realized
> character. And we are starting to
> understand who she is already. But
> the situation gives you all the
> eye-gags and misunderstandings and
> hyperbolic frenzy as well, if you
> want.

>   IMPLIED YOU
> I think I want.

10. Assistance

This beat is not the movie's Crisis, but it brings us to it.

Your protagonist will need all the help they can get now because the stakes have been raised once again.

Just about every screenwriting teacher has noted that this crisis often brings your protagonist into a close brush with death. In a violent genre story your protagonist might nearly die, or someone close to them could actually be killed or at least threatened with death. In an emotional drama, "death" might mean something more like the loss of all hope or seemingly blowing your chance to make good. If girl met boy (or other girl, for that matter) earlier in the story, this is likely where girl has lost boy and has to seriously reexamine her sad self if she wants to get him back, or find a way to move on. However you conceive it, somewhere through this beat and the next (Crisis) you need to bring your protagonist up against the hardest truth and make it hurt.

Typically, Assistance has a double function.

1. It continues and accelerates the slide through crisis begun at the midpoint.
2. It expands the context of that crisis and shows us where our protagonist is in their story relationships.

Do they have any support? Who is kicking their butt to make them change? Who do they turn to when things get really bad and what does that tell us about their state of mind?

The "help function" of Assistance is actually less set in stone than some other beats. Not all movies articulate this beat in this way. Sometimes it is just another, steeper section of the slope down which Acceleration is heading for Crisis. However it is still an important reminder that most heroes don't work in a vacuum. At some point we should play to this.

For Hiccup it all comes to a head in the arena. He won the right to make his first kill in front of the entire village, remember? Well now he has the perfect opportunity to show them what he has learned. Of course when you are dealing with wild dragons and even wilder Vikings things could go badly wrong. Also, he's Hiccup. Things go badly wrong.

Cut—we are in the arena. Stoick gives an embarrassing speech about how he was as shocked as everyone else when he found out Hiccup didn't suck: "Today my boy becomes a Viking. Today he becomes one of us."

```
                    IMPLIED YOU
         Speaking the theme much, Stoick?


                    FRIENDLY ME
         Shh - he'll hear you. He's only just
         over there in the movie - ah, too
         late.


                      STOICK
         Who's that wee runt?


                    FRIENDLY ME
              (to Stoick)
         Nobody. Nobody at all.
```

> IMPLIED YOU
Hey!

> FRIENDLY ME
Great speech, by the way. We were
just saying. But don't let us stop
you, Stoick. Not when you were being
so nice about Hiccup and all.

> STOICK
Aye, a father's job is never done.

> FRIENDLY ME
True. True. Don't mind us, you go
right back to your proud fatherly
speechifying. Go Hiccup! Who knew,
am I right?
> (through gritted teeth)
Just. Stop. Staring at me . . .

Friendly Me is all fixed grin and cheerful wave
until Stoick turns back to the villagers.

> FRIENDLY ME
> (aside to Implied You)
We've been over this. Sometimes on
the nose is funny. Sometimes it
plays to the pleasure of parallels.
When we get the set-up we are even
more keen to see the payoff.

> IMPLIED YOU
Yeah, I get it. Sometimes we need
The Terminator to tell us: "I'll be
back," so we enjoy the payoff of his
return.

> FRIENDLY ME
Besides, are you crazy — did you see
the size of Stoick's hammer?

Waiting in the entrance tunnel, Hiccup hears the speech and looks resigned. But he knows his duty now. *Duty* is the theme that lies underneath acceptance in *How to Train Your Dragon*. Remember, movies can engage with more than one theme but only one, central theme drives and resolves the protagonist's story. In this way duty isn't the core theme of the film, rather it is a secondary theme that the core theme reveals. From his own experience of Vikings and dragons—and from the salutary B Story example of dutiful Astrid—Hiccup comes to understand that he has a duty to his friends and his people that is more important than the selfish motivation of fitting in. The movie's theme is still acceptance, however, because the exercise of Hiccup's new-found sense of duty will be to enable a new spirit of acceptance between the species.

Right now Hiccup's position on his transformational arc has shifted towards (heroic) sacrifice. His new sense of duty to the dragons prompts him to risk any chance he had of acceptance from the Vikings, right when his efforts had given him the best opportunity to gain it. At this point in the story he knows he has to: "Put an end to this." See how far his arc has taken him? Astrid agrees to protect Toothless if things go badly—and we're off.

Hiccup faces down a huge fiery dragon in the arena, reassuring it with a public statement of how far he's come since the story began:

HICCUP

```
      I'm not one of them.

GASPS and MURMURS race through the crowd.

ON STOICK, as all eyes turn to him. He's welling
with upset.
```

Hiccup has calmed the dragon. Now he turns to the crowd and starts his lesson: "They're not what we think they are. We don't have to kill them." Stoick has heard enough (in other words: nothing) and calls for the fight to be stopped. He smacks his hammer against the arena bars in anger. The noise spooks the dragon and it attacks Hiccup.

Now, when he really needs Assistance, Hiccup finds he has friends. Even though he is in a very bad situation, even though it is going to get a whole lot worse before it gets better, this is an important moment. Remember, we see the clearest evidence of progress in the *story* through relationships. That's why Assistance can be a key marker of *story* progress. In *How to Train Your Dragon* Hiccup still has a distance to fall, but we see that he has the nucleus of a team to support his struggle to change the world.

So plucky Astrid makes her way into the arena as Toothless rushes from the forest, having heard all the commotion. The Night Fury blasts his way into the arena and defends Hiccup. He even pins Stoick, but relents when Hiccup begs him not to hurt his father. Sadly the only reward for the dragon's courage and loyalty is to be captured by the Vikings.

So much for Hiccup's plan to teach his people the truth. He has failed (down angle). His best friend has been captured and may be killed because of him (down angle). The whole village thinks he is a traitor (down angle). He's about to find out just how bad his story's Crisis can feel . . .

Lesson Break: Supporting Characters and Story Theme

The most important lesson to learn about all of your significant supporting characters is that they need to have a direct impact on your protagonist's attempt to resolve their story (Astrid and duty). In other words every major character needs to pay their way. Nobody gets to be window-dressing.

If your characters all need to affect the A Story, they need to have distinct and specific attitudes to the theme. That way you know what their jobs are. More than this, every significant supporting character should have some kind of transformational arc of their own—imagine they are parallel clothes rails in your wardrobe.

Let's lay it out for the important characters in *How to Train Your Dragon*, starting with the protagonist and the antagonist:

Character	Status	Key Trait	Need
Hiccup	Outsider	Progressive	Needs to Change the Status Quo
Stoick	Insider	Conservative	Needs to Keep the Status Quo

That's a clear protagonist/antagonist opposition. In order to resolve his theme (in order to gain acceptance) Hiccup needs to change the world. That puts him in conflict with Stoick, who follows the old ways in an attempt to save *his* world. We see clear evidence of the bankruptcy of Stoick's position in act three when he has no answer to the Red Death. Only Hiccup offers a solution and that solution is the very embodiment of social change.

Incidentally, I have read analyses of this movie that suggest that even though Hiccup is the main character he is actually the antagonist and

Stoick the protagonist. This argument is mistaken for many reasons, chief among them: *for a story to develop you can't have a protagonist who doesn't develop*.

Stoick believes one thing doggedly until almost the very end. He submits without complaint to what he considers to be an unavoidable necessity—getting rid of the dragons. In other words he is, as his name suggests and in the terms of the movie, stoic. This means that for most of the movie Stoick can't accept Hiccup or his ideas because his beliefs do not allow him to do so. When Hiccup proves himself, Stoick simply changes his mind. It is an arc of sorts—after all there is change in there—but it's not a complex protagonist's arc, it's a straightforward expression of an antagonist's resistance until he is forced to change by the example of the protagonist.

Now let's look at the key supporting characters. Their attitudes to the theme make them models of good action for Hiccup and Stoick:

Character	Status	Key Trait	Need
Astrid	Insider	Pragmatic	Needs What's Best for the Village
Toothless	Outsider	Loyal	Needs What's Best For His Friends
Recruits	Insider	Egotistical	Need What's Best for Them

Astrid and Toothless offer variations on insider and outsider status. Astrid is a lesson in what Stoick should be and offers Hiccup hope that changing the Vikings is possible. If she can accept him, then surely any Viking might do so. Toothless forces Hiccup to see the importance of his theme in *selfless* terms. Without Toothless, Hiccup would just be a whiny, self-obsessed emo kid. Between them, the examples of these two characters help make Hiccup a hero.

Astrid is an insider by inclination. She understands the value of community and trains in dragon combat when she believes it is for the good of that community (duty). Unlike Stoick, she is pragmatic enough to accept the new truths she learns from Hiccup and Toothless. She also comes to accept Hiccup for who he is, not merely what he does. That sets her apart from the rest of the Vikings and offers another object lesson.

Toothless is the ultimate outsider. He puts Hiccup's little problems into perspective and shows him selfless friendship. Toothless is loyal to his friends and this is part of the lesson Hiccup has to learn in this angle—as we shall see, Astrid also helps remind him of this in Revelation.

The other recruits—whom I have lumped together because their story role is the same—also provide an important story function. First, they serve to highlight Hiccup's initial inadequacies and idiosyncrasies. Their immaturity also flags Astrid's maturity and her own separation from the Viking herd. We discussed this previously in relation to the B Story.

Secondly, the recruits embody the unavoidable kids-movie logic that awesomeness overcomes tradition. If you were a Viking teenager and someone gave you the choice between killing a dragon and riding one into battle which would you pick? Besides, for all their stupidity and self-regard, they are brave kids. In story terms, bravery will be their redemption.

The purpose of this little discussion is to help you see how all of these characters are doing important and interlinked story jobs. They each have a role to play in exploring the theme and demonstrating its depth and breadth to the other characters and to the audience. Once again: nobody gets to be window-dressing.

Case Study: Assistance Beats

The Town – assistance in the negative

The Town plays its Assistance beat *in the negative*. Bank robber Doug MacRay wants out, but the slide towards crisis peels away his support network. Jem, his friend and fellow gang member, morally blackmails him to stay and take the job, revealing he killed a man who was coming to kill Doug. What's more he served time for it. Fergie, the local crime boss, threatens Doug with violence if he doesn't take part in the job and his girlfriend breaks up with him (for reasons explained in the previous Acceleration case study). Finally, all alone and out of viable short-term options, Doug will agree to take part in the robbery. That's for a future beat, right now Doug's losing any chance of immediate Assistance.

Note that, just like beats that play by proxy, many story beats can work beautifully when played in the negative. In this case stripping away Assistance is as resonant as proving a protagonist has friends. Both versions play the protagonist's increasingly desperate situation externally—into the story world—and that's the point of the beat (other than to raise the stakes once more).

Captain Phillips – assistance raises the stakes

In *Captain Phillips* the Assistance beat is marked by the arrival of the three American warships. The *Maersk Alabama* now departs, after shadowing the lifeboat to ensure the USS *Bainbridge* finds it, leaving the Somalis under the guns of the Navy and with no avenue of escape open to them. At almost the same moment, the team of Navy SEALs arrive on the *Bainbridge*, prepared to offer a military solution to the hostage drama. The Americans tell the Somalis to surrender if they want a peaceful resolution. This precipitates frantic debate amongst the Somalis in the movie's Crisis.

                    FRIENDLY ME
        Who's the villain in Temptation?

                    IMPLIED YOU
        Well I have a kind of rival and I
        also have a kind of moveable
        obstacle. The rival is Bryce's ex.
        So I guess she would be the
        antagonist.

                    FRIENDLY ME
        Two women fighting over a man, now
        who's being sexist?

                    IMPLIED YOU
        I figured she wouldn't be a rival in
        that sense. But Lucy assumes she's a
        rival because, at the start, Lucy's
        still kind of a kid and makes snap
        judgments.

                    FRIENDLY ME
        Hot Halloween sex with a stranger.

                    IMPLIED YOU
        Yuppers. So she acts on that messed
        up assumption. But Tara, the ex, is
        just trying to warn Lucy about Bryce.

                    FRIENDLY ME
        Comedy from mistaken motivations.
        That could be fun. So Tara is a
        red-herring antagonist. Really she's

exposing that Lucy is her own worst
enemy?

                    IMPLIED YOU
It's just she was with Bryce before
he was ready to move on and she got
hurt.

                    FRIENDLY ME
Tara was his relationship trial
balloon.

                    IMPLIED YOU
Yeah, because she'd love to be
described that way. So, when Lucy
hears about them she gets freaked
out from the other side of the
trust equation. This happens in
Assistance. It's like Assistance
in the negative, right? There's
also stuff from Katya and others
here.

                    FRIENDLY ME
Katya seems to be receding. Are you
sure Tara isn't the B Story?

                    IMPLIED YOU
Oh. I hadn't thought about that.

                    FRIENDLY ME
Well Tara is the one Lucy can deal
with about Bryce. Once she gets over
the misplaced jealousy.

                    IMPLIED YOU
Yeah. I guess so. Pfft. More
stuff to think about. I'd have to
back-fill Tara into the story and
work out something else for
Assistance . . .

                    FRIENDLY ME
Let's move on for now. So, who's the
"moveable obstacle"?

                    IMPLIED YOU
Bryce's father, Dan. He's
protective. A caring dad. But he's a
farmer and kind of conservative in
his way.

                    FRIENDLY ME
So Dan is the dragon Lucy has to
slay to keep Bryce?

                    IMPLIED YOU
If by dragon you mean "nice guy" and
by slay you mean "convince," then
yes.

                    FRIENDLY ME
I mean Dan's the antagonist. In the
Stoick the Vast sense. Lucy has to
fit in to the family. Or to change it
to fit her somehow. Either way, she
has to prove to Dan that she's
worthy.

                    IMPLIED YOU
Ah. Right. So, in this beat Tara and
Dan push Lucy from different angles
and she is getting deeper and deeper
into her comedy deceptions, like you
suggested before.

                    FRIENDLY ME
Remember you need to seed all the
Dan stuff in earlier.

                    IMPLIED YOU
Yeah. Wow, we're really racking up
major character stuff to do now.

```
              FRIENDLY ME
    That's how it works. As you figure
    out your story, you learn what each
    of your characters needs to do.
    You'll go back and forward, over and
    over, until you have it strong
    enough to write a first draft.
```

F – Crisis

This half-angle takes your protagonist to the very depths. Through experiencing a Crisis they earn clarity and are able to see their way forward. By the end of this half-angle your protagonist should have completed enough of her arc of change that she has a chance to resolve her story in the third act to come.

11. Crisis

The Crisis beat brings everything that has happened to this point to a head. Plot and story collide in a moment of greatest threat and greatest honesty.

In *How to Train Your Dragon* this is a short beat. It brings the disaster of the Assistance beat into full focus. Furious and embarrassed, Stoick has dragged Hiccup to the great hall. Once again they don't communicate properly. Hiccup tries to explain about the dragons but Stoick is blinkered by his anger, embarrassment and responsibilities and can't hear what he needs to hear.

The only information that gets through to Stoick is that Hiccup has been to the dragon's nest and that Toothless can lead the way back there. Hiccup tries to warn Stoick that he is completely unprepared for what he will find in the nest, but his father isn't listening. The beat ends in a terrible denouncement:

```
                 HICCUP
    No. Dad. No. For once in your life,
    WOULD YOU PLEASE JUST LISTEN TO ME?!
```

He throws Hiccup off his arm, SWATTING him to the
floor.

[NOTE: This parallels Stoick throwing Hiccup out of the way in the Story World beat.]

Icy stillness. Hiccup stares back, stunned.

```
                          STOICK
       You've thrown your lot in with them.
       You're not a Viking.
            (beat)
       You're not my son.
```

Stoick calls for the boats to be readied and in the next scene the Vikings set sail, with Toothless tied up on the deck of Stoick's longship. Hiccup watches them leave from a platform high above the village. Stoick can't bear to look at Hiccup. He turns to Toothless: "Lead us home, Devil." Hiccup has failed. Absolutely and utterly—or at least that's how it seems during the Crisis. Fortunately he still has Assistance from Astrid and she's never been afraid of kicking his butt. Now it's time for the B Story to resolve and for Astrid to do her job in helping the A Story (Hiccup) see the wood for the trees.

That's what will happen in the Revelation beat...

Case Study: Crisis Beats

The Crisis near the end of act two is the culmination of a lot of the storytelling work you have already been doing. It does not emerge from a vacuum. Rather it should be the logical result of your protagonist's struggle to address their theme (and your antagonist's attempts to thwart them).

The Crisis can happen any number of ways in any genre you can think of, but your audience should always feel it comes out of the arc of the story. Even if it is finally brought about by a plot event, it should never be imposed arbitrarily by the plot. In a well-written plot-driven movie, the Crisis is the result of your protagonist being drawn ever deeper into a world of danger. This kind of Crisis may be about physical danger—bad guys threaten—but the situation should still be motivated by story.

Phone Booth – crisis as the hardest choice

In *Phone Booth* (2002, scr. Larry Cohen) the protagonist, philandering Stu Shepard, is given a stark choice by the unseen sniper who has him trapped in the public phone booth of the title. He has to choose whether his wife or his girlfriend should be the sniper's next victim. Stu solves the problem by calling his wife, Kelly, secretly on his cell so she can hear his conversation with the sniper that is taking place simultaneously on the booth's landline. Kelly gives the phone to the cops and now they know the truth—that Stu is being framed by a killer who is also on-scene. The choice the killer gives Stu emerges from his "crime" of infidelity and his way out of this Crisis is to trust the relationship to which he originally committed, his marriage.

When Harry Met Sally – crisis as the worst idea

Some movies add a level of explicit thematic focus to this kind of choice by setting up a direct question which the characters have to work at throughout the story. In *When Harry Met Sally* (1989, scr. Nora Ephron) that direct question is: can a man and a woman just be friends? The second act Crisis sees Harry and Sally finally making the mistake of sleeping with each other, potentially ruining their friendship.

Brick – crisis as collapse

Sometimes a story works to break down a character physically, emotionally or both at the same time. In this kind of story, the Crisis is the moment at which that breakdown is finally achieved. The idea in these stories is that until the protagonist has been stripped of all defense and pretense they will not be ready to hear or uncover the truth, face up to themselves and/or face true change. In *Brick* (2005, scr. Rian Johnson), unlikely tough guy Brendan is beaten to a pulp, witnesses murder and learns unpleasant truths that shatter his illusions about his ex-girlfriend. At the end of the act he is so vulnerable as a result of his story crisis that he does something he promised himself he would never do. He lets the femme fatale in. It is a mistake emotionally, but it gives him the final clue he needs to solve the mystery. (Note: You can find an extended case study of the structure of *Brick* in Chapter Six of *Write What You Don't Know*.)

These are only a sampling of story possibilities, but you can see that each uses its Crisis to address theme and character, not just plot. This should be a pretty obvious thing to do if you think about conventional storytelling as a process of character testing. Change is hard and crisis earns change.

> IMPLIED YOU
> In <u>Temptation</u>, the Crisis comes when
> Bryce finds out about the eyes. We
> already talked about that.

> FRIENDLY ME
> But that's not the thing that drives
> them apart. He's falling in love

with Lucy by now, so the eyes alone
wouldn't have mattered. It's all the
other dumb stuff she's done. Now he
feels like he's made a terrible
mistake and the woman he thought he
knew isn't real.

> IMPLIED YOU
> Now it's trust, not love. In
> fairness, it wasn't before our
> conversation, but it is now.

> FRIENDLY ME
> That's why Tara is such a good idea
> for you. She helps to reinforce
> Lucy's dumbass thinking.

> IMPLIED YOU
> Also, what Bryce wants is a serious
> relationship with a serious
> person. He's not messing about
> anymore. Not after his wife died.
> Lucy's crap just makes him think
> she's a flake and not worth
> commitment.

> FRIENDLY ME
> And of course Dan sees Bryce's
> Crisis as proof positive that any
> relationship is bad for his poor,
> emotionally damaged son. You need to
> set up something in Dan's life and
> experience that Lucy can work with
> in making her way back from the
> Crisis by the way. She needs to get
> him to stop infantilizing Bryce.
> And Bryce needs to realize that he
> needs to grow up there as well. He
> doesn't have the monopoly on
> maturity.

                    IMPLIED YOU
Stoick needs to listen to Hiccup. I
get it. That's going to be part of
the Plan. I guess a very Hollywood
version would be that Dan is a
widower himself. He is projecting
his own experience of losing his
wife onto his son.

                    FRIENDLY ME
Yeah, that would be a standard way
to play it. With good character
writing it could still work. By this
point, your audience could know,
before Lucy does, how to convince
Dan she's a good thing for Bryce.
It's fun for them as she works it
out in Revelation.

                    IMPLIED YOU
We could see something that reminds
us how good they are together. That
would answer all of Dan's
objections, if only he could see it
too?

                    FRIENDLY ME
Something like that. More
importantly, I think, Dan needs to
have a mirror held up against his
own nature as an over-protective
father.

                    IMPLIED YOU
Everybody learns. Everybody goes to
Disneyland . . .

                    FRIENDLY ME
Or they learn, but that doesn't save
the relationship. Or it does, but it
causes a major split between Bryce

and Dan that may not fully be healed
by the end of the movie. A darker
kind of comedy. But for now all that
is in the future.

12. Revelation

The Revelation beat pays off the Crisis. Revelation is the clarity Crisis buys.

Once again this is a short beat in *How to Train Your Dragon*. It takes up about two pages in script form. Hiccup is deflated but he's about to find that he has already set up his path towards redemption. His struggles have already borne fruit because there is Astrid behind him, ready to lay out her own home truths. She is acerbic to be sure, but she has a way of cutting through Hiccup's self-pity. That's exactly what Hiccup needs right now.

Astrid starts by sticking the knife in as only she can: "You must feel horrible. You've lost everything. Your father, your tribe, your best friend." Her purpose, of course, is to push him into an honest emotional response. She wants him to acknowledge his *difference*—his heroic uniqueness. Face up to that—in other words accept himself—and he can externalize his failure and move beyond it.

She repeatedly asks him why he didn't kill Toothless when he had the chance. Her goading transforms his self-pity outward into anger and then he sees it—Revelation. Hiccup opens up. He didn't kill the dragon: "because he looked as frightened as I was. I looked at him and I saw myself." In other words he empathized with the enemy. *You* remember all this, right? Because we've been over this part before. Good, well now so does Hiccup.

Now Astrid seals the deal by bending the emotional arc for Hiccup. She connects that moment with this and that connection prompts Hiccup to climb out of his self-indulgent wallow and step into action to help his friend—Revelation.

```
                    ASTRID
        I bet he's really frightened now.
          (provoking)
        What are you going to do about it?

Beat.


                    HICCUP
        Probably something stupid.
```

                          ASTRID
              Good. But you've already done that.

Another beat.

                          HICCUP
              Then something crazy.

Astrid smiles.

                          ASTRID
                 That's more like it.

Now we really love Astrid (another kind of Revelation, perhaps). It took a while—all that unbending duty got in the way—but now she has earned her place as a leader in the exciting new world Hiccup is going to create. Remember, if the writers hadn't played the B Story arc Astrid wouldn't know enough about Hiccup and Toothless to do her job in this beat. They have, she does, and now all Hiccup needs is a crazy plan, some crazy friends to help and some really crazy luck and skill to pull it off. Fortunately that's what the third act and second up angle is all about.

Lesson Break: Revision – A Stories and B Stories

Revelation is the beat where the B Story pays off. The act-long arc from the B Story beat to Revelation that gradually brought Hiccup and Astrid closer bears fruit as Astrid helps enable the resolution of the A Story. At the risk of repeating myself, in structural terms this is why Hollywood movies have B Stories in the first place.

Let's lay it out clearly:

A Story – This is your protagonist's main story. The A Story follows your protagonist as they address and attempt to resolve their theme. In this case study the A Story is all about Hiccup trying to fit in.

B Story – This follows a key supporting relationship between your protagonist and another character. B Stories do not have to be romantic, but romantic relationships involving the protagonist are typically referred to as B Stories (unless the romance is the A Story of course, as with a romantic comedy or drama like *The Fault in our Stars*) In the absence of a romantic subplot a B Story might be a friendship, family or mentoring relationship—as between a callow young moisture farmer and a wise old Jedi master perhaps?

Whatever the emotional basis of the B Story, its purpose is twofold:

1. The B Story is our easiest method of checking how our protagonist's attitude shifts in relation to their theme. They talk about their feelings with those they are close to and their actions betray their true emotions more eloquently than words. In *How to Train Your Dragon*, this begins at a distance as Hiccup's unexpected and unaccountable progress draws attention and interpretation from Astrid.
2. The B Story should play an *active* role in helping your protagonist resolve their theme. In other words you don't write a B Story just so that your protagonist has somebody to whine at, or to be whined at by. On the contrary your B Story character should influence your protagonist's thematic development (transformational arc) in a significant way. This is underwritten in *How to Train Your Dragon* but, as we have seen, it still operates in the Revelation beat.

C, D and E Stories – you may hear these talked about sometimes. There is no rule here exactly, all the letters after "B" are just a convenient shorthand to refer to other relationships or key subplots you may have in your story. In a conventional Hollywood narrative it is the B Story that is assigned the special and transformative function.

Case Study: Revelation Beats

Alien – revelation as manipulation

In *Alien* (1979, scr. Dan O'Bannon), the story is pretty simple: it is all about survival. Appropriately enough, it is the earned Revelation of terrible knowledge which makes that survival seem impossible. At the end of act two the surviving characters learn the cynical truth about their mission from the ship's computer "Mother." Also, their fellow crew-member, Ash, is revealed to be an android working for their employers the Weyland-Yutani corporation: "I can't lie to you about your chances, but... you have my sympathies." That sets up the enormity of the final struggle against the alien nicely and plays the Revelation to the theme of survival as it does so.

Safety Not Guaranteed – creepy revelation and unlikely reinforcement

The Revelation beat of *Safety Not Guaranteed* causes Darius to question every good feeling she has for Kenneth. The morning after they bond and kiss for the first time she discovers that he lied about his motivation for traveling into the past. The woman he told her he wants to save turns out to be alive and well. The journalists also encounter government agents who have been watching Kenneth, suspecting he is a spy. In the third act she has to weigh her instincts about Kenneth against the evidence of the Revelation beat in order to decide whether to keep helping him on his crazy time travel mission.

The Hunt for Red October – revelation as confirmation

The plot-driven Revelation beat in *The Hunt for Red October* (1990, scr. Larry Ferguson and Donald Stewart) emerges directly from the Crisis over whether to give Soviet submarine captain Ramius the chance to defect. The American protagonist, Jack Ryan, makes a desperate 50:50 gamble to persuade his colleagues to try to contact the Soviets rather than destroying them. His gamble pays off and in the Revelation beat' there is a tense communication between the two submarines periscopes using Morse code and active sonar: "one ping only." This results in Ramius indicating that he and his officers do indeed wish to defect.

The Revelation plays off the tense dance between Ramius' plan and Ryan's attempt to work it out that has driven the second act in a movie that intercuts parallel American and Soviet storylines all the way through. Although Ryan is nominally set up to be the lead, the story really plays off double protagonists and recruits Ryan as Ramius' B Story helpmate in the world outside the submarine *Red October*. Ryan initiates the Americans' arc towards contact and the resolution of the defection plot. He pays it off in the Revelation beat.

```
              IMPLIED YOU
In Temptation, Lucy is now in full
"I give up" mode. So this is the big
moment when Katya - wait, Tara now
- kicks her butt and tells her that
she needs to sort things out.


              FRIENDLY ME
Remember that, in conventional movie
storytelling, Tara needs to express
```

her own arc to get to the point
where she can do so. Same with Lucy,
in terms of her attitude to love and
trust. Why does Tara want to help
Lucy get back with Bryce? Also, what
has the story "taught" Lucy about
love and trust by this point?

                    IMPLIED YOU
Well trust is easy. She knows she
made a mistake.

                    FRIENDLY ME
But the Tara issue brings another
trust lesson with it.

                    IMPLIED YOU
So, Tara's arc could be to learn her
own lesson about trust. She
communicates it to Lucy? Or shows
her by example. Better. But what is
it? Maybe she's also in a
relationship?

                    FRIENDLY ME
That relationship probably shouldn't
be romantic. Especially if Lucy is
going to be jealous of her with
Bryce. Oh, wait. What if you do play
Tara as a semi-real threat
romantically?

                    IMPLIED YOU
Semi-real?

                    FRIENDLY ME
Well, what if Dan decides that Tara
is a much better option than Lucy is
for Bryce. Even though their
relationship is over, Dan tries to
set fire to the embers between Bryce

and Tara to stop him taking things
forward with Lucy? If Dan is sneaky
he arranges to meet with Tara and
apologizes for how he behaved to her
previously, when she and Bryce were
together. Oh and, by the way, "you
kids should give it another go."

                    IMPLIED YOU
Should he really be that evil? I
mean I know we need tough
opposition, but I thought Dan would
basically be a good guy. He's Stoick
in Carhartt jackets, right?

                    FRIENDLY ME
He still can be. First, comedy gives
you a license to be evil, up to a
point. You can redeem villains more
easily and push them further, as
long as you don't cross obvious
criminal and moral lines, than you
can in a drama.

                    IMPLIED YOU
Sure, I get that.

                    FRIENDLY ME
Second, you need to build a
pragmatic reason for Dan to be
worried. He's a farmer right?

                    IMPLIED YOU
Yeah. I was thinking cows and corn.

                    FRIENDLY ME
Cultivating methane and diabetes. He
really is a supervillain.

                    IMPLIED YOU
Harsh.

                    FRIENDLY ME
I live in San Francisco, so I have
drunk deep of the Kale Kool Aid. But
what if Tara is a country girl, Lucy
is from the city. See where this is
going?

                    IMPLIED YOU
Lucy-fish is flapping and gasping a
long way from her home water. A new
vista of physical comedy just opened
in front of me. Cow poop for the
win!

                    FRIENDLY ME
Have fun with that.

                    IMPLIED YOU
So, in the new version, Tara's arc
would resolve with her figuring out
what Dan is doing. And realizing she
and Bryce have no future
romantically and that's alright.
Let's see. She'd also need to
realize Lucy and Bryce should be
together, so she helps Lucy to sort
things out. Meh, she sounds like an
angel. She's poor Suzanne Pleshette
in "The Birds."

                    FRIENDLY ME
Well, you get to write the
complexity of course. Hey,
alternatively, maybe Tara's a
mother, dealing with a young kid.
Maybe Lucy thinks the kid is Bryce's
to begin with?

                    IMPLIED YOU
Maybe both.

                         FRIENDLY ME
          Sure. Or maybe it's a work
          relationship that gives Tara a trust
          arc. Whatever it is, we see Tara
          mirroring or responding to Lucy's
          need for growth. You could play Tara
          any number of ways. Just some more
          of those spitballs.

                         IMPLIED YOU
          And Dan needs to learn to trust
          Lucy. I'm still thinking here – and
          to trust Bryce. So that's another
          couple of trust arcs.

                         FRIENDLY ME
          See how the internal logic is
          starting to come together as you
          explore it? You haven't decided on
          the actual events yet. That is the
          next big stage. But you have a good
          idea of the work those events have
          to do in terms of your story
          structure.

                         IMPLIED YOU
          Yeah I do. It's like those spitballs
          are kind of useful strategically,
          even if they mostly suck as scene
          ideas.

Did you spank your hero/ine today?

Astrid just summed this one up nicely for us. At the end of the second down angle Hiccup has lost his tribe, his father and his best friend. I think that counts as a bit of a spanking by his writers.

Second down angle in *Let the Right One In*

In this angle, Oskar learns to take Eli's advice about using violence as a tool. He hurts Conny on the ice when the bullies try and intimidate him. This is a temporary victory which is paid back in the next act by Conny's brother and the gang in the swimming pool. For now, however, we see Oskar taking an important step on his path towards externalizing his capacity for violence. In a creepy way this is offering us an instance of character growth. It is also taking him further down the path towards becoming Eli's next human servant.

Another key function of the angle is for Oskar to understand and to process the truth about Eli's vampiric nature. At first he is understandably disturbed, but he comes back and eventually helps Eli to kill Lacke at the end of the act. At the same time Oskar is cutting ties with his family and becoming more and more dependent on his relationship with Eli just as she is forced into more dangerous action to feed herself in the absence of Håkan. This causes her to attack Virginia, and leads Lacke to make the connection to her in the resolution of the loose B Story.

The angle ends with Eli leaving her home in the aftermath of Lacke's murder. We don't know whether Eli has gone for good, but for the short term at least she is out of the picture. At the end of act two, Oskar is now truly alone, just at the moment when the normal world is planning his demise.

The story beats of the third angle of *Let the Right One In* work like this:

E – Commitment

9. **Acceleration:** On a school ice skating field trip the bullies confront Oskar once again and he takes Eli's advice to fight back. Oskar hits Conny with a pole, injuring him. In the B Story, the frozen corpse of Jocke is found in a pool.
10. **Assistance:** Emboldened by his first act of violence, Oskar tells Eli that they should be blood "brothers" (this is Assistance in terms of bonding them closer). He cuts his hand to make the pact and Eli is overcome by the presence of Oskar's blood. This initiates the crisis in that Oskar now understands that Eli is truly different.

In this beat Oskar also goes to stay with his divorced father. His father's rural home was previously a space of fun—of acceptance. Only this time there is another guest, Oskar's father has a male friend—we assume a gay lover—and Oskar has lost the last place in his old life in which he felt wanted and special. As with our previous case study example of *The Town*, this is Assistance *in the negative*, a peeling away of support to leave Oskar more and more isolated in his friendship with Eli, right at the moment he is coming to realize the truth about her.

This peeling away is a common horror film tactic, sometimes achieved by the simple expedient of an increased body count. Often, by the end of act two, most of the minor characters have died. This leaves the heroine—in some subgenres described as the "final girl"—alone to face the monstrous threat.

F – Crisis

11. **Crisis:** Oskar confronts Eli about her nature and learns she is a sort of vampire. Eli tells him they are alike—that he is also an outcast wishing to commit violence on the mundane world—but initially Oskar rejects this easy assertion.
12. **Revelation:** Soon after, Lacke finally finds Eli asleep in her apartment (it is his Revelation that moves the resolution forward). Oskar sees him and is prompted to defend Eli. This is part of the Revelation because it resolves Oskar's uncertainty from the Crisis. Eli kills Lacke, with Oskar's support, but that means Eli must leave her home (Revelation) and Oskar is left alone again.

Second down angle in *Winter's Bone*

This angle builds the relationship between Ree and Teardrop as he comes to take more and more of a protective and supporting interest in her. His respect for her determination, and sympathy for her situation, has brought him to help and into mortal danger. Ree is punished for that same determination and it is only with Teardrop's arrival and his promise to take responsibility for her in the future that Thump Milton agrees to release her.

Once again, Ree's progress is blocked at the Crisis of the act. She will even consider the unthinkable act of breaking up her family in order to save it. This is one more example of the paradoxical power of plot paralysis, when used in thematically appropriate ways. The very Crisis of the movie speaks directly to Ree's seeming inability to move her culture to help her. Even the threat of Teardrop's intervention seems to have no effect. The third act will give those assumptions the lie, of course. Ree's actions are causing wheels to turn offscreen. The writers are again taking risks by putting Ree (and with her the movie's story) in this position, but those risks are consistent with character and culture and so we have reasons to accept their unconventional choices. This would not work in most movies.

The story beats of the third angle of *Winter's Bone* work like this:

E – Commitment

9. **Acceleration:** Ree is badly beaten by Thump Milton's "women" for her presumption. Her fate is not certain at this point as the clan considers killing her and tells her as much.
10. **Assistance:** Teardrop arrives at Thump's place and agrees to "stand for" Ree in order to rescue her. Now he tells Ree that she "owns him" as he will be punished for her future wrong actions.

F – Crisis

11. **Crisis:** With nowhere left to go and no way to find her father, Ree considers allowing her brother to be brought up by the neighbors. The Crisis has her seriously contemplating splitting up the family for the first time. She had rejected this possibility in the strongest terms when it was first suggested in act one.
12. **Revelation:** At this second moment of impasse, Teardrop comes to help Ree find her father. He and Ree bond further and the Revelation is that blood does still mean something. Family does still mean something— especially when Ree's strength has impressed this on Teardrop so forcefully in what has happened previously.

Questions to ask *yourself* as you write act two – second down angle

Acceleration

Q: Am I making things tougher for my protagonist immediately after the Midpoint?

Q: Am I showing this in more than one way in my storytelling?

Q: Does this Acceleration speak both to the theme and arc of my protagonist and the nature and goals of the antagonistic force in my story?

Assistance

Q: Am I raising the stakes again?

Q: Am I making sure that the B Story and the supporting cast of my story interact with the impending Crisis?

Q: Assistance can also refer to my protagonist's own inner strength—how am I testing this?

Crisis

Q: Is this Crisis a real crisis—does it threaten my protagonist with the worst possible future my story could provide?

Q: Am I helping my protagonist towards seeing the truth of their task clearly through the pain?

Q: How is my antagonistic force driving the Crisis and working it to my theme?

Revelation

Q: Does my protagonist "get it" now?

Q: Am I making sure that my B Story is essential in moving my protagonist from Crisis to Revelation?

Q: Can the audience see enough of the way forward such that they get the significance of what just happened?

Questions to ask *your first draft* of act two – second down angle

After you have finished a first draft of your screenplay, re-read it and ask the following questions:

Acceleration

Q: Looking back through the story, is the payoff of the Midpoint clear and powerful enough?

Q: Does this beat pick up the pacing of my storytelling—and do I ever let it slip from now on?

Q: Does the parallel between the Decision and Acceleration beats bookend the turn of the story satisfactorily?

Q: How can I write all of this just as effectively with fewer words and in fewer pages?

Assistance

Q: Have I kept up the new, second half pace of my story—established in the previous beat—or, ideally, increased it still further?

Q: Does the parallel between the Challenge and Assistance beats show the value of the preparatory work of the previous up angle—is it paying off now?

Q: How can I write all of this just as effectively with fewer words and in fewer pages?

Crisis

Q: Does my Crisis emerge organically from my theme and my protagonist's arc?

Q: Looking back, does the parallel between the Progress and Crisis beats show—or at least suggest—how my protagonist's first steps led her here?

Q: How can I write all of this just as effectively with fewer words and in fewer pages?

Revelation

Q: Looking back, could my protagonist have got here without the Crisis?

Q: Does the parallel between the B Story and Revelation beats prove that without the B Story relationship my protagonist would not have made it through?

Q: How can I write all of this just as effectively with fewer words and in fewer pages?

Act Three: Second up angle (resolution)

By the end of act two we will be at the very bottom of the *second down angle*. In a conventional movie, things were at their worst until our protagonist finally learned the lesson of their trials and saw a way forward. Now all that remains is to follow them up the steep slope of the second up angle that constitutes act three to eventual success (an "up ending") or failure (a "down ending").

Typically, the Revelation at the end of act two drives the protagonist into making a plan to achieve the resolution of her theme. Of course the opposing forces have not been idle and they will resist her every step of the way. That's what makes third acts fun, so don't stint on the resistance. After all, there wouldn't be so much pressure in that Death Star trench if all you were facing were some noob slacker flak cannons. It is when Darth Vader appears in a fighter behind the attacking rebel ships that things really heat up for them.

At the end you have a choice whether to have your protagonist succeed or not. Of course most mainstream movies end in success for their heroes or heroines. Our heroine has *redeemed* her past failings and has restored a better world. Your choice as to how to resolve your story should come organically from the way you have written your protagonist and their theme. It should be the final statement of your purpose in telling this particular story.

A trap many young writers fall into is thinking that just by killing off their protagonist at the end they have somehow written a radical story. (I know who you are, sitting in the metaphorical back row in your imaginary hipster hats...) This is almost always *not* the case. Unless their failure is in itself dramatically, thematically and emotionally satisfying (as with James Cole's thematically necessary—and indeed inevitable—death in *Twelve Monkeys*, for example) we will "hear the typewriter" behind the scenes and call out your "twist" for the empty and sophomoric gesture it probably is.

On the other hand, down endings can be incredibly effective when handled well. Historically, tragedies have their own internal logic in which an otherwise admirable or sympathetic protagonist has a tragic flaw which dooms them to an awful fate. (This is loosely related to the concept of *hamartia* in **Aristotle's *Poetics*.**) In Shakespeare's play the admirable soldier, Macbeth, is doomed by his tragic flaw, ambition. What's more he understands his own nature, declaring in a soliloquy: "I have no spur to prick the sides of my intent, but only vaulting ambition, which o'erleaps itself, and falls on th'other." At the end of the play. Macbeth the jaded monster is killed by a Shakespearian "gang of light" led by Macduff.

Of course one doesn't have to write a Shakespearian tragedy to earn a down ending. Nevertheless, the link between character and fate we are shown in such classic stories offers an important lesson. In *Brick* the protagonist, Brendan, solves the mystery of his ex-girlfriend's murder. However he ends up badly damaged as a person both physically and emotionally. The story punishes Brendan for his failings as a man, even as it allows him to succeed as a detective.

Remember also that whether your protagonist succeeds or fails, the story world we are left with at the end of the movie has changed. Perhaps for the better, maybe for the worse but it can't be the same as it was at the beginning or your story had no effect. In objective terms, the story world of *Brick* is restored at the end of the movie. In subjective terms, it is broken. At the end of the final story angle you might need to give us some time—maybe only a few moments, maybe a scene or two—to observe and reflect upon this change.

The story beats of the second up angle of *How to Train Your Dragon* work like this:

G – Confrontation

13. **Plan:** This is a tale of two competing plans to deal with the dragons, Stoick's old way and Hiccup's new way.

14. Pushback: Stoick and the Vikings encounter the Red Death. In the face of this awesome pushback, Stoick's old-school plan suddenly seems lacking. Fortunately, Hiccup is there to save the day and father and son are reconciled. Now all that remains is to defeat the Red Death.

H – Resolution

15. Resolution: Hiccup and Toothless lead an epic aerial fight with the Red Death. It ends in victory, but Hiccup is badly hurt. Heroism has a cost.

16. Resonance: Hiccup wakes at home to find he has lost a leg but gained a better world. Viking and dragon are now partners and Hiccup is a hero to all. As we leave the changed world of Berk we see further evidence that his theme is resolved.

G – Confrontation

This half-angle sets up the final struggle between your protagonist and the story's antagonistic force. You test both these forces almost to the limit here. By the end of these two beats everything should be ready for the story to be resolved.

13. Plan

Stoick and the Viking longships enter Hellheim's Gate. Gobber—who has clearly taken screenwriting classes—nervously asks Stoick whether there is, you know, a plan. Apparently Stoick's plan is to "find the nest and take it." Gobber's response helpfully reminds us of the story status of Stoick's thinking: "The old Viking fallback. Nice and simple." Gobber performs his key thematic function here. In the story world his task is to be "Stoick Lite." Gobber reassures us that even old-school Vikings might be open to change.

Stoick's plan is the kind of plan you come up with if you never had to think about making plans. We are Vikings. We hit stuff with other stuff. That makes hitting more stuff with other stuff a respectable plan. Remember that the audience has already seen the Red Death, so we share Hiccup's concern that the Vikings are in for a rough time.

Meanwhile, back in the arena, Hiccup pauses outside the door to the dragon pens. The other recruits turn up, led by Astrid: "So what's the plan?" Hiccup just looks at them and smiles.

So now we have competing plans, one old-school and one—well we don't know exactly what it is yet but you can bet it involves dragons. This sets the angle up very nicely as a contest between the old ways and the new. Sure enough, out come the dragons and Hiccup shows the recruits how to relate to them. It's a cute moment of calm before the storm. He throws them a rope: "You're going to need something to help you hold on."

At the start of act three Hiccup is falling naturally into a leadership role. He never could have spoken to the other recruits like this before. His arc of change, otherwise known as act two, had to be played out first. Now he's on top of his game. It's a good thing he is, because the Vikings have just found the dragons' nest. They blast open a hole with their catapults and Stoick steps into the breach: "No matter how this ends, it ends today."

Hiccup's plan isn't exactly brain surgery: fly dragons + pwn in the boss fight. It is still immensely satisfying however, because it is both the only way for the Vikings to defeat the Red Death and is simultaneously proof positive of Hiccup's heroic, transformational status. Its simplicity has been earned by Hiccup's struggles. I guess what I'm saying here is, contrary to much of the advice you will read about what makes a good third act, the climax of your story doesn't have to be overly complex, *it just has to be right.*

We are back to parallelism again: show us what your story has made us want to see. Do it with style and eloquence and we will be happy. That doesn't mean you shouldn't be raising the stakes in the final angle. On the contrary, things should look very dicey. Your forces of opposition should be at their most brilliant and dangerous:

                    PORKINS
        Yeah, so we checked out that Death
        Star trench. . . and we'll be taking
        the next shuttle out of here.

                  PRINCESS LEIA
        But. . . the rebellion and all . . .

                    PORKINS
        Maybe next time you'll think before
        you call the fat guy "Porkins."
        Later days, princess.

People often say that "screenwriting is all about the ending." And they are right. Of course screenwriting is also all about beginnings and middles. Without great structure from the start, your ending will be a damp squib because we won't care a damn what happens. Having said that, a great ending relies on powerful opposition to your protagonist and their Plan. At the end of the beat, all the smaller dragons fly out and away in a great flock. Some of the Vikings cheer, thinking the battle is over before it has begun. Stoick feels the ground shake and splinter: "This isn't over." Indeed it isn't—the Pushback is on its way. . .

Case Study: Plan Beats

Captain Phillips – the plan gradually revealed

In *Captain Phillips*, the plan is revealed gradually as we watch the US Navy take a series of steps to make the rescue possible. The Somalis are distracted while a listening device is placed on the lifeboat. Their leader, Muse, is removed, ostensibly to discuss the situation on the American warship with elders from his tribe. The lifeboat is placed under tow, bringing it directly under the guns of the SEAL snipers who intend to execute the pirates. Captain Phillips is warned to stay in his original seat—so that the snipers will know where he is. The beat plays out as a slow reveal that allows us to appreciate the tactical sophistication of the armed forces and the psychological manipulation they use to place the pirates where they want them.

The narrational choice to position the movie's audience between the opposing forces in terms of knowledge is smart. We play catch-up with the Navy as they execute their plan, but we are given a more privileged position in terms of access to information than either the captain or the pirates. In this way, we are invested in making connections and recognizing patterns in the actions of the military—in working out their plan as it manifests in the plot—and we are privileged enough to be able to empathize with those on the receiving end. We know what is coming. The captain expects the result, but does not know the exact tactics. The remaining pirates assume treachery, but hope for reprieve.

The Hunt for Red October – between multiple plans

The Hunt for Red October draws together the threads of a whole handful of Plans in this beat. First we are shown Ramius' plan to get the crew off his submarine alive by faking a reactor leak. Next he dives the boat, ostensibly to scuttle it. Meanwhile Jack Ryan's own plan matures as his US Navy group enters the *Red October* submarine via a small rescue sub. Independently, an American surface vessel drops a torpedo on *Red October*, but the weapon is detonated prematurely by Admiral Greer. This provides more "evidence" that *Red October* has been sunk, hiding the truth that it has in fact been handed over to the Americans.

Things are about to get even more intense in the Pushback beat, but for now the Plan beat sees a complex, tense and intriguing intersection of strategic and tactical thinking from all the major players in the story. In a plot-driven military thriller like *Hunt for Red October*, having multiple plot threads pulling together around the beat in this way is particularly effective. It is like *Captain Phillips* on overdrive. In this case, the audience is already well aware of the intentions of Ryan and Ramius. The basic dramatic alternatives (defection or destruction) are already on the table, so the more additional complexity and perspectives the writers throw at this problem to enrich our expectations the better.

>   FRIENDLY ME
>   Now tell me the plan in <u>Temptation</u>.
>
>   IMPLIED YOU
>   I'm working it out again, now that
>   we made all those major changes.
>   Lucy has to persuade Bryce she's
>   not a flake, and that she's learned,
>   and that she's serious about him.
>   All that big stuff. So she can do
>   that directly, or through Dan,
>   or . . .
>
>   FRIENDLY ME
>   Working backwards through your story
>   to think about how we might get
>   here, did you consider making Dan
>   the catalyst for the Crisis?
>
>   IMPLIED YOU
>   How would that work?
>
>   FRIENDLY ME
>   Well, you told me about how Dan is
>   over-protective. What if he's so
>   concerned about Bryce and Lucy that
>   he follows her. Dan in the city. Or
>   he finds out about her from Tara, who
>   is no longer a threat to him. And
>   this works especially well if Dan
>   is playing gullible Tara to run

romantic interference between Bryce
and Lucy, like we discussed.

                IMPLIED YOU
So, he's doing that to get her on
side. And if she doesn't know about
the eyes. . . That would be cool.
Tara only meets Lucy separately from
Bryce. She's only seen her with her
natural green eyes.

                FRIENDLY ME
Nice. Because, given how things start
between them, Lucy wouldn't confide
in Tara about her big deception. At
least not before all of this goes
down. Maybe in her cups in
Revelation. She takes her contacts
out and shows Tara. Then she drowns
them in her glass of booze.

                IMPLIED YOU
So Tara could tell Dan how impressed
she is that Bryce has got over his
issues there. And that sets up Lucy.
Dan weaves a tale for Bryce that
plays Lucy as the flaky, deceitful
city girl who is just using him.
Nasty Dan!

                FRIENDLY ME
Ok, here's Hollywood Moment 337. Gag
over it at your own pace please:
back in the Crisis, Lucy believes
she's meeting Bryce to talk about
moving in together, or about taking
their relationship to the next
level. And that was the idea before
Dan poisons Bryce on Lucy, after
talking to Tara. So the big set-
piece becomes a nightmare.

                    IMPLIED YOU
Thanks for the warning, because
I did throw up a little in my
mouth there. As you said before.
It depends how I can turn it.
But I like the idea that Dan is
scared Bryce will leave the farm
and go live with Lucy in the city.
Also, not sure that would be
Bryce's way of doing it. He's
meant to be the decent, mature
one.

                    FRIENDLY ME
You're right. He wouldn't. Bad idea.
But he could ruin the big moment
anyway. He just wouldn't be so
confrontational and crass.

                    IMPLIED YOU
I've made a note though. I like the
hope denied.

                    FRIENDLY ME
That reminds me, we need to work
Bryce much harder on our next pass
through the story. We don't know
what makes him right for Lucy yet.
But Dan's set-up also gives Lucy
some moral permission to dig into
Dan herself. She also wants to find
out how to help Bryce.

                    IMPLIED YOU
Lucy goes to Dan's country. She
talks to his neighbors or people
in town. Tara could go with her,
to help make amends. After the
Crisis, she will understand what
she did.

FRIENDLY ME

How about they find something: an
example of how Dan broke trust with
his wife or his community. Maybe
something he's doing right now? But
then Lucy realizes she's going about
it all wrong. Tara is gung-ho but
Lucy thinks . . .

IMPLIED YOU

"I can't destroy this family to
join it." I mean she's not
necessarily thinking about marriage,
but still. And she backs off.
That's her Hollywood arc of change
and sacrifice, or whatever: Lucy
becomes Charmander, then becomes
Charmeleon. She decides to give up
the chance of a future with Bryce
rather than mess up his world. It
needs work, but I could do something
with it.

FRIENDLY ME

Oh, so Lucy's sacrifice is her
Pushback against herself? It's the
next beat.

IMPLIED YOU

Maybe. But how come when we are
working on one beat we seem to figure
out what to do about a different
beat?

FRIENDLY ME

Happens all the time. That's why
having a structural model can be so
useful. When you are thinking about
what one piece needs, you reveal
something about the others.

14. Pushback

We've had the Plan(s), now we get the Pushback. Predictably Stoick's Plan doesn't survive contact with the real enemy, but our knowledge of storytelling makes us confident that Hiccup's will—if only he arrives in time. In the meantime, the Red Death has arrived, however. The Vikings find their catapults are useless against her and the Red Death burns their boats with a single fiery breath.

Stoick may not be a master planner, but he knows he can be a master heroic sacrifice. Nobody ever accused him of being a coward. He and Gobber stay to distract the Red Death to allow the rest of the Vikings to get away. They do their best, but soon enough the monstrous dragon gets the drop on Stoick (Pushback).

Suddenly a bolt of dragon fire hits the Red Death in the head, distracting her. It's Hiccup and the other kids and they are all riding dragons! What's more, Hiccup is in total command, giving tactical instructions to the other riders in the middle of combat. This is where even the most cynical amongst you shout: "Woohoo!"

Talking of self-esteem, Gobber looks up at Hiccup: "Every bit the boar-headed, stubborn Viking you ever were." Stoick just nods, speechless at Gobber's evident need to speak the story—again!

What follows is the beginning of a dynamic "boss fight" action sequence, full of derring do, as the recruits try and work out the Red Death's weaknesses. Meanwhile Astrid drops Hiccup onto the burning deck of Stoick's longship. He starts to free Toothless from his bonds. Before he can untie the dragon, however, the Red Death's foot smashes down and Toothless is knocked into the water.

Hiccup dives in to save him but isn't strong enough. Just when all seems lost, Stoick grabs him and pulls him on to shore. Then Stoick dives right back in to save... Toothless. Big deal, right? Hiccup mounts up and he and Stoick share a moment. There are apologies, there is forgiveness. Hiccup is officially Stoick's son again, and then:

```
Hiccup spurs Toothless on, charged with his
father's belief in him. They rocket into the sky
as Stoick watches.
```

There's still the Red Death to defeat.

Lesson Break: The Thematic Power of Monsters

The ~~Death Star~~ Red Death will be in range in. . .

Not all antagonists are monsters. If we have been paying attention we already know this from the example of Stoick. For that matter, neither are all monsters antagonists. Sometimes they are just malign or mindless forces that need to be defeated or neutralized for our protagonist to prevail. They are merely brutal bumps in the road, not fully motivated supervillains.

A non-antagonist monster is the troll under the bridge in all its forms. Its function is to test the worthiness of our heroine to progress to the more dangerous battle against the real antagonist who waits on the other side of the river. Of course in *How to Train Your Dragon*, the Red Death isn't a troll under the bridge as much as a dragon under a mountain, but the same principle applies. Although they are mortal enemies, the Red Death is also Stoick's proxy. Only through its defeat—only through Hiccup's Plan—will he learn his own lesson.

The Red Death is huge and vicious and holds the other dragons as thralls. On those terms it fully deserves a smack on the nose with a rolled up newspaper. It is also a *thematically appropriate threat*.

By now you will hardly be surprised that I am referring every important story choice back to theme. That's because your story is nothing without your theme so everything in the story should serve it. This is how it works:

- *The Red Death is the embodiment of all that the Vikings fear about dragons.* If there wasn't a Red Death, then the other dragons would be no threat to the Vikings and we wouldn't have a plot. It is vicious and voracious and it wants their sheep.
- *The Red Death is the antithesis of what Hiccup knows about the other dragons.* In the terms of the story, we have already learned that the other dragons are not true monsters. By virtue of its huge size, grotesque appearance, cannibalistic instincts and insatiable appetite (a common movie shorthand for monstrosity as perverse excess) the Red Death is. In structural terms its very monstrosity excuses the milder eccentricities of its smaller cousins.
- *The Red Death is the brutal twin of Stoick.* Just as Stoick represents all the forces holding the Vikings to the old ways, so the Red Death is what keeps the dragons raiding the Vikings. They are both forces of conservatism in their communities and, thus, need to be overcome in order for the world to change enough for Hiccup to fit in.
- *The Red Death is a necessary monster.* We would feel its lack as a structural absence for all the reasons above and because it allows the story to be light. Without the Red Death as an excuse, it would be much

harder to integrate the Vikings with the dragons because their economic interests (sheep = tasty) would still clash. With the Red Death in play, the writers can allow the other dragons to eat fish—but not eels of course—and be happy.

In sum, the Red Death is not a random brute but a carefully worked component in the thematic puzzle of the story. When you design oppositional forces for your story remember that the more closely you weave them into your protagonist's theme and into the problem of your story world the more we will enjoy them.

Case Study: Pushback Beats

The Town – pushback as test

The Pushback beat in *The Town* is set up early within the Plan beat. We follow robbers Doug and Jem as they infiltrate Fenway Park baseball stadium in Boston, disguised as police officers. Then, before their whole plan has been revealed, the script cuts away to a hospital ward, where FBI Special Agent Frawley is putting pressure on Doug's ex-girlfriend, Kris, to reveal their scheme. Although we don't know the outcome of that conversation up front, when we cut straight back to watch the robbers negotiate their way into the stadium's cash room we have more reason to assume the Plan is going to go awry, no matter how clever it might be or how smartly it is being executed.

The audience has their cake and eats it as the smart plan plays out. We admire the thoroughness of the robbers' preparation and know that all that preparation will be as nothing compared to what happens if the FBI finds out about it. When the Pushback begins in earnest, we see the robbers forced to react to events as they play out. They have been tested in planning the job, now their test is in playing the moment and responding on instinct. Pushback pressures them in new ways and that's the fun of the beat.

The Hunt for Red October – staggered pushback

The Pushback beat in *The Hunt for Red October* intersects the interlocking Plans of the good guys with the ongoing need of the bad guys to destroy the submarine. After all the tension and suspense has paid off into communication and understanding between the Americans and the defecting officers—just as it feels like success is at hand—the Soviet forces strike back. A Soviet attack sub arrives and fires torpedoes at *Red October*.

Defeating this threat will demonstrate the talent of Ramius as a sub commander and the need for collaboration between the scratch American and Soviet crew. To top this external threat, a lurking KGB agent on the *Red October*'s crew attacks and threatens to blow the ship up by detonating one of its nuclear warheads.

So Pushback is well plotted in delivering action threats both internal and external to the submarine. The Plan beat has been used to get the Ryan and Ramius groups in the same place to face off together against whatever threats will be incoming in the beat. The revelation of these threats is then staggered, so that we are engrossed in watching the good guys addressing the first problem right when the second attack is launched.

Another way in which the plotting is especially effective in this sequence is that the external threat emerges before the internal one. This gives us the illusion of a safe space for collaboration within the submarine. The internal threat is then deployed by the writers to peel away that illusion. What's more, each of the threats is powerful enough on its own to ruin all the best laid Plans of our heroes. In combination, the double attack raises the stakes to the highest. We understand that it will take the combined skills and heroism of our principal characters to overcome both. That, of course, is what happens in the Resolution beat.

> IMPLIED YOU
> Temptation is becoming a city-girl-on-a-farm-movie. I hadn't planned it that way.

> FRIENDLY ME
> It's also a farm-boy-in-the-city-movie, if that helps! But we've been following the clues you already seeded into your own idea. You made Bryce a farmer, right? These ideas have emerged from what you already know about your movie. Does that worry you?

> IMPLIED YOU
> I don't know yet. It's a lot to think about. It's feels like Jennifer Aniston bushwhacked Sandra Bullock and stole her story.

                    FRIENDLY ME
Jennifer Aniston. Really?

                    IMPLIED YOU
Cow poop jokes.

                    FRIENDLY ME
Right. But look, here's another way
you can conceptualize the story as a
whole: it's a collision of cultures
and visual frames. That is assuming
the city-girl-in-cow-poop thing
doesn't put you off in the long
term.

                    IMPLIED YOU
Dammit, you're going to make me
start from scratch, aren't you?

                    FRIENDLY ME
Not at all. Act one is, and always
has been all about the city. True?

                    IMPLIED YOU
True.

                    FRIENDLY ME
Lucy and Bryce meet. Lucy is in
control in her space. Bryce is kind
of under her aspiring-to-be-a-bit-
sophisticated spell. Which fits with
the deception plot.

                    IMPLIED YOU
She's Carrie Bradshaw, but
recognizably human. Exactly.

                    FRIENDLY ME
Act two, up to the Midpoint, is
country. They take a trip . . .

                    IMPLIED YOU
But it's not to visit old Auntie
Plot-Device, it's to see Bryce's
family farm: Plot-Device Acres. Of
course.

                    FRIENDLY ME
They meet Dan and Lucy sucks out
on the farm. Still, she is charming
and Bryce is drawn. So, the Midpoint
is: "I love you." Bryce has moved
beyond his late wife and Lucy
finds – shock – that she means the
words for once.

                    IMPLIED YOU
It's a big deal for both of them.

                    FRIENDLY ME
In terms of your story, it's a
double Midpoint win: Lucy is set up
for the fall and them falling in
love scares Dan. It is a catalyst
for more desperate action.

                    IMPLIED YOU
I got it. Let me take it from here.

                    FRIENDLY ME
By all means.

                    IMPLIED YOU
Act two, from the Midpoint to the
end of the act? It's the city again.
So now Bryce tries out Lucy's world.
He meets all her friends and so
forth. Meanwhile, Dan is creeping on
Lucy's past and Tara is part of that
set-up.

                    FRIENDLY ME
Lucy thinks she's on safe ground
now, but in fact it's starting to
collapse around her.

                    IMPLIED YOU
Right. Then it all comes to a head
in the city. The Crisis undermines
Lucy in front of her own friends and
in her own space. Bryce has gone
back home. Dan is ruling the roost.
Tara will help her but, in act
three, Lucy has to go deal with
the pesky country again to win
him back.

                    FRIENDLY ME
City; country; city; country. It's
very Donnie and Marie.

                    IMPLIED YOU
Huh?

                    FRIENDLY ME
Ignore me, I'm old. And Lucy;
Bryce; Lucy; Bryce. Act one is
Lucy and Bryce alone, mostly. Act
two to the Midpoint is mostly Lucy
in Bryce-world. From the Midpoint
to end of act two Bryce is mostly
in Lucy-world. In act three the
worlds collide and resolve.
It's a neat structure and it
also works symbolically, in
terms of power and arcs and so
forth.

                    IMPLIED YOU
Yeah. I like it, but I want to think
about it some more.

FRIENDLY ME
That's wise. Let me put one more
thing in your mind. It's for later
in the writing process, but it's
very important.

IMPLIED YOU
Shoot. I'm all Moleskinned up and
ready to go.

FRIENDLY ME
As you write the screenplay, you can
set up a whole image network that
illustrates the collision of worlds.
As Lucy and Bryce get together, we
see country images blending
naturally into the city and, in
turn, the city imagery blends
naturally into the country.

IMPLIED YOU
Oh I see. Music will be doing the
same thing.

FRIENDLY ME
Yup. But, when they are on the outs,
those images will feel out of place
or sound more discordant. That's how
Temptation becomes worthy of being a
movie, not a radio play. Writing
imagery is for later though. Now
it's time for the Pushback.

IMPLIED YOU
Well the Pushback is Dan's final
defense against Lucy, Tara and the
truth. But I'm more interested in
the bigger structure right now. I
mean now I get why we're going
through the beats. It's not to plot

them out, but to let them ask us
questions of the whole story.

                    FRIENDLY ME
Yeah. A fallback model lets you test
your ideas against it in concrete
terms: if I want to get here by this
beat, then how does that work in
practice? What do I need to know
about my characters to plan this?

                    IMPLIED YOU
I was thinking, what if Lucy does
have skills the farm can use? Like
she could set up a website for them
to sell their produce, their
diabetic methane, or. . . No, that's
lame. Wait, what if Bryce is the
tech guy?

                    FRIENDLY ME
That's interesting. He's the
American Adam with an Apple
computer.

                    IMPLIED YOU
He's not that good of a farmer,
truth be told, but he's a tech
wizard. So Dan is scared that the
farm will be lost to the family
because Bryce is going to go work in
Silicon Valley.

                    FRIENDLY ME
Maybe Dan went to the local Aggie
College to please his dad, but
really he's been all hyped-up for
computers and online stuff. He's
basically self-taught. Maybe he took
some classes at college. Also, he
married his high school sweetheart

and she died after only a year? That
gives the young-version timeline
some credibility. The lure of the
big city at the start makes more
sense now.

IMPLIED YOU
He was there for a job interview!

FRIENDLY ME
Great. That also gives Dan a really
human reason for his antagonism and
makes him redeemable. He's really
scared about the future. And people
do the dumbest things when they are
scared. So all you need to do now is
decide on the resolution . . .

H – Resolution

This half-angle pits protagonist and antagonist against one another in the final struggle. This is where you test them to the absolute limit and set the terms of the movie's Resolution. After that Resolution comes Resonance, and you allow your audience to dwell on what the ending means for your protagonist, their world, and also for your audience in the world outside your story.

15. Resolution

This is the beat where anybody who still needs to get some... gets some. This is what we have been waiting for throughout our protagonist's struggles. In other words this is the big parallel payoff so you better make it fun. Typically Resolution also contains the obligatory moment that responds to the story's inciting incident (see below).

Hiccup makes the Red Death chase Toothless through the skies. They climb up and hide in the clouds and smoke, ambushing the monster with bolts of Night Fury fire. Then they turn and lead the Red Death back down through the clouds. The Red Death's little wings start to rip, she is having trouble controlling her dive—clearly she shouldn't have eaten so many sheep. Toothless turns to fire a final bolt into her mouth, distracting her so she can't react in time to save herself from crashing to earth in a huge explosion.

Toothless shoots skyward, trying to escape the flames. He almost makes it but, at the last moment, he gets hit by a final flail of the Red Death's tail. Hiccup falls off and the last thing we see is Toothless diving back towards the fire in a desperate attempt to catch Hiccup.

Cut to the beach. Stoick desperately searches for Hiccup in the smoke. There's Toothless, collapsed on the beach but alive. No sign of Hiccup. Stoick mourns: "Oh son... I did this..." He also apologizes to the dragon ...

```
Toothless unfolds his wings, revealing Hiccup,
unconscious, clutched safely against his chest.
Stoick's eyes widen.
```

Here's the movie's obligatory moment. Toothless has fallen to earth once again, but this time to save Hiccup. The crowd of Vikings and dragons roars with relief and delight. Stoick thanks the Night Fury for saving his son. Gobber: "Well, you know... most of him." What does that mean? We'll have to wait for Resonance, the next beat, to find out ...

Lesson Break: Writing Action

Writing action sequences is a tricky thing to do. Every writer has their own approach and style of course and different kinds of movies require different levels of detail.

As we saw previously, the screenwriter Shane Black (*Lethal Weapon, The Last Boy Scout, The Long Kiss Goodnight, Kiss Kiss Bang Bang*) used to add in ironic or factual asides about the type of gun his hero was using or the way he expected industry readers to respond to his scenes. I have already warned you about copying another writer's style, however you might follow his advice in this at least: "The worst of the action films are the ones where everything is one shout from beginning to finish. And there's no differentiation between beats, like small or big, or quiet or expansive. It's all just one loud shout." Well-written action sequences have their own internal logic and longer ones even have story beats. Some of them—to follow Shane Black's lead—are certainly louder than others.

Remember also that *narrative economy* should always be in the back of your mind as you are writing any sequence. Say as much as you can in as few words as possible. Here are a few thoughts to get you started:

- **Clarity:** Whatever your genre and whatever the level of technical complexity involved that may need some explanation, you have to find a way of hitting a balance between blandly over-simplifying and When

Details Attack. That is a nice judgment of course. One cannot generalize other than to say: you are writing a story so, if in doubt, make sure story trumps detail. Also remember the difference between a spec screenplay and a shooting script. The former plays more to clarity of concept and story, the latter may add a different kind of clarity through detail.

- **Flow:** That means you have to keep the narrative flowing throughout. Don't let the pace of the read drop away through over-writing or you will lose the very excitement, the kinesis-on-the-page an action sequence should be about. We need to be focused on *why* we are watching action at least as much as *what* we are watching. I'm all for cool explosions, but they don't fill my heart with movie love on their own.

- **Character:** The way to make sure narrative flows through action is to play that action to character. Action happens because our characters initiate it or are the victims or objects of it. That means we should care about what happens to them. Don't hide them behind props and special effects.

Every action scene should be led by character and should speak directly to their arcs and relationships. The characters involved will use, perhaps even discover, skills and take instinctive decisions, reacting to danger in ways that tell us something about who they are, where their thinking is, their strengths and weaknesses and what they are trying to do in the larger story.

Think about the opening sequence of *Raiders of the Lost Ark* (1981, scr. Lawrence Kasdan) in which we follow Indiana Jones as he explores an ancient tomb. As our hero navigates the tricks and traps left by the original builders we learn that he is smart and well educated in such matters. His whole demeanor speaks his experience and his care to look after the other members of his team speaks to an underlying decency. Indy could have used them as cannon fodder to trip the traps, but he takes his own risks to protect them all. This moral sensibility isn't shared by his back-stabbing accomplices who double-cross him and die as a result. The sequence is not just an exciting tomb raid, it is a primer on Indiana Jones.

This applies both in modest and multi-million dollar sequences. If you compare the set-piece action sequences from *The Avengers* (2012, scr. Joss Whedon) to the *Transformers* movies (2007, 2009, 2011), for example, you will see a far greater emphasis on character and story development through action in the former than the latter. Bloated and largely redundant sequences that repeat inconclusive action over and over like the battle on the pyramids in *Transformers: Revenge of the Fallen* are examples of how not to do this. On the other hand, think about how the final sequence of *The Avengers* plays to the underlying

narrative of team formation. Each superhero is used according to their strengths and, in doing so, the parts become greater as a whole. This is the point of assembling the Avengers after all and this sequence is to be found in the next case study.
- **Justification:** The way to make sure you are being honest with your audience and focusing your action through character is by making sure your action sequences have weight. In other words you need to justify them through story, not just have them ambush the plot. (See the earlier lesson about monsters for a discussion of how the Red Death fits into this context.)

Of course there is a great deal more to say about how to structure action sequences as spectacle. All I am trying to do here is to give you a framework for your thinking to keep you honest to your overall story goals while you write. Always try to avoid writing action for action's sake, but revel in the kinetic, dramatic fun you offer us when you write action well.

One final note: when writing action sequences in a spec script, *white space is your friend*. Don't write in big dense paragraphs, crammed with detail. Encapsulate a moment of kinetic drama in a sentence or two, leave a blank line, then give us the next. It makes for a faster, more exciting read.[42]

Case Study: Structuring Tentpole Action in *The Avengers*

The climactic battle sequence in *The Avengers* is structured like a small movie within a movie. It tells a little story that replicates, in miniature, and also resolves the narrative of the bigger film. It follows its own internal story logic, turns at a Midpoint and even has its own little B Story to ground all the high-stakes superhero derring do in real-world peril. In this sequence the proof of the Avengers concept is proven as the disparate superheroes meld into a team and begin to use their individual skills as part of a whole that now becomes more than the sum of its parts.

Joss Whedon has mentioned in interviews that he wrote this sequence in "five acts." What follows is my interpretation of those sections and the lead-up to them. I don't know where Whedon marks his act changes, but this is the logic of the sequence as I see it. My purpose is not to second guess the writer, but rather to build on our previous discussion of the Red

[42] Note: A version of this lesson was previously published in Craig Batty, *Screenplays: How to Write and Sell Them* (Harpenden: Kamera Books, 2012).

Death fight from *How to Train Your Dragon* to explain how a big-budget action sequence has the potential to be structurally complex as well as dynamically exciting.

Prologue

After a series of short prologues that follow individual Avengers and small groups as they converge on Stark Tower, Tony Stark squares off with Loki to set up the premise of the sequence. Stark reminds him of the power of the individual Avengers, which leads to this short, iconic exchange:

                    LOKI
         I have an army.

                    TONY
         We have a Hulk.

Now it's time to test the movie's (and S.H.I.E.L.D.'s) premise that the potentially powerful, yet disparate, unfocused and often conflicted alliance that *The Avengers* has so far proved to be has the potential to save the world. In comics it was ever thus.

Act One

The alien army appears from the dimensional rift in the sky above Stark Tower. Iron Man engages them alone.

Act Two

The Leviathan appears and Thor reaches the Tower to battle his brother, Loki. The "act" ends as Thor forces Loki away from the Tower (and control of the rift). Loki escapes on a flying chariot.

Act Three

Captain America takes control of the group as Iron Man battles the Leviathan. The big question is: how can they close the rift? The act ends with this terse exchange:

                    NATASHA
         How do we do this?

```
                         CAP
             As a team.
```

This is the structural Midpoint. Now Cap is bringing them all together and focusing their efforts like a good commander should. Before this moment individual Avengers were fighting hard, but we are being shown that victory will need Cap's leadership.

Act Four

The Hulk and Thor beat the Leviathan while the other Avengers take on the chariot-mounted aliens. Whedon writes what he calls a "tie-in shot" in this section, showing the hero-team coming together as a unit. This is how it reads in the shooting script:

```
Iron Man dives towards the Park Avenue ramp,
barreling through a mass of alien footies before
joining Cap on the viaduct where he blasts his
repulsors into Cap's Vibranium shield — the two
working together to take out a horde — we circle
around them and then follow Iron Man as he rockets
towards a Chariot, smashing it and leaving us an
angle on Hawkeye who fires an arrow that we chase
as it takes out another Chariot, which flies into
the Leviathan that Hulk has commandeered, where
Foot Soldiers pop from their pods and Hulk smashes
them as Thor joins him and the two relentlessly
wrest the Leviathan into the side of a multi level
mall's giant window —— ending the tie-in shot.
```

Act Five

Despite the progress being made by the Avengers, the Council of S.H.I.E.L.D. decides to nuke the city. The sequence ends as Iron Man directs the missile through the rift instead, as Natasha closes it behind the incoming blast. This raises the stakes from fighting Loki and small aliens, through the Leviathan and then trumps that impressive threat with a sort of blue-on-blue nuke attack.

B Story

The B Story in the climactic battle tracks the increasing peril and heroic rescue of a Waitress and her group of survivors. We have seen her before and she becomes the icon of the ordinary people who the Avengers are meant to be protecting. I call it a B Story because the Waitress has a distinct story function in representing the purpose behind the Avengers assembling. This is who they are fighting for and her eventual rescue resolves that part of the narrative linking superheroes and their story world.

> FRIENDLY ME
> I have one question for you about the Resolution. What are you trying to say about love and trust?

> IMPLIED YOU
> Because the answer is the resolution?

> FRIENDLY ME
> It's what we could be building to. Are you selling us love at first sight? Is there really a happily ever after? What does "getting the guy" mean? Ok, that's three more questions. But they are about the same thing.

> IMPLIED YOU
> I don't believe in love at first sight. Lust at first sight: oh yeah baby. Lucy wants Bryce. Bryce wants Lucy. Om nom.

> FRIENDLY ME
> Yeah. Put that on the poster.

> IMPLIED YOU
> No, but most relationships start from desire, then develop how they develop.

> FRIENDLY ME
> Not sure about most, but some, yes.

IMPLIED YOU

To your question about happy
endings, I guess that depends on the
genre and the budget and the market.
That's cynical, I know. But you tell
me. For a mainstream movie I sell
that harder than for indie?

FRIENDLY ME

Maybe, but most indie movies are
full of fantasy. Attitude is in the
telling more than the tale. They're
mainstream stories in a hipster hat.
But put all of that to the side.
Stop evading. What do you want to
say with this story?

IMPLIED YOU

Do I have to say anything big? I
mean two people like one another;
get to know one another; fall for
each other; deal with crap.
Afterwards, they still like each
other enough to want to be together,
for now. That's kind of a modern,
first world miracle.

FRIENDLY ME

I see the shape of your hipster hat,
but is that what you want to write?
That edge of realism to your romantic
fantasy? I mean that's fine but, to be
honest, it doesn't feel like the
conversation we've just been having.

IMPLIED YOU

Realism would be: Lucy gives up
because, "like, it's too much
hassle." Bryce gets back with Tara.
He stays on the farm and they pump
out grandkids for Dan. Maybe he sells

the farm after Dan dies. He goes for
a middle-aged second life, following
his dream. But it's too late by then,
because the tech world has moved on.
So they have to rely on Tara's income
as a. . . let's say a veterinarian?

> FRIENDLY ME
> Actually that could be fun for
> earlier.

> IMPLIED YOU
> Another cliché, no? Anyway, at the
> same time Lucy goes through an
> endless series of internships and
> relationships with no future, before
> ending up in a service job or in a
> cubicle. Eventually, she settles
> for an unchallenging guy who makes
> enough to keep them in a modest
> apartment in a modest neighborhood.
> One day she goes to see a movie
> like this and doesn't realize it's
> about her.

> FRIENDLY ME
> Ouch. Or she enjoys the fantasy of
> love and escape, in a different
> version, and it makes her think
> about Bryce?

> IMPLIED YOU
> No. Occasionally Lucy and Bryce
> think of one another. But they slide
> into sluggish lives of marginal
> discontent as metaphors for a
> broader American decline.

> FRIENDLY ME
> And you tell their wasted love
> story as a bitter-sweet memory

> sparked by a random meeting when
> they are old.

>   IMPLIED YOU
> Or Lucy gets inspired to get back in
> touch after she becomes an empty
> nester and, somehow, Meryl Streep.
> It's nice to reminisce, but their
> moment has passed. It's all about
> carpe diem and holding onto that diem
> no matter what. That's what the story
> is about. The romcom version I mean.

>   FRIENDLY ME
> You mean in terms of trust?

>   IMPLIED YOU
> Yeah. Happiness comes when you fight
> past your mistakes. Blah. Meh. Pfft.

>   FRIENDLY ME
> Writing gives complexity, remember?

>   IMPLIED
> Oh please let's hope so. Maybe I
> want to write the bleaker version. I
> don't know.

16. Resonance

Toothless nudges Hiccup awake. He's back in Stoick's house in the village. At first things don't really compute: "does my dad know you're in here?" The dragon is full of energy and leaps about, impatiently. Hiccup starts to get out of bed, then stops. Something is wrong.

Hiccup has a metal prosthesis in place of his lower left leg. He takes it all in. Considerable time must have passed since we last saw Hiccup on the beach. He pulls himself up and tries to walk. Toothless supports him. Together they make it to the door...

Outside, the world has changed. The village is full of Vikings riding dragons. Stoick comes over, along with many other villagers, excited to see Hiccup up and about. He offers an appropriately resonant moment of parallelism:

                              STOICK
                    (sweetly)
          Turns out all we needed was a little
          more of. . .
                    (gestures non-specifically at Hiccup)
          . . .*this.*

                              HICCUP
                    (playing along)
          You just gestured at all of me.

There's some good-natured discussion with Gobber about his new leg and then Astrid punches him (*repetition with variation* again): "*That's* for scaring me." Then she follows up with a big kiss on the lips. The recruits mount up and fly through the village as we end on a reprise of Hiccup's opening narration: "This is Berk. It snows nine months of the year... and hails the other three. Any food that grows here is tough and tasteless. The people that grow here are even more so. The only upsides are the pets. While other places have... ponies or parrots, we have... dragons."

The return of Hiccup's narration is a nice reminder of his journey. If subjective narration speaks to personality we are happy that Hiccup hasn't lost his dry wit. We are also happy that he can now see a way to being happier about his home.

The world has shifted to meet Hiccup's wants and needs and he was the public intellectual who gave it the shove. He fits in, he is accepted, Viking and dragon have reached a happy accommodation. His theme is resolved. Despite his injuries, the emotional drive of the ending is most definitely *up* and we can leave Berk happy that, for now at least, all is well. At least until the sequel (see later).

Lesson Break: The Resonance of Endings

Endings are treats. Endings are rewards to your audience for their kind attention and investment in your storytelling. They speak very clearly to the pleasures of structure. Even when your story has an unhappy ending remember that your audience has traveled the road with you and your characters. That means they have earned its resonance so don't deny them.

Having said that, the shortest route to undercutting all your hard work is to play an ending too strong or too long. Don't let your audience leave with the wrong kind of bad taste in their mouths. Less is usually more here and deciding how long to let your ending "breathe" is another one of those tricky judgment calls.

Here are a few pointers to help you think it through.

- *Play your ending as a reprise of your opening.* Show us a changed world or show us your protagonist in a new relationship to that world. The iconic end of *The Searchers* (1956, scr. Frank S. Nugent) is a perfect example. There's Ethan framed in the doorway, a reference to the film's opening image. He is an outsider, unable to be part of the family he has restored. An up ending for the story world. Not so much for Ethan.

  In *How to Train Your Dragon*, the change in the world speaks through the loss of a single letter. In Hiccup's bookending narration "pests" become "pets," signaling that the dragons are now a welcome part of the Viking world (see also the section on how this movie works as a ring).

- *Play your ending as a new beginning. How to Train Your Dragon* does this and references the opening in Hiccup's narration as well. At the end of *Let the Right One In,* Oskar is on the train to a strange new life. His vampire love is in a box on the floor next to him.

- *Leave us in uncertainty.* At the end of John Carpenter's *The Thing* (1982, scr. Bill Lancaster) the last two survivors face off. They don't know if they are both human or... not. More importantly, neither do we. They are outside in the smoldering ruins of the polar research station as the temperature drops. MacReady says: "Why don't we just wait here for a little while? See what happens." And that's it. This kind of ending works for high-concept genre plots, but perhaps less well for other kinds of dramas.

- *End on a reveal.* The ending of *The Usual Suspects* (1995, scr. Christopher McQuarrie) solves the puzzle of the movie in the final frames. Verbal Kint is revealed as the inventor of "Keyser Söze" the antagonist master criminal, and we are out. The audience leaves on a big deal. You can bet they are talking about it right after.

- *Deny us resonance as a kind of resonance.* Sometimes a film should just end at the moment of its thematic resolution. Bang. Story's over. Deal with it. Speaking of bangs, the ending of *Butch Cassidy and the Sundance Kid* (1969, scr. William Goldman) goes out on several. Butch and Sundance are cornered and they decide to go down fighting. They burst out of their hiding place, shooting. The image freezes and turns sepia like an old photograph with the sound of gunfire over. Without actually seeing their deaths the myth is somehow sustained.

- *Trick endings and codas.* These come in all sizes, famously including the discovery that the monster has stowed away on the shuttlecraft at the end of *Alien*. *Phone Booth* has its own tricky coda, thanks to the writing of the great Larry Cohen. We believe the killer has died by his own hand but, as Stu is going under from a sedative in the back of an ambulance, the killer appears to offer a final goodbye and a warning about Stu's future conduct: "you don't have to thank me, nobody ever does. I just hope your new-found honesty lasts." Both of these "tricks" are Resonant because they are thematically embedded, not mere mechanical plot twists. The alien has been defined by its intelligence and adaptability. Like Ripley it is a survivor in a movie about survival, so why wouldn't it end up on the shuttle? In *Phone Booth*, Stu will have to correct his behavior for real now that he knows the killer is still out there watching and judging him.
- *End on an Emotional Payoff.* Show us the future the story has bought. This is a variant on the ending as beginning, particularly resonant in romantic movies. Our couple is married, they have kids, they get divorced (comedy)... Movie cycles and series sometimes have emotional payoffs for their entire arcs as well. At the end of *Harry Potter and the Deathly Hallows: Part Two* (2011, scr. Steve Kloves), for example, we are given a short epilogue set years in the future. We see many of the surviving characters collected on Platform 9 and ¾ of King's Cross Station, putting their children on the train to Hogwarts. The world has healed after the death of Voldemort, we are being told. Our wizarding friends seem happy enough and life goes on. Now we can feel safe in leaving them to their destinies. At least until Ms. Rowling decides to write another Harry Potter book ...

  A recent example of an emotionally ambivalent ending can be found in Wes Anderson's *The Grand Budapest Hotel* (2014, scr. Wes Anderson), in which the perfect hotel concierge, Gustave H. has died and his protégé, Zero (aka Mr. Moustafa) has survived and found love. However we know that his wife and child will soon die and that for all his worldly success he ends up a lonely old man. The successful resolution of the crazy plot will provide him only temporary solace and our pleasure at it is tempered somewhat by our knowledge of his future.

This is only a sample of the many possibilities. Whatever choice you make just remember that it should resonate with your theme and be a fitting payoff for your audience's attention. Don't fall into the trap of being cute or playing false for no reason other than to overturn expectations. That's another common sophomoric trap that catches young writers.

Case Study: Act Three of *Edge of Tomorrow*

Edge of Tomorrow (2014, scr. Christopher McQuarrie and Jez Butterworth & John-Henry Butterworth) is a straightforward alien invasion war movie with the addition of a time-reset twist. Its third act is worth a case study not because it is innovative in its structure, despite the time travel device, but rather because its beats operate so typically that they offer a clear example of how Hollywood tends to think resolution in the era of tentpole movies. The plot and context, however, are rather more involved. So bear with me while I set things up.

Swarming alien creatures have invaded Earth and humanity has united in its defense. Reluctant hero Cage has teamed up with heroic warrior Rita, because they have unique insight into the nature of the alien threat and into its potential vulnerability. It works like this: Cage killed a rare "Alpha" creature and, through contact with its blood, has gained a unique ability to reset time backwards one day upon his death. This is how the aliens are avoiding defeat—they can reset a battle and respond to the tactics used by their opponents the next time round. Previously, Rita had gained the same ability and used it to win the last battle against the aliens. Subsequently she lost the power after a blood transfusion when she was injured, but she is able to explain to Cage what is going on.

Another plot device consequent to the alien's blood has Cage getting visions of the location of the controlling alien "Omega" creature. He and Rita settle on the destruction of the Omega as a means of winning the war. Much of the second act has them learning incrementally, through reset after reset and death after death, how to approach the Omega through alien-occupied France. The Crisis emerges from the growing affection Cage feels for Rita. He gets blocked at a stage on their journey after which nothing he does can save Rita's life. Cage's solution is to try the journey without her, given the knowledge bought from previous resets. He makes it to the place of his vision, but finds it was a trap.

On the next reset Rita's friend, the disgraced scientist Dr. Carter, tells them in the second part of the Revelation beat that he developed technology that would link Cage to the real Omega and help him fix its location. The only problem is that his work is locked in the army commander's office in Whitehall. At least now they have a . . .

PLAN

Cage and Rita go to Whitehall to retrieve Dr. Carter's technology. Using the knowledge gained through multiple time resets they get where they need to go and obtain the tech.

PUSHBACK

On the way out, however, they are attacked by security troops. During their escape attempt, Cage interfaces with Dr. Carter's device and discovers the Omega's location. The security troops stop them, injuring both Cage and Rita. Cage wakes up, restrained in a medical facility after a blood transfusion. He has lost the power of the Alpha's blood, but now he knows where they need to go to defeat the aliens. The only trouble is they will have one chance to get it right. No more resets.

RESOLUTION

Cage, Rita and their squad head for Paris and the Omega. After battling the defending aliens, Cage and Rita make it to the Omega but they have to sacrifice themselves to destroy it. Rita distracts an Alpha long enough for Cage to get to the Omega and then he is himself attacked by the Alpha just after priming explosives to destroy the Omega. The resulting explosion kills the Alpha and we see its shiny blue blood covering Cage once again as he dies.

RESONANCE

Cage wakes up after a reset, enabled by his second exposure to an Alpha's blood, to find the alien threat destroyed and he goes to find Rita to rekindle their budding romance.

This is typical of Hollywood genre storytelling:

1. Making a *Plan* to resolve the story is prompted and enabled by choices made as a consequence of the *Crisis*: Cage's affection for Rita leads to him learning the truth. In doing so it also resolves the *B Story* into romance.
2. *Pushback* raises stakes to the highest: no more resets, one chance to get it right.
3. The *Resolution* requires great sacrifice: Cage and Rita are killed, believing their deaths will be final this time.
4. That ultimate sacrifice is paid back by a new reset through *Resonance* as the threat is defeated and our redeemed hero gets a second chance at happiness.

Did you spank your hero/ine today?

You have to ask? Poor old Hiccup lost half his leg. Move on now, shoo. . . nothing to see here. Pesky rubberneckers.

                    IMPLIED YOU
So, in <u>Temptation</u>, the resonance is
the message of the resolution given
time to breathe? Lucy and Bryce
happy on the farm, or in the city.
Or both.

                    FRIENDLY ME
Or we stop, bang! We know there is a
future of some kind for them, but
you don't spell out the terms. Old
school, you end on the kiss.

                    IMPLIED YOU
Or, I go the bleaker route and they
part as friends and nothing more. Or
the Meryl Streep version. Or they
never meet, when they are older.
They are both too afraid to get
together after all that time and the
movie has been about the reasons why
they don't. Now I don't know what I
want to write. So, thanks for that.

                    FRIENDLY ME
Well, there are lots of stories
milling around now. Some of them
might end up not being about Lucy
and Bryce. Some of them may be
written later. Or you may have a
series of stories about the life-
long, on-off relationship between
these two people, starting from
youthful romantic idealism and
exploring the more realistic expectations that come with age and
experience. You just have to decide
which to write first.

                    IMPLIED YOU
Easy to say.

                    FRIENDLY ME
Here's a tie-breaker. Right now, do
you think you can write funny?

                    IMPLIED YOU
Yes. Everything I've written so far,
in prose and short scripts, has been
funny somehow. I feel kind of at
home with wry humor. I guess it's my
default in life as well.

                    FRIENDLY ME
I noticed. So write funny. Get
Jennifer Aniston into the cow poop.
Or Jane Levy. Or that great unknown
actress for whom cow poop humor will
be her big break.

                    IMPLIED YOU
So we're back where we started.
Thanks.

                    FRIENDLY ME
Hardly. You know so much more about
your characters and your story. You
just have to start making hard
decision now. That's your job not
mine. My job is to help you explore
possible consequences of those
decisions in story terms. But now
you get to make them from a position
of more knowledge. You're not going
to be writing in a vacuum.

                    IMPLIED YOU
That's fair. I guess I have more
hard thinking to do.

                    FRIENDLY ME
That never ends, trust me. And
welcome to being a writer.

Second up angle in *Let the Right One In*

Act three and Oskar is alone, in danger and living in a story world over which he has no control. His situation is even worse than that of Ree in *Winter's Bone* because he doesn't fully realize when antagonistic forces are conspiring against him. Like Ree he has an ally, however. What's more, she promised him she would help. Eli has left her apartment—she has left the scene of Lacke's murder, but we will discover that she is still looking out for Oskar.

He doesn't know this yet—at least he acts as though he doesn't. There is still a vestigial, childish part of Oskar that is hopeful and trusting so, when one of the bullies plays traitor and pretends to be friendly, Oskar seems pleased. It is all a set-up however, to draw Oskar into a trap. This Plan belongs to the bullies and Oskar is their bait.

Eli has left, Oskar has lost faith in his father and he has discovered that the world is so much more terrifying than he had imagined. He has even been an accomplice to murder. There are monsters in the world. One of them was his friend and protector, but now she has gone and Oskar is at the mercy of monsters of a more quotidian variety. Perhaps it is no great surprise that he grasps at the tiniest show of affection that comes his way.

In act three the forces of mundane and supernatural evil collide for possession of Oskar's fate. Eli will win that battle, of course, and her prize is to cement Oskar in the role of traveling companion and day-walking servant for the bloody adventures that no doubt await them. The entire world will be against them and we have learned from Håkan's example that Oskar will be obliged to do terrible things to keep his place at Eli's side. It's an up ending of a kind, but equivocal and ambivalent for sure.

Let the Right One In takes risks by removing its protagonist from control over his own destiny. The W beats are there but, at crucial moments in the story, they "belong" to different characters. I have already suggested why I believe this works well in a horror film.

The story beats of the fourth angle of *Let the Right One In* work like this:

G – Confrontation

13. **Plan:** Pretending both apology and friendship, Martin—one of the bullies—sets up Oskar for Conny's brother. He wants to get revenge for the injury Oskar did to Conny on the ice. They find out that Oskar will be going to the swimming pool and plan to attack him there. The pleasurable payoff is that we are now waiting to see how Eli's arc will pay off. We can see the Plan beat as Martin's deception, however we can also see it as the structuring absence of Eli's Plan (to say nothing of Oskar's). She has gone, but we understand stories well enough to

know we haven't seen the last of her. The Plan beat speaks at least as much to her presumed imminence as it does to the bullies' explicit presence. We are faced with two competing thoughts: "poor Oskar" and "where's Eli?"

14. **Pushback:** As the Plan belongs to the antagonists in this movie, there is no Pushback from them. Oskar meekly accepts Martin's overture of friendship and goes like a lamb to the slaughter. Oskar is forced to hold his breath underwater for an impossible amount of time or have his eye cut out with a flick knife. He goes under and Conny's brother grabs his head, preventing him from surfacing. This isn't Pushback so much as acquiescence, the inversion of the beat that suits the inversion of the power dynamic in the first half of the act. The true Pushback will come from Eli as she attacks in the next beat.

H – Resolution

15. **Resolution:** In the swimming baths, Oskar has been under water a very long time. Just when it seems as if he might really die, Eli returns and kills all the bullies (bar one, who had no part in the final attack) efficiently and bloodily.
16. **Resonance:** In a train compartment a happy Oskar is traveling to who knows where. Eli hides from the killing rays of the sun in a big box on the floor next to him. They communicate by Morse code through the box as they go off together to an uncertain future. Finally, Oskar has earned acceptance from Eli, but what a strange new life he has signed up for...

Second up angle in *Winter's Bone*

Once again progress begins out of Ree's hands. However Teardrop is with her now. People are frightened of him and his threatening presence adds to the disturbance she has made in the hills. All of this pressure leads to a break as Thump Milton's people decide finally that their best action is to make the trouble go away and give Ree the evidence of Jessup's death she has been searching for.

This is a short act. Ree is taken to Jessup's body and they cut off his hands as evidence of death. The sheriff accepts the evidence and gives Ree the money remaining from Jessup's bond. Her home is safe and she has cash in hand. Back at home, however, Teardrop turns up to tell her he has found out who killed his brother. This takes a big edge off the up ending of the story, but Ree has achieved what she set out to attempt.

Winter's Bone takes risks in this act especially, particularly if we have any doubt as to whether Ree has earned her victory. If we accept that it is thanks to her actions—thanks to her determination, her bloody minded refusal to back down—that her world bent towards her in the end, then the story works. Indeed, I appreciate the authenticity and believability of the moments in which she despairs at her own impotence. There's a messiness, a human haphazardness to them that feels deeply appropriate.

The structural model holds in this movie—the beats of the W still occur in the order we have come to expect. However, as with *Let the Right One In*, it is around control and ownership of the story that *Winter's Bone* pushes that paradigm to the limit. If we judge the story's structure strictly according to the conventions of typical Hollywood storytelling, it falls down. If we value the alternative and perhaps more truthful vision of human endeavor in an uncaring world that it offers, then we can see why it was a critical and, relative to its small budget, a commercial success.

The story beats of the fourth angle of *Winter's Bone* work like this:

G – Confrontation

13. **Plan:** Thump Milton's women turn up to take Ree to find her father's body. The clan has had enough of her and Teardrop making waves and want things settled.
14. **Pushback:** The kicker is that Ree's father is dead and lying at the bottom of a lake and now Ree has to help cut off his hands with a chainsaw as evidence of his death. This is the final test of her resolve and responsibility.

H – Resolution

15. **Resolution:** The hands are delivered anonymously to the sheriff, proving Ree's father, Jessup, is dead and thus releasing his bond. Ree's quest is over and, as an unexpected bonus, she is given a bag full of cash that an anonymous donor had paid to complete her father's original bond. It is implied that the donor was Thump Milton, who wanted Jessup released so he could be killed to keep him quiet, but this is never resolved categorically.
16. **Resonance:** With their home saved, life goes on as before, only now uncle Teardrop is closer to Ree. However we learn that he has found out who killed his brother. That means he is honor bound to seek revenge and is likely to die in the new cycle of violence he is now fated to initiate.

Questions to ask *yourself* as you write act three – second up angle

Plan

Q: Am I making the Plan as clear as possible without revealing too much plotting?

Q: Is my protagonist's Plan in character—is it the perfect way *she* would interpret the potential fix?

Q: Is the Plan an appropriate response to the Revelation and is it dramatic enough to keep the second half Acceleration of my story on track?

Pushback

Q: Am I raising the stakes yet again—is my antagonistic force truly earning its pay?

Q: Is my antagonist also responding in character, based upon their take on the story's theme?

Resolution

Q: Is the antagonist being overcome in a manner both necessary for story resolution and dramatically satisfying?

Q: Is the Resolution paying off my protagonist's wants and needs?
Note: this does not necessarily mean straightforwardly achieving them.

Resonance

Q: How has the Story World changed since the start of the story and is this change clear?

Q: Should this be an up ending or a down ending, or should it be mixed and somehow ambivalent?

Q: If the ending is ambivalent, am I being clear how this is played in terms of story, plot and theme—for example are plot goals achieved but story goals not achieved, or vice versa?

Questions to ask *your first draft* of act three – second up angle

After you have finished a first draft of your screenplay, re-read it and ask the following questions:

Plan

Q: Can I make the revelation of the Plan more exciting or dramatically resonant in some way?

Q: Is the Plan clear in terms of potential thematic resolution, if not in "tactical detail"? In other words, does it show how the story can be brought to a satisfactory conclusion?

Q: Does the parallel between the First Commitment and Plan beats eloquently express the protagonist's journey from *willing* to *able*?

Q: How can I write all of this just as effectively with fewer words and in fewer pages?

Pushback

Q: Can I make the Pushback any more surprising, shocking, exciting, unexpected, cunning, nefarious, multi-faceted, terrifying—in short can I make it more fun for the audience and more challenging for the protagonist?

Q: Does the parallel between the Hesitation and Pushback beats show—in hindsight—how my protagonist might well have hesitated before laying herself open to the struggles to come?

Q: How can I write all of this just as effectively with fewer words and in fewer pages?

Resolution

Q: Was the Resolution truly hard won?

Q: Looking back, does the parallel between the Desire and Resolution beats show—or at least suggest—how my protagonist's initial wants and needs led her here?

Q: How can I write all of this just as effectively with fewer words and in fewer pages?

Resonance

Q: Have I wrapped things up efficiently while leaving enough time for the end of my story to "breathe"?

Q: Does the parallel between the Story World and Resonance beats show the meaning of the story imprinted in its world and characters?

Q: How can I write all of this just as effectively with fewer words and in fewer pages?

How to Train Your Dragon as a ring

We have just spent a good while trekking through the story of *How to Train Your Dragon* as it unfolds in a linear fashion, from beat to beat, angle to angle and act to act. I hope that this journey has helped you to appreciate how a well-written conventional movie is structured. What we haven't yet done is to explore the full potential of parallelism in the film.

To do this we can reorganize our view of the W as a kind of story ring, similar to how we discussed *The King's Speech*, but with more beat-to-beat detail. This is *like* a ring composition, but strained through a contemporary screenwriting grid. The beats are all the same as the W, but we are going to look at them from a different perspective. In this form we can see that the story is told in two halves: beats 1 through 8 and 9 through 16, split by the midpoint.

If we lay those halves out alongside one another we can look across and back between their story beats and see how they are *paired*—how they speak to one another. This will tell us a great deal about how—or even if—all of the set-up work you have been doing in the first half of your story pays off in the second. The more eloquently your beats interact in parallel, the greater the pleasures your story structure will be giving your audience.

In the diagram below, I have included a significant moment or a line of dialogue that speaks to the story function of each beat. Just reading across from line to line should begin to highlight the parallels—the required story development at each stage of the ring.

First Half		Second Half
↓		↑
1. Story World	←→	**16. Resonance**
"... problems are the pests"		"... upsides are the pets"

2. Desire   ←→   **15. Resolution**
"I'll kill a dragon"   Hiccup kills the Red Death

3. Hesitation   ←→   **14. Pushback**
"... look after Hiccup"   Hiccup comes to the rescue

4. First Commitment ←→   **13. Plan**
"You think like us"   "so what's the plan?"

5. B Story   ←→   **12. Revelation**
Hiccup alone: "Nope, just you."   *"That's* more like it." Astrid an ally

6. Progress   ←→   **11. Crisis**
"So why didn't you?"   "... thrown in your lot with them"

7. Challenge   ←→   **10. Assistance**
"Everything we know... is wrong" "I'm not one of them"

8. Decision   ←→   **9. Acceleration**
"I am so leaving"   "We need her to like us"

MIDPOINT
Second Commitment
Hiccup accepts responsibility

Parallel beat pairs in *How to Train Your Dragon*

1 & 16: Story World is paired with **Resonance**. This pairing gives us a clear opportunity to witness the impact of Hiccup's story on his world. I think it is safe to say that his impact has been pretty dramatic. Sometimes beat pairs offer us direct references in dialogue that encompass the story work that has been accomplished between them. Not all beats do this, but you find it most often in the pairs the audience is always paying attention to. One such pairing is between the opening and the final beat of the story and, as discussed in the previous chapter, we get just such a correlation when we compare Hiccup's opening and closing narration.

It may seem like a small change to transform the word *pest* into *pet*. In losing one letter the entire story world is made anew. As we have seen, in the first scene of the movie Hiccup tells us: "The only problems are the pests. You see, most places have mice or mosquitos. We have... dragons." In the final scene this has changed: "The only upsides are the pets. While other places have... ponies or parrots, we have... dragons."

This is an eloquent and efficient summation of all he has been through. In saving the Vikings from crisis, he has changed the attitudes and the social relations of his culture and he has become a hero in the process. That's quite an achievement and it is expressed in the connections the writers draw between these parallel beats as dragons fly, once again, through the Viking village, only this time with riders on their backs.

2 & 15: Desire is paired with **Resolution.** This beat pair sets up the protagonist's wants and needs and then shows how they finally achieve them (or finally fail in the attempt). Remember that, as with all the structural correspondences in your screenplay, the need to pay off this parallel is already locked into the minds of your readers and audience. As soon as we know what your protagonist wants, we are invested in seeing how they go about getting it.

Once again the set-up has a clear payoff, but the meaning of that payoff is transformed. In Desire, Hiccup dreams of killing a dragon because he sees that as the way to gain acceptance and Astrid. He shoots at the Night Fury to help improve his own situation. In Resolution he is forced to save the day by defeating the Red Death but that action is no longer selfish and is more about rescuing his people and freeing the other dragons from servitude than it is about fulfilling his selfish needs.

This is an eloquent parallel in *How to Train You Dragon*. It enacts the *external event* that Hiccup always desired—he kills a dragon in the plot. What has transformed for Hiccup between these beats is the *internal story meaning* of that external plot event.

3 & 14: Hesitation is paired with **Pushback.** This parallel tests out a huge move on the part of your protagonist from rejection to engagement. In Hesitation, Hiccup is dismissed as a destructive misfit by the Vikings. Looking after him is a punishment for cowardice. In Pushback, it is Hiccup who comes to save—to "look after"—the Vikings and, as a consequence, is reconciled with his father. The transformation we have seen from the *child in need of care* to the *heroic caretaker* is played out very clearly in this parallel.

4 & 13: First Commitment is paired with **Plan.** The former establishes a need for decisive action from a protagonist ill-equipped to take it. The latter shows us the first decisive move of a newly equipped protagonist towards final story resolution. All that comes between them is the whole of the second act and we have already established that *second acts are all about change.* This parallel checks whether your second act has done its job.

In *How to Train Your Dragon* we are given a nice dialogue shorthand to check our progress. In First Commitment, Stoick tells Hiccup that now he is going into dragon training he has to conform: "you think like us." By the time we get to Plan, the others are looking to him for how to think. Astrid puts it into words: "so, what's the plan?"

NOTE: I hope that by now you get a sense of why we are working with a ring model of story structure and taking note of these corresponding beats. Each parallel offers us direct evidence of vital story work accomplished between them. They all pay off and, in doing so, lock us in ever more tightly to the pleasures of the story's structure.

The parallels between beats in the first and third acts are pretty clear. In the second act we are sometimes looking at how much the stakes have been raised. Some of the parallels in this act can serve less as specific micro-resolutions and more as markers of degree.

---

5 & 12: B Story is paired with **Revelation.** We have already discussed how these beats bookend the key functions of the B Story. Again this parallel is an important marker of your protagonist's arc. At the start of act two they are willing but hopeless, at the end they are ready to become the man or woman with the plan. On the way it is likely that they have been prodded, pushed, pulled and generally supported by at least one developing and significant relationship.

Of course in *How to Train Your Dragon*, Hiccup's B Story is with Astrid. These two parallel beats show us how she rejects his opening gambit in the arena at the start and pushes him to take decisive action at the end. The work of the act has been to bring the two of them together so that they can form something of a team. Astrid is able to pick Hiccup up after the shock of Crisis only because by now she understands him. In other words, Hiccup isn't the only one who gets an arc from the B Story. Astrid gets one also and it is just as important for the structure of the movie. She is also active and decisive in both beats, much more than a passive love-interest figure.

6 & 11: Progress is paired with **Crisis.** This is the first of the act two escalation parallels. We will work back down the scale towards the Midpoint, but for now this is the biggest story shift. Again, it follows internal story logic. This parallel is required by the story because it exposes the seemingly irreconcilable nature of the conflict between protagonist and antagonist.

In *How to Train Your Dragon* this parallel bookends the transformation in Hiccup's thinking leading from a single question: if dragons always go for the kill, why didn't Toothless? This question leads to a whole lot of investigation and to his eventual rejection of Viking tradition. That leads, in turn, to Stoick's condemnation of him after he attempts to tame the dragon in the arena in Assistance rather than killing it.

7 & 10: Challenge is paired with **Assistance**. This parallel bookends Hiccup's final abandonment of Viking "thinking." In other words it enacts the crisis of the previous parallel. In Challenge he becomes convinced that "everything we know about [dragons] is wrong." In Assistance he calms a dragon by denying his kinship to the other Vikings: "I'm not one of them."

Again in plot terms this is another escalation parallel, but it also plays out its own internal story logic by having Hiccup enunciate the lesson he has learned from his experiences with the Night Fury. It takes real courage to say what Hiccup says in the arena in front of his whole village, but we would expect no less from our *hero*. Again this teaches us the importance of first half set-ups: if Hiccup has learned the truth before the Midpoint, we expect him to go on and speak it after the Midpoint. The first half of the movie is all about the learning, the second half all about the speaking.

8 & 9: Decision is paired with **Acceleration**. These beats bookend the Midpoint. They take us from Hiccup on the verge of running out on his problems to the first results of his commitment to address them. This parallel is always a useful test for a writer because it checks that your Midpoint—your story's fulcrum—is working correctly. Being discovered by Astrid is the final catalyst for his Midpoint decision. Bringing her on side is the first test of that decision. It will be a first test of his Second Commitment. The plot payoff emerges directly from that story event: Toothless leads them to the discovery of the Red Death.

Midpoint – Second Commitment: Hiccup accepts responsibility. We've discussed this already, so I'll just note here that Hiccup's decision not to run, but to take responsibility for his knowledge and actions, turns the story in the following ways:

First half		Second half
Hiccup wants to fit in	➔	*He wants to change the world to fit him*
Hiccup is learning	➔	*Hiccup is teaching*
Hiccup is a loner	➔	*He becomes a leader*
Hiccup is the protagonist	➔	*Hiccup becomes a hero*

So there you have it, *How to Train Your Dragon* as a ring. Remember that I'm not suggesting that contemporary movies are true ring compositions in the strict context of ancient literary forms. I'm reminding us that most relatively conventional movie stories turn at the middle and work back towards a transformed ending. I'm reminding us that there are explicit causal connections between every beat of your story. I'm suggesting to you that the ancient principles of pattern recognition and literary parallelism are deeply inscribed in our storytelling, even if we don't always write with parallels in mind. I'm suggesting that looking at your story as a ring is the best way of testing out and checking on the work every element of your story is doing.

I'm arguing that it is in the simplest structural devices that we come closest to the oldest, deepest and most primal sources of the pleasures of story.

Now let's see how both *Let the Right One In* and *Winter's Bone* work as rings in their own right.

Let The Right One In as a ring

Here's a diagrammatic representation of the movie's structure as a ring:

First Half		Second Half	
↓			↑
1. Story World	←→	**16. Resonance**	
Oskar alone		Oskar and Eli	
↓			↑
2. Desire	←→	**15. Resolution**	
Oskar wants friendship		Eli saves Oskar	
↓			↑
3. Hesitation	←→	**14. Pushback**	
"I can't be your friend."		Bullies can't be his friends	
↓			↑
4. First Commitment	←→	**13. Plan**	
A puzzle and a problem for Eli		The bullies' plot	
↓			↑
5. B Story	←→	**12. Revelation**	
Eli kills Jocke		Eli kills Lacke	
↓			↑

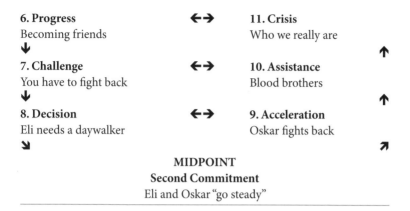

6. Progress	←→	**11. Crisis**
Becoming friends		Who we really are
↓		↑
7. Challenge	←→	**10. Assistance**
You have to fight back		Blood brothers
↓		↑
8. Decision	←→	**9. Acceleration**
Eli needs a daywalker		Oskar fights back
↘		↗

MIDPOINT
Second Commitment
Eli and Oskar "go steady"

Parallel beat pairs in *Let the Right One In*

1 & 16: Story World is paired with **Resonance**. At the start of the story we meet Oskar in the blur of his own loneliness. His distorted reflection in his bedroom window introduces us to a boy who is disconnected from the world and looking for purpose and even revenge. At the end, Oskar has new purpose, a new connection with Eli and a new life that will take him into a perverse reflection of the mundane world of love and commitment and no vampires. With the special knowledge gained from his relationship to Eli we understand that Oskar has transcended his separation. He sees things with a new focus and he is happier for now and more confident in his strange new life.

2 & 15: Desire is paired with **Resolution**. Despite his confused and violent impulses, Oskar is clearly interested in an initially reluctant Eli. For the most part, the arc of their relationship bends from her, not him. Although the Crisis asks him to take on board new hard truths for the rest of the movie it is Oskar who needs and Eli who decides. She is influenced by Hakån's slide into failure, but also by affection. The arc pays off when Eli intervenes with Conny's brother and the bullies at the swimming pool. She told him she could help and she does. This violent act cements them together as nothing else could.

3 & 14: Hesitation is paired with **Pushback**. This pair emphasizes Oskar's continuing vulnerability and dependence on the decisions of others. In Hesitation, Eli tells him they can't be friends—although soon enough we learn about Hakån's "duties" and Eli begins to come round to the idea. In Pushback, with Eli seemingly gone, Oskar is vulnerable once more and looking for any sign of acceptance (his theme) in a lonely world. He goes along with Martin's plan, walking into a trap in a kind of negative Pushback. Oskar's Pushback is not to push back, which is itself a kind of sad denial of his progress in the rest of the story. The lesson of the pair in character terms is that Oskar's development is still so very contingent that he needs the strong presence of Eli to give it any kind of permanence. A perfect set-up for a master and servant relationship in the future perhaps.

Of course another reading of the Pushback beat is that Oskar knows Eli will help him and is leading the bullies to their doom. However, there is no clear evidence for this interpretation in the story itself. Indeed there is a kind of gap, a lacuna around the terms on which Eli leaves that the third act fills with the surface of Oskar's doomed acquiescence.

4 & 13: First Commitment is paired with **Plan**. We can think of this pair as a double problem for Eli, even if one problem is played in her absence. In First Commitment she has reason to come to question Hakån's competence and to look elsewhere for her future security. In Plan, we see everything she worked for with Oskar (emotionally and pragmatically) in danger of being undermined or even destroyed. In a story that systematically disempowers its protagonist like *Let the Right One In*, the audience is being given a double taste of that function in this parallel. In the first beat we learn something that Oskar doesn't (Eli is a vampire). In the second, we are positioned with Oskar, wishing Eli hadn't left and hoping she will return to use her vampire strength to help our strange little friend. This is Eli's absence understood as story potential again.

5 & 12: B Story is paired with **Revelation**. The arc of the B Story is bracketed by two murders—two dark events that move the plot and story of this dark tale forward. In the first beat, Eli kills Jocke and sets his friend Lacke on a heartfelt, if intermittent track towards revealing Eli. Versions of this "hunt the monster" subplot are common in vampire movies. Of course the poor man has no idea what he's getting himself into and the second beat of the pair ends with Eli killing him in her home with Oskar's help after he does, indeed, find her lair. Lacke's death in Revelation pays off his investigative arc. The B Story's key function of initiating the resolution of the A Story is also enacted here, because now Eli has to leave her home. The story Revelation is that Oskar is still with Eli after he knows her true nature. It is also a plot Revelation that they cannot stay as they are, in this place that seemed safe. The emotional choice is subverted by the pragmatic necessity. As we have already seen, that leaves Oskar at least temporarily vulnerable.

6 & 11: Progress is paired with **Crisis**. This pair brackets the development of Oskar and Eli's friendship. In the first beat he is happy to be getting closer to his new friend—he is making Progress towards his thematic goal of acceptance. In the second beat he finally understands exactly what it is that he has been getting close to. The movie's Crisis is all about that revelation and what Oskar will do about it.

7 & 10: Challenge is paired with **Assistance**. In this pair of beats, the advice to fight back that Eli gave Oskar in Challenge is paid off in Assistance as a more confident Oskar wants to cement their friendship with blood. He is emboldened by his success in hurting Conny and his desire to be blood brothers is a demonstration of his commitment to her—it is *his* pledge of Assistance. Of course it leads directly to the revelation that Eli is a vampire in Crisis. In this way, the story is binding earlier storytelling decisions into the onrushing resolution of the relationship arc. Eli's nature—and her needs—inform her advice to Oskar. Oskar takes that advice, has some success and thinks that makes Eli his equal now in friendship. He responds as a boy might and, as a result, finds that the gulf between him and Eli is wider and deeper than he could have imagined.

8 & 9: Decision is paired with **Acceleration**. This is a very significant pairing because it links Eli's urgent need to replace Hakån with clear evidence of Oskar's progress in becoming that replacement. In Decision, Hakån dies and Eli goes to Oskar's bed, confirming their special bond at the Midpoint. In Acceleration Oskar fights back, hurting Conny on the skating trip.

Midpoint: Eli agrees to "go steady" with Oskar. This binds him to her and provides the emotional backup for his hesitant arc towards bravery, physical self-improvement and violence. Let's take a look at how the Midpoint acts as fulcrum for Oskar's development as a character:

First half		Second half
Oskar hates the world	➔	*He wants a new world*
Oskar is helpless	➔	*Oskar starts taking action*
Oskar is a loner	➔	*He gains a kind of partner*
Oskar is the protagonist	➔	*Oskar becomes a servant*

As we can see, Oskar's progress is contingent on Eli. It is undercut by the nature of their relationship and much of his progress is hinted at as future potential, rather than present success—he is still pretty helpless in the third act, for example. Looking at *Let the Right One In* as a ring—seeing how the parallels operate—helps us to understand the strangeness of the relationship at the heart of the story.

Winter's Bone as a ring

Here's a diagrammatic representation of the movie's structure as a ring:

First Half		Second Half	
↓			↑
1. Story World	←→	**16. Resonance**	
Ree's family insecure		The family more secure	
↓			↑
2. Desire	←→	**15. Resolution**	
Needs to find Jessup		Delivers Jessup's hands	
↓			↑
3. Hesitation	←→	**14. Pushback**	
Denied help		Takes Jessup's hands	
↓			↑
4. First Commitment	←→	**13. Plan**	
Goes to see Little Arthur		Taken to Jessup's body	
↓			↑
5. B Story	←→	**12. Revelation**	
The clan pushes back		Teardrop makes waves	
↓			↑
6. Progress	←→	**11. Crisis**	
The search progresses		Considers splitting the family	
↓			↑
7. Challenge	←→	**10. Assistance**	
Teardrop hasn't forgotten Ree		Teardrop "stands for" Ree	
↓			↑
8. Decision	←→	**9. Acceleration**	
"I don't know what to do."		Ree goes after Thump	
↘			↗

MIDPOINT
Second Commitment
Eviction looms

Parallel beat pairs in *Winter's Bone*

1 & 16: Story World is paired with **Resonance**. At the start of the movie, we see that Ree is the primary caregiver and the glue that keeps her poverty-stricken family together. At the end, she has managed to secure their home and provide a little financial security for her family. In the process she has brought her uncle, Teardrop, into the family frame. The ending shows he is not likely to survive much longer and the future violence he will be involved with may cause Ree major problems. The ending also leaves Ree stuck in relative poverty, but at least they still have their land and a roof over their heads. She has earned an up ending, in the conventional term, but it is qualified by an uncertain future.

2 & 15: Desire is paired with **Resolution**. Ree needs to find Jessup in order to keep her family in its home. This Desire pairs with its Resolution when the sheriff accepts Jessup's hands as evidence of his death, freeing his bail bond. These beats bookend the "quest" plot and resolve Ree's wants and needs, in a straightforward sense and for the short term at least.

3 & 14: Hesitation is paired with **Pushback**. Part of the Hesitation beat plays defiantly in the negative. Ree has no Hesitation in going to see her school friend for help. The Hesitation lies in how the story world treats her. Her friend's husband refuses to lend them his truck, for example. The only real hesitation Ree shows is in the Pushback beat when she can't bring herself to cut off her father's hands. She ends up holding them while someone else removes them with a handy chainsaw. It is because of the actions she takes starting in Hesitation (set-up) that she is finally in a position to be squeamish in Pushback (payoff).

4 & 13: First Commitment is paired with **Plan**. Ree is warned not to bother her uncle Teardrop but she goes right ahead, establishing her bona fides in terms of her theme of determination. She will need Teardrop in due course and he wouldn't have come around if she hadn't, literally, come round to see him in First Commitment. Despite further warnings, Ree goes beyond Teardrop—beyond her remaining immediate family—and starts visiting more dangerous members of the local clan, starting with Little Arthur, to find information and help. These two beats set up and resolve the clan narrative—the struggle between Ree and her world. Moving beyond family into the closed-off world of her neighboring Ozarks hill folk eventually leads to the clan deciding (Plan) to help her to get her to stop making waves.

5 & 12: B Story (Progress) is paired with **Revelation**. As we have already established, the B Story doesn't fully engage in this beat. We see instead the parallel between Ray's attempt to fool Ree and her and Teardrop's respective responses to the story's Crisis. Ree's personal Crisis sees her despairing of ever finding Jessup and saving her family home. It prompts her to try the only other course of action that might be open to her, joining the army and using the joining bounty to pay off their debt. An interview with a sympathetic recruiter disabuses her of that possibility however and Ree realizes (Revelation) that there is no avoiding her present circumstances. She has taken the only kind of action she can in the moment, now it's up to Teardrop to take on his adopted role as family protector (a role that has been Ree's creation, to some extent).

Teardrop has become tired of waiting for "shit to come down" and brings Ree with him to "poke 'em where they're at." In other words Teardrop's plan is to carry on doing what Ree has been doing the whole movie. Only people are scared of Teardrop and of the potential for violence that lies behind his words. Teardrop smashes the windshield of one of Thump's cronies with an axe and leaves to calls of: "It's on now!" He gets things moving again and provides the final nudge that motivates the clan to give up Jessup's body. So the split B Story pays off where it should and the parallel plays between the clan's first and penultimate responses to the Dolly family's aggravating persistence.

6 & 11: Progress (B Story) is paired with **Crisis**. Ree shows her smarts in Progress. She also shows more evidence of her determination not to be sidetracked or put off her quest. The moral pressure she put on Gail in Hesitation pays off as she turns up with the truck, getting the B Story assistance thread underway. In Crisis Ree has come to another halt, beaten and defeated she is still determined but, until Teardrop turns up again, she has no place to go for more progress. It is at this low point that she contemplates what was previously unthinkable: splitting up the family. The parallel resonates because all her talent and strength and sheer effort has led to the world shutting her down. What can she hope for if all of that good work leads nowhere? Of course the alliances she has already made will be her payoff into Revelation, but right now she is at her lowest point.

7 & 10: Challenge is paired with **Assistance**. This pair of beats marks moments at which the B Story comes into a closer, more supportive alignment with the A Story. In Challenge, Teardrop visits Ree. He tells her he hasn't forgotten her and brings her news of her father's probable death. In Assistance, Teardrop turns up at Thump's place to get Ree back after she has been beaten.

Teardrop agrees to "stand for her" and be responsible for her actions from here on out. After Assistance, Ree and Teardrop are united, in the minds of the locals at least.

8 & 9: Decision is paired with **Acceleration**. This pair bookends Ree's Midpoint decision to do the most dangerous thing and go find Thump. Decision finds her at a loss, once again, as to how to proceed. Her determination is wavering, and her mother can't help. She is looking for the Decision to make. The bail bondsman will focus her mind again. Acceleration finds her calling out Thump Milton in public. That action will have immediate and violent consequences. It will prove the danger—the story value—of her Midpoint commitment—and it will set the story on a faster track to resolution as Thump's women come after her.

Midpoint: The bail bondsman turns up, accelerating the clock and acting as final catalyst for Ree to go find Thump Milton.

Case Study: Writing Sequels with *How to Train Your Dragon 2*

By a strange coincidence, the sequel to *How to Train Your Dragon* was released in cinemas in the United States on the very day that I completed the first draft of this book. That was on June 13, 2014—a Friday, no less—to save you the bother of looking it up. Just in case your thirst for more discussion of animated Vikings hasn't been entirely quenched by what has gone before, I'm going to end the case study section of the book with a quick sketch of the ways in which *How to Train Your Dragon 2* (2014, scr. Dean DeBlois) develops the story begun in the first.

Conventionally, sequels take on the thematic baggage of their antecedent movies. No matter how completely the first film in a cycle or **franchise** resolves its story, the sequel treats both the protagonist and their story world as distinctly "unfinished" and eminently breakable. Whatever was resolved hesitantly is open to further exploitation, whatever was seemingly wrapped up can be undermined. Sometimes this leads to a smooth segue into the sequel plot, but too often sequels get bogged down in all of that business and it hurts their storytelling. This is at least in part the case with *How to Train Your Dragon 2*.

In the *Harry Potter* movies, at the end of each entry in the franchise the antagonist, Lord Voldemort, is defeated, delayed, or deflected for a time. In films like these, however, we are under no illusion as to the partial and contingent nature of each movie's resolution. Indeed, the anticipation of future unfinished business is intrinsic to the pleasure the audience gets from the cycle. With a film like *How to Train Your Dragon* there is no extant antagonistic power the likes of Voldemort still "out there" planning new mischief. There is a family that has experienced more than its fair share of trauma, however, some of which has not been explained. That provides more than enough story material for the sequel to build upon.

The first major motion picture to use "Part II" as part of its title also had no franchise baggage. Instead, it had the complex story work undertaken in the first film as a primary resource to develop. In *The Godfather Part II* (1974, scr. Francis Ford Coppola & Mario Puzo) we are shown the longer-term consequences of Michael Corleone's violent rise to power at the end of *The Godfather* (1972, scr. Mario Puzo and Francis Ford Coppola). Threats to the Corleone crime family, from sources both internal and external, combine to test him as a leader. From within the family Michael's older brother, Fredo, betrays him. Fredo hasn't forgiven Michael for sidelining him and taking the position of Godfather that would otherwise naturally have been his. Other business and crime relationships outside the family are also inflected by Michael's murderous rise to power. Friends and associates of those he had killed are now circling, looking for their own chances to undermine him and take revenge. In this way the sequel continues the work of *The Godfather*, revealing interesting ways in which its story could be seen to be unfinished.

Back in the equally deep and artistically resonant story world of cartoon Vikings and dragons, *How to Train Your Dragon* left Hiccup a hero. His thematic goal of gaining acceptance (and a little romance) had been realized and the hide-bound culture of his village had been transformed, through his example, into a partnership of a kind with the dragons. In the sequel, set several years later with Hiccup now aged 20, a graying Stoick pushes his son to take over from him as chief. Thus the theme picks up the work of the first film and transfers it thematically from a search for *acceptance* to the acceptance of *duty*.

It is refreshing to see an animated film acknowledge the passage of time and the maturation and aging of its characters. This is certainly unusual and it distinguishes the franchise from most of its competition. In an interview for the *Los Angeles Times*, director Dean DeBlois describes Hiccup as poised to become his father: "He is the town hero and has achieved all the things he wanted in the first movie, but he's stepping into a new stage of his life where he has to set aside the freedom of childhood and essentially become his father. . . He doesn't really feel cut out for the job."[43]

---

[43] Susan King, *Director Dean DeBlois sought depth in his solo flight on 'Dragon 2'*, LA Times online, http://www.latimes.com/entertainment/movies/la-et-mn-dragon-director-dean-deblois-20140613-story.html#page=1 accessed June 21, 2014.

Stoick's dynastic plans play counter to Hiccup's ongoing quest for adventure and romance—it was ever thus. Accompanied by Toothless and Astrid, he spends his time exploring and mapping the world further and further out from his island home. The tension between the pull of the unknown and the counterweight pull of responsibility and duty to the village plays strongly in the first act and angle.

In developing the more mature theme of duty, the sequel places Hiccup on the same thematic page as Astrid. In DeBlois' words his themes are more "sophisticated, rich and grown up" in this movie. As Hiccup observes at one point, dutiful Astrid always knew who she was and now he has to find a way to live up to the serious expectations of leadership. Sadly there is never a moment in which Astrid's arguably greater potential as an alternative candidate to become community leader is even discussed.

In the resolution of the transformational arc of duty, Hiccup dutifully learns his lesson, in true Hollywood style. In the movie's Crisis beat, Stoick dies heroically to save the life of his son. It is through Stoick's sacrifice—his ultimate lesson in love and duty—that Hiccup will come to terms with his own destiny. Fortunately he now has a B Story Revelation from his long-lost mother, Valka, to explain this all for him. Long thought dead, she has apparently been hanging out with wild dragons like a crazy old cat lady for the last twenty years, after her repeated pleas for change and tolerance fell on Stoick's once-deaf ears.

Valka is a strange character. She was originally designed, in DeBlois's words again, as a similar kind of "sympathetic antagonist" to Stoick in the original film, Valka's character still bears the eccentric traces of that iteration, but now has little to do in plot terms other than to speak the emotional closure of the family narrative. The movie spends a lot of time developing her only to hand the plot over to the actual—and arbitrary and underwhelming—antagonist Drago. From then on Valka is rather sidelined. She helps in the final battle, but her presence as a strong woman in the film speaks more to story potential unfulfilled. In terms of cultural politics, this feels like another instance of the all-too-common tendency in Hollywood movies that seem too scared to use the strong female characters they create.

While clear, the thematic arc is not as strongly plotted, nor as vital to the storytelling in the sequel. Arguably this reflects in part Hiccup's changed status at the start of the second movie. The story plays the leap from hero to leader as a lesser move than that from outsider to hero enacted in *How to Train Your Dragon*. Hiccup begins the sequel with the support of friends, family and community. All he has to do is decide to grow up a bit. His arc works logically, but doesn't really satisfy in comparison to his personal struggles with loyalty and identity in the first movie.

For all its adventure plotting, the first film played the emotional and moral choices that drove Hiccup towards heroism with commendable power. *How to Train Your Dragon* was strongly story-driven. In the sequel, much of the early plotting focuses on establishing his mother's backstory and temporarily restoring the family unit. It then gives over a great deal of screen time to a villain whose motivations are underdeveloped and whose ability to control a monstrous dragon is taken as a given and never explained satisfactorily. This move towards increasingly plot-driven storytelling is pretty common in tentpole sequels. Although *How to Train Your Dragon 2* is visually stunning and avoids some of the worst pitfalls of this tendency (for an example of which see *Transformers: Revenge of the Fallen*—or rather don't), its structure is missing some of the charm and drive of the original.

Section Three

Screenwriting, A Critical Glossary

Rather than organizing this glossary of screenwriting terms alphabetically, I have split it into broad thematic sections. The idea is to provide a certain continuity of reference. For example, if you want to follow the thread on important terms relating to screenplay style and format, or the development process, you can find information in the same place. I have also provided a list of contents under each major heading to make navigation easier.

Where appropriate, the entries also offer brief historical and critical contexts for how and why a concept has developed through the history of screenwriting and how it may be the focus of debate among professionals and in the critical literature. Terms in **bold** have their own entry in this glossary.

Part One: Screenplay

Screenplay Format; Spec Screenplay; Shooting Script; Slug Line; Transitions; Master-Scene Format; New Spec Format; Parentheticals; Screenplay as Blueprint; Scriptment; The Transcended Screenplay; Courier Font; Experimental Formats

Screenplay is a general term used to refer to the script of a motion picture. In the past, movie scripts have gone by other names, including scenarios, plots and photoplays, but screenplay has long been the default. Not all movies have conventional screenplays (see the entries for **scriptment** and **experimental formats** below), but all screenplays are written to be made into movies. The length of screenplays depends on the intended length of the films they will be made into, but most *feature* screenplays run to between 90 and 120 pages. In Hollywood a single, professionally formatted screenplay page is calculated to be equivalent to one minute of screen time (see **Courier font** below). Thus a screenplay of 100 pages will result in a movie close to 100 minutes long. (See also the lesson about acts and length in Section Two, above.)

Screenplay format

Screenplays are literary documents, they tell stories; however, unlike most other literary texts, they have a hybrid function. They also provide important practical information that is needed by your professional colleagues in every production department. The information contained in a screenplay will guide the entire crew. For this reason, screenplays are formatted so that your fellow professionals can access the information they need from your document easily and quickly.

Here's a simple example: in a conventional screenplay, the first (and only the first) time a character is mentioned in description (in "action"), their name is capitalized, thus: COLE YOUNGER. This makes the job of the casting department easier as they hunt through the screenplay, making up their master-list of all the characters that will need actors to play them. As we write our way into the story, we go on to mention characters by name—but no longer in capitals—in every subsequent scene in which they appear. That way the assistant director will be able to prepare her call sheets for the actors and crew, and the costume department will have the appropriate costumes prepared for a given day's shoot. The list of departments that need that information to be present goes on, and on. In order to make sure she has the correct equipment on set, for example, a cinematographer needs to know if a given scene will be filmed during the DAY or at NIGHT. That's why we provide this information at the end of **slug lines**.

The way a screenplay is presented on the page has changed over the course of the history of filmmaking. The long arc of that history has bent towards standardization, at least in terms of the format of the **spec screenplay** and **shooting script**. Some established writers still have more leeway in their formatting, because they already have a track record and often long relationships with the professionals who will be reading their scripts.[44]

Spec screenplay

A spec screenplay is a script written *spec*ulatively in the hope of a sale or possibly as a writing sample to demonstrate a writer's skill. A writer develops and writes a screenplay and then shops it to potential buyers, agents and managers, or enters it into competitions in the hope of gaining recognition. A spec screenplay is written with the expectation that it will be read, in the first instance by the industry's gatekeepers. The first level of **gatekeeping** is usually

---

[44] The most complete resource for screenwriters on Hollywood formatting is: Christopher Riley, *The Hollywood Standard*, 2nd edition, (Studio City: Michael Wiese Productions, 2009). See also the entries on the **scriptment** and on **experimental formats** below.

a **script reader** (the lowest hanging branch of the **development** tree) who has neither the time nor the inclination to plow through dense pages of detailed description. For this reason, amongst others (see **screenplay format**) the formatting of spec screenplays has trended over time towards minimizing description and excising unnecessary elements. See **master-scene format** and **new spec format**.

Shooting script

In current usage, a shooting script is a screenplay version prepared late in **development** in anticipation of the film's production with additional information added in preparation for that process. Typically shooting scripts will include elements such as scene numbers and **transitions** that are not used in **spec screenplay** format. There is no point numbering your scenes as you draft and re-draft your spec script. It will just be confusing as the scenes move around and get cut. Besides, there is a complex system of numbering scenes used by the industry during script revision in pre-production. But that comes much later.

Shooting scripts may also include additional descriptive information for reasons of detail and clarity at the request of the film's director. They often include more detail in the description of action sequences. This is especially true of big-budget genre movies (see also **screenplay as blueprint** below).

Looking back through the history of Hollywood screenwriting, we can see that a particular variant of the shooting script was once the dominant format for movie scripts. It was the precursor to what is called **master-scene format** in the development of the screenplay towards its contemporary form. Before the 1950s, scripts were written more often in what we might now describe as sequences of shots rather than strictly by scenes. The job of the screenwriter was as much to outline the visual continuity of the story through camera choices as to provide dramatic description. This began to change in the 1930s, when the coming of sound necessitated the inclusion of dialogue in screenplays, but the new master-scene format didn't become the standard until decades later.

Nowadays, however, when you do need to number your scenes, you type the number both at the left and the far right margins of the **slug line**.

Slug line

In **master-scene format**, every scene in your script begins with what is called a slug line. The slug line tells us whether the scene is set inside, INT. or outside, EXT., where it takes place, BEDROOM, and in the daytime, DAY, or at night, NIGHT. It looks like this:

```
INT. BEDROOM - NIGHT
```

Note that slug lines are in caps and that there is a period after the first word and a dash after the location. You use the abbreviations, always `INT.`, never `INTERIOR`.

Transitions

Every time you change scene in a screenplay, you can choose how that transition will be accomplished both technically and creatively. The default is `CUT TO:`, in which one scene is edited straight onto the end of the previous with no effects like dissolves or fades or wipes. In a **spec screenplay** the convention is that you *don't* add this particular transition because a reader will assume a cut is your intention and you are just wasting words and space on the page. If you need to express a more complex kind of transition *that affects how we understand your story*, you would format it on a line of its own at the right-hand side of the page, thus:

`DISSOLVE TO:`

Master-scene format

Master-scene format is a catch-all term for the layout of screenplays that became, over time, pretty much universal practice in Hollywood. The principles of master-scene format are still in use today, although the style has been refined somewhat in recent decades (see **new spec format** below). The key change from the previous style of screenplay formatting was that now the master-scene script was divided by scenes rather than camera shots and the action of the entire scene was described as far as possible without reference to specific shots and similar technical issues. It was understood that directors and cinematographers would "translate" the drama of the scene into a *coverage plan* (see note below) later in the filmmaking process.

Steven Price suggests that it is likely that the shift to master-scene format was precipitated by the coming of sound and the inclusion of dialogue in screenplays on the one hand and by a formalization of the **treatment** towards master-scene description on the other. In this latter case, he argues, the development of a master-scene screenplay from a treatment necessitated only the addition of slug lines and dialogue.

Master-scene format divides the screenplay into a series of distinct scenes separated by **slug lines**. The description of the action in these scenes is written as if viewed in a wide or "master" shot, hence "master scene." In this way, you describe the action clearly and simply as if your reader were observing from a distance and could see everything that is happening. You do not break the action down by signaling individual shots or the sequence of shots that will actually be filmed, unless this is absolutely necessary (as with inserts, for example).

When you do specify a specific perspective or a shot, it will be unusual, your reader will notice it, assume it is important and pay attention. Given their technical requirements, action sequences in **shooting scripts** are often described with clearer reference to shots. In big-budget movies these additions usually come after the input of directors, visual effects specialists and previsualization teams.

Planning shots is the work of the director and the cinematographer, the job of the Hollywood screenwriter is to present the dramatic intent of the scene in such a way as to guide and inspire, but not *overtly* to direct, that process. A professional **script reader** noted in 1981 that, "as far as stage and camera direction, they should be as simple and precise as possible. They should be used to enhance the feeling you are trying to achieve. But don't go overboard because you are a writer, not a director or cinematographer." Dore Schary also wrote of the distinction between a **shooting script** and a screenplay in master-scene format in the late 1940s:

> *The Next Voice* happened to be divided into 172 scenes. But a shooting script which would reach the screen in exactly the same length might contain up to 500 scene numbers, if the writer and producer felt it necessary to write out each camera angle in advance. But most directors justifiably consider the handling of the camera as in their province. . .[45]

Of course, any professional screenwriter worthy of the name endeavors to write their scenes in such a way that the director "discovers" the appropriate style and tone intuitively. We writers like to let directors think they have vision, it keeps them happy!

Note on coverage plan: Here the term coverage refers to the shots filmmakers plan and execute to ensure a scene is "covered" for editing. A well-covered scene means that the editor will have flexibility in how to work the drama and the actors' performances in post-production. Also the director's vision for the scene will be encapsulated in appropriate camera angles. The other meaning of **coverage** in the movie industry refers to the analytical reports **script readers** produce for each screenplay they read.

---

[45] Schary and Palmer, *Case Study of a Movie*, 59–60.

New spec format

This is a loose and contested term, used by some screenwriters and commentators to refer to a gradual process of winnowing down screenplay format, most notably from the early 1980s, to make scripts faster and easier to read. New spec format is a variant on **master-scene format**, using the same basic formal elements but paring description to a minimum. New spec format also allows the inclusion of brief statements in **parentheticals**. It also encourages a more liberal use of white space on the page. For example, David Trottier, author of *The Screenwriter's Bible* observed that:

> ...throughout the 1990s, there has been a movement toward "lean and clean" screenwriting: Shorter screenplays, shorter paragraphs, shorter speeches, more white space and the omission of technical instructions. It should come as no surprise that this gradual evolution continues to refine spec style.

These changes signify a broad tendency, not a set of absolute rules. However, spec format is slowly becoming more standardized through a number of parallel processes emerging from the transition to a **freelance paradigm** for professional screenwriters in Hollywood and the uptake of word-processing and **screenwriting software**, the advice of the screenwriting industry (aka the para-industry) and the need to keep those poor **script readers** awake.

In sum, spec screenplays are now increasingly being *written to be read.* That sounds blindingly obvious—of course a script is written to be read—and yet when you compare the style typical of screenplays from the classical period with that popular today, the difference is marked. The development of a new spec format, however hesitantly we acknowledge the term, echoes an important change since the heyday of the studio system in how a typical screenplay addresses its readers. As noted above, this stylistic development is, in part, the offspring of the change from writers being employed on contract by studios to a **freelance paradigm** that emerged in Hollywood after the closure of in-house story departments. Writers had to learn to become better salesmen in the freelance world and formatting for an easier read has been an important part of that process.

Parentheticals

In screenplay format a parenthetical is a short statement, enclosed in parentheses, either between a character's name and the first line of their dialogue, or between lines of dialogue. The parenthetical is used to provide context to the following speech in some way. A common example is when lines are to be spoken in a foreign language, but are written in English for the convenience of the reader, thus:

                         JEANNE
                      (in French)
                    Good morning.

As noted above, one of the developments associated with the **new spec format** is to accept more direction or action description in parentheticals. Personally I find this distracting and often ugly when it is overdone. Bad screenplays frequently overdo it, and I try to avoid it in my own writing, but it is acceptable nowadays. I think Kevin Delin articulated the heart of the issue very well in a recent piece for *Script* magazine: "...actors assume they can trust your writing. So why don't *you* trust your writing? If you feel your intent requires a parenthetical clarification (of any kind), that's a subconscious warning signal. Go back and rewrite until the parentheses are no longer needed."

Personally, I would exempt the foreign language note from this observation, but otherwise he's dead on. Another reasonable, clarificatory use of parentheticals is to indicate when a character changes who they are talking to in the middle of a speech. Sometimes this is obvious but, if in doubt, it is better to be clear.

Of course many good writers do use parentheticals as occasional direction, and good movies are made from their scripts. Just be careful. Here's an example from Lisa Cholodenko & Stuart Blumberg's screenplay for *The Kids Are All Right*:

                         NIC
             What a good idea. We should try
             That. Right, honey?

                         JULES
                 (taken aback by Nic's
                 cheerfulness)
             Mmm-hmmm.

Screenplay as blueprint

As we have already discussed, screenplays are *hybrid documents*, with both literary and practical applications. They are also hybrid in that, unlike a novel, their purpose is to be transcended by the movie that will be made from them. It used to be fashionable to refer to the screenplay as a kind of "blueprint" for the finished movie, in a similar way one might think of architects' plans in relation to the finished house. Once again, Dore Schary provides us a clear example from the classical studio era. Converting a treatment into a screenplay "…would call not only for creative writing talent, but for a technique equivalent to that possessed by an architect, attorney, or other professional practitioner."[46] While there is certainly some truth in this analogy, it tends to imply a strict demarcation between the period of writing and the period of production. Recently, this periodization has come under increased scrutiny, both academically from within screenwriting studies and professionally, as writers and filmmakers blur the boundaries of these periods in more fluid development and production processes.

This kind of overlapping happens in the microbudget scene as well as in high-budget tentpole cinema. As the technologies of filmmaking, and especially special effects, transformed from the late 1990s, the style of writing action sequences began to defer to the new capabilities of the medium. To generalize somewhat, each effects shot had to be written very specifically to the limits of analog effects technology in advance. The scale, design and construction of elements was often dependent on the exact movement, articulation or interface their practical and cinematic elements would be required to undertake. Matte paintings, armatures, models and other properties had to be manufactured well in advance.

This required a very specific approach to writing these shots and sequences in terms of establishing perspective, camera position, movement and so forth. Here's an example from the **shooting script** of *Star Wars Episode V: The Empire Strikes Back* (1980, scr. Leigh Brackett and Lawrence Kasdan):

```
INT. WALKER No. 3 COCKPIT

Two pilots watch the distant gun emplacements as
they maneuver their war machine forward.

Luke's speeder banks in from the side and heads
straight for the viewport, blasting away. A huge
explosion hits the window and dissipates. The
speeder roars over the window
```

---

[46] Schary and Palmer, *Case History of a Movie*, 27.

```
EXT. ICE PLAIN - BATTLEFIELD - HOTH

FULL SHOT - Moving across the top of the walker as
Luke's speeder skims across it. Trucking with the
speeder then it flys [sic] overhead.
```

In the era of immersive digital special effects this became less the job of the screenwriter. All of these issues were still important, but the process of inscribing them cinematically was increasingly "handed off" from the screenwriter to other members of the creative development team. There are still practical effects of all kinds and animators still build their own digital models, of course, but the potential flexibility of these computer animated constructions transcends that of analog practical effects.

In an interview with *Wired* magazine in 1997, George Lucas raved about his new digital working practice on *Phantom Menace*:

> Instead of making film into a sequential assembly-line process where one person does one thing, takes it, and turns it over to the next person, I'm turning it more into the process of a painter or sculptor. You work on it for a bit, then you stand back and look at it and add some more onto it... You basically end up layering the whole thing. Filmmaking by layering means you write, and direct, and edit all at once.[47]

While Lucas' process is not typical, it speaks to a trend in contemporary genre screenwriting in which increasingly the writer acknowledges the work of previsualization as part of story development. Often action screenplays are less proscriptive in writing description, handing it over to colleagues for a layer of previsualization storytelling as a second order of writing.[48] The blueprint metaphor is also being transcended at the microbudget level of screenwriting with the increasing use of **scriptments** and other partial screenplay documents.

Scriptment

This term has emerged most recently from the world of microbudget film production. Many filmmakers no longer go into production with a traditional

---

[47] Kevin Kelly and Paula Parisi, "Beyond Star Wars: What's Next for George Lucas", *Wired*, February 1997, http://www.wired.com/wired/archive/5.02/fflucas_pr.html accessed February 2014.
[48] For a fuller account of the blueprint debate see Steven Maras, *Screenwriting: History, Theory and Practice* (London: Wallflower Press, 2009).

screenplay as their centering document. Instead, they develop variants on a composite document combining elements of a prose **treatment** with scripted scenes. In this way, the movie's story is clearly laid out, but not every scene is "finished" in the way that it would be in a conventional screenplay. Not every scene in a scriptment has dialogue written in advance. The assumption is that the director's working practice will include improvisation and that the prose narrative will help to keep the actors on track without imposing too much specificity on them.

Travis Mathews, the acclaimed writer and co-director (with James Franco) of the hybrid narrative/documentary feature *Interior. Leather Bar.* (2013, scr. Travis Mathews, *Sundance* and *Berlin* film festivals 2013) felt that the style and intent of his film would not be best supported by the imposition of fully realized dialogue. When I interviewed him for *Filmmaker Magazine* he put it like this:

> It just made sense to put in guideposts, rather than dialogue, because it was important for it to seem honest. . . There were a few things I felt were important for them to cover, but once they started talking they were just bouncing off each other.

Not every scriptment looks or reads the same way. The term is an attempt to account for a non-traditional, but increasingly popular alternative to the screenplay proper in a generic rather than proscriptive manner. For example, some scriptments move beyond the written document to include audio and visual materials that help in establishing atmosphere and context for the director and actors.[49]

The transcended screenplay

Another approach that is fairly common in independent and microbudget filmmaking is to write a full screenplay—a property that is typically required to secure financing—but to view it as already transcended when the film goes into production. Again common sense and experience teaches us that screenplays are always transcended by the movies made from them. Such is the consequence of their hybrid nature. However, there is a difference between this general condition and the approach of directors who understand their screenplays as indicative, rather than proscriptive documents and work improvisation and other techniques into their practice in order to move beyond the script as a matter of creative principle.[50]

---

[49] You can read the rest of my interview with Travis Mathews here: http://filmmakermagazine. com/63105-gay-porn-auteur-travis-matthews-talks-interior-leather-bar/

[50] For more information, see the lesson on improvisation in Section One.

Independent filmmaker Travis Mathews (see **scriptment** above) used this approach for his first narrative feature film, *I Want Your Love* (2012, scr. Travis Mathews), another project on which I worked as a **story consultant**:

> It was a full-on, 112 page script. I knew that it was going to get totally ripped to shreds but the core of some of the story elements were necessary to continue with... I wasn't married to what I had as long as it felt as if it was realistic... I would give [the actors] the script and they would see their character and we would talk about it because, from the very beginning, I wasn't married to any piece of dialogue. There were some things that I thought were special and I loved but, for the benefit of being natural I wasn't going to be locked to it. We talked a lot about the trajectory of their characters and then we workshopped it. If it didn't sound right I would try to get a different performance but if it felt like it wasn't going to happen, nine times out of ten I would ask: "how would you say this?"

I have referred to Mathews' working practice twice in this glossary to reinforce the idea that independent filmmakers often adapt their screenwriting or scripting practice on a project by project basis.

Courier font

Since the 1950s, Hollywood screenplays have been written in Courier font. It's the classic font we now associate with the generic style of the typewriter, although not all typewriters were built around Courier (which was designed in the 1950s). Despite the fact that almost all screenwriters now write on computers rather than typewriters, professional spec screenplays are still presented in some digital variant of Courier font, such as Courier New or Courier Final Draft (see **screenwriting software** below). Tradition has something to do with this, but Courier was also a very computer-friendly font because it does not require "kerning" (the adjustment of spaces between letters). This saved memory in the early days of personal computing, but the predictability of spacing also helped to ensure that the important equation of one screenplay page to one minute of screen time would be maintained in the computer era. [51]

Experimental formats

Of course not all screenwriters and filmmakers follow **master-scene format**. When filmmakers work outside the Hollywood or the international

---

[51] For a fuller discussion see: Kathryn Millard, "After the Typewriter: the Screenplay in a Digital Era", *Journal of Screenwriting* Vol. 1, No. 1, 2010.

mainstream, they imagine, structure and present their scripts in whatever form suits their creative and working practices. It is impossible to generalize or to account for all these variants in this short entry. Versions of the common two-column documentary format—one column for sound and the parallel column for images—are popular. So are simple prose descriptions, or linear documents in which pacing on the screen is implied by spacing on the page.[52]

Part Two: Development

Freelance Paradigm; Tentpole; Franchise Movies; Representation; Gatekeeping; Script Reader; Coverage; Packaging; Option; Treatment; Outline; Breakdown; Pitch; Elevator Pitch; Logline; Story Consultant; Rewrites; One-step Deals; Polishing

In Hollywood, development begins when you sell your **spec screenplay** or when somebody buys your **pitch**. It is the process through which that initial property is "developed" into a movie. There is no hard and fast sequence to the development process. It will depend on how the producers and the development executives with whom you are working operate. Although many of the creative aspects of development are relatively constant, the institutional context for development has changed since the classical era of studio production.

Freelance paradigm

In Hollywood, after the Paramount Case of 1948, the studios entered a period of contraction. They were obliged to divest themselves of their theater chains and downsizing would also transform their internal organization. This contraction included getting rid of the old story departments. Where once writers had been salaried, on contract to a studio like actors and directors, now they became freelance. As freelancers, screenwriters were obliged to **pitch** projects to the studios. They wrote **spec screenplays** and hoped for writing assignments.

Over time the illusion of access implied by the freelance paradigm encouraged more and more new writers to try their luck in Hollywood. They

---

[52] For a fascinating series of case studies of experimental scripts see Scott MacDonald, *Screen Writings: Scripts and Texts by Independent Filmmakers* (Berkeley: University of California Press, 1995).

were also being sold the narrative of "breaking in" by the screenwriting industry. At the same time, the number of movies being made by the studios decreased as producers increasingly put more money into fewer, bigger productions. From the early 1970s, the studios retooled once more towards the blockbuster and the competition for sales and development deals got fiercer. One consequence of this pressure was an increasing reliance on **gatekeeping** to keep the flow of screenplays manageable.

There was a short-lived "spec boom" in the late 1980s and early 1990s, when the studios famously splurged with a series of high-profile seven-figure script sales. A few writers, notably Joe Eszterhas (*Basic Instinct*) and Shane Black (*Lethal Weapon*) made a lot of money and gained notoriety for their deals. This boom was also fueled by the increasing power of agencies and the practice of **packaging**. However, as Rhonda Gomez, an agent at Triad, noted in 1990: "A few years ago, a lot of writers could make a living. Now it's getting like the Screen Actors Guild, where a few stars are getting lots of money and the majority are starving."

The boom lasted about as long as it took the studios to make movies from these high-profile spec screenplays and to lose a bundle on many of them. By the late 1990s the spec boom was over and studios were increasingly initiating project development in-house, leading (in part and by degrees) to the **tentpole** model that operates today. Fred Dekker, screenwriter on *Robocop 3*, gave an epitaph for the multi-million dollar sale in 2001: "Screenwriters are back to being the bastard children of Hollywood... There was a bit of a backlash to all the big screenplay deals in the late 80s and early 90s. We're paying for it now."

Tentpole (or tent-pole)

In contemporary Hollywood, studios initiate a few big-budget movies every year that are designed to "hold up the tent" in commercial terms for everything else (including smaller, perhaps riskier movies) that the studio produces or buys in to fill its slate. Increasingly, however, the tentpoles have to hold up less and less as studios focus their energies and resources on the big films and produce fewer lower-budget movies.

Franchise movies

Big-budget, high-recognition movie series that lend themselves to **tentpole** status. *Harry Potter, Batman, Spiderman, Transformers, Lord of the Rings, The Hunger Games* and *X Men* are all recent examples of franchise properties. The advantage of successful franchise properties for the studios in terms of marketing, cross promotion and functional repeatability is obvious.

Representation

Many screenwriters are represented by other specialist creative industry professionals. These are the *agents, managers* and *entertainment lawyers* who variously take an interest in developing a writer's careers and/or become involved in their business and financial dealings. While not all successful writers have relationships with all of the above, a successful Hollywood screenwriter will certainly have representation of some kind.

1. *Agents* – Agents are primarily focused on deal making and promoting their clients for work opportunities. They negotiate contracts, sell scripts and act as an intermediary between the writer and the industry. An agent takes a 10 percent commission for her work and (in California) is licensed by the state. Reputable agencies are typically certified by the Writers Guild of America.
2. *Managers* – There is some overlap between the roles of agent and manager (indeed writers may be represented by one or the other), however managers typically take more of a holistic interest in their client's career development. Unlike agents a manager is allowed to develop creative projects such as movies or TV shows and so they can collaborate in ways an agent cannot. Managers take a base 15 percent fee.
3. *Lawyers* – Legal services for entertainment professionals are typically focused in areas of contract law, intellectual property and copyright, taxation, publication, litigation, and liability. A reputable agency or management company may be able to handle the legal issues arising from their clients' work but some writers also like to have relationships with lawyers, specialist or otherwise, independently from their other representation.

When screenwriters are starting out, they do not need and likely will be unable to obtain representation. Getting an agent is necessary when there is a deal to be made; and when there is a deal to be made an agent (or even a swarm of them) will miraculously appear. Until that time an aspiring writer is better served developing her craft and reputation rather than expending too much energy trying to get an agent. Developing an early relationship with a manager may be a more effective way of getting representation, but again an established manager is unlikely to be interested in a writer with no track record.

Gatekeeping

Gatekeeping is the process by which producers, agents and other industry types separate some of the wheat from the chaff and avoid having to deal with most of the worst speculative screenwriting. As one studio vice-president noted in an interview in the late 1990s: "There are so many [screenplays] to read, even a recommended script can take a while. There's just so much out-and-out bad writing out there. Everyone is writing a script. It's a jungle. You've got to machete it down in some way."

First most screenplays will never be read by anyone with decision-making power because their authors have no contacts, **representation**, or track record. For legal reasons, unsolicited screenplays sent in hope to agencies and studios are thrown out or returned unopened. If you have written a screenplay, the next thing you need is a reason for anyone to want to read it. Having the right contacts is an obvious shortcut to access but, failing that, winning or placing in *recognized* screenwriting competitions might also be a reason. Having a track record as a filmmaker, or as a writer in other media might get your screenplay read and so on.

Once you have passed this first step and you have made a connection with a producer or agent who has agreed to read your screenplay, it is very likely that your script will first be read by a **script reader**. The reader is a gatekeeper for the producer. She writes **coverage** on the screenplay which is, in turn, read by her boss. On the basis of that coverage, the producer or agent will decide whether they need to read the script themselves or simply respond on the basis of the reader's report.

Script reader

A script reader may be an experienced professional or merely this week's intern. Often script readers are also aspiring screenwriters. Whatever the case, they occupy the bottom rung on the movie **development** ladder, but are also the most important gatekeepers (see **gatekeeping** above) your screenplay has to get past on its journey towards a sale and production. That's because the **coverage** they write on your screenplay will be archived in their organization.

Readers are given stacks of scripts and other original materials such as novels, stories, plays and journalistic articles, to "cover" for their agency or production company bosses and their job is to analyse and identify promising material and writers and to keep the unpromising away from anyone higher up the ladder. Typically organizations will give their script readers instructions as to the kind of material they are looking for. Here's a fairly generic example from Karen Moy, Executive Director of Creative Affairs for Columbia Pictures in 1999:

> ... they're to look for fresh takes on mainstream commercial material, but they should also acknowledge good quality of writing in the more

esoteric or small pieces. This latter type is unlikely to be made at a studio, although some of these writers do get hired to work on writing assignments for the studio.

Since the classical studio era in Hollywood, the basic process of gatekeeping hasn't changed much other than in the reorganization of in-house departments. Dore Schary explains how things worked at MGM in the late 1940s. *The Next Voice You Hear* was adapted from a story originally published in *Cosmopolitan* magazine (August 1948) by George Sumner Albee:

> Dorothy Pratt sifted through the morning's grist on her desk and assigned the story to one of the fifteen story analysts in her department. The analyst drew off a synopsis, put down a personal opinion, and relayed the file along the corridor to editor Marjorie Thorson... These synopses are designed to capture the producer's interest and give him the essential bones of the stories: they provide the only means by which an executive can even begin to cover the field in the hours... he can set aside for his reading. When a synopsis intrigues him he calls for the original book or story or play and reads it in full. Often our reader's synopsis, particularly of a long novel, is better than the original for our purposes; crisper, the story line cleaner, and the characters standing out in sharper relief.[53]

In this way Schary was acknowledging that the classical Story Department did not buy stories so much as sell them to the producers higher up in the studio's hierarchy.

Coverage

Coverage reports are written by **script readers** or sometimes junior development executives. They are concise, analytical and evaluative documents that producers and agents will read instead of, or at least before they read actual screenplays. There is no single format for coverage reports, each company or agency will have its own version. However, most coverage reports ask the reader to provide a short summary of the screenplay's plot and to assess the quality of the writing, focusing in particular on story structure and character development. The report may also comment on the film's potential budget and on its likely commercial viability. It will highlight perceived problems or deficiencies and sometimes offer suggested fixes. In

---

[53] Schary and Palmer, *Case History of a Movie*, 8.

this way the producer reading a coverage report can get a sense of the project in a few pages and gage whether it is worth her while to actually read the script. For the screenwriter, the most important part of the report is the reader's final grade: "Recommend," "Consider" or "Pass."

Most screenplays get a Pass, which means the script is not deemed to be of sufficient quality or interest. Sometimes even good scripts may get a Pass if they are simply not what the institution is looking for—a romantic comedy at a company specializing in low-budget horror movies, for example. A grade of Consider implies that the script is well written, or at least potentially commercial, and may be of interest to the reader's boss. A Recommend is extremely rare, as it indicates exceptional quality in the opinion of the reader and that the producer should read it as a priority. A Recommend also entails some potential risk for the reader if their boss disagrees and feels their time has been wasted reading the script. Recommends tend to get read at a higher level, while not all Considers get that privilege. Due to the nature of the industry it is certainly the case that many readers, especially inexperienced readers of the "this week's intern" variety, keep their heads down and tend to avoid giving Recommends.

Most coverage reports grade the writer as well as the screenplay. It is quite possible for a script to get a Pass but the writer to be graded Consider or Recommend. The company isn't looking for a script in that genre, but they recognize the quality of the writing and might have assignments in the future for a good writer—or at least they will be more open to reading her next screenplay. The important thing to remember, as an aspiring writer, is that the coverage—and most importantly the grade for both writer and screenplay—are filed away in the agency or company and will be referred to in the future. In this way, your coverage is your reputation, so don't send out a screenplay until it is as good as you can make it.[54]

Packaging

Packaging is a strategy in which agencies assemble "packages" of talent so as to sell studios "shovel ready" movie projects. These packages typically include actors and directors wrapped up in a screenplay. The effect of an increase in packaging was to shift the balance of power in deal making from the 1950s away from the studios and towards the bigger agencies.

---

[54] For those wanting more information, or help in preparing for work writing coverage reports, this is a good place to start: Asher Garfinkel, *Screenplay Story Analysis, The Art and Business* (New York: Allworth Press, 2007).

Option

Sometimes scripts are not sold outright, rather the license to develop them is sold for a specified period (typically one or two years). In this way, producer A options screenplay B at price C for period D. The writer is paid for exclusive rights to attempt to attract financing, attach talent and place the script into development and production. An option fee is variable, but typically much less than the price of buying the script. The writer gets a payment (writers like payments) and hopes that the producer will be able to move the development process forward. The incentive for the producer is that she gets the chance to do so exclusively and for a much lower initial investment.

For example, a screenplay I wrote with a writing partner a few years ago was optioned by a producer in New York for one year. He managed to attach a well-known British director and tried to get financing. In the end he was not successful. It's a story that is all too common for screenwriters—and producers for that matter. After the end of the option period, all rights on our screenplay reverted to its authors. The other advantage (small as it may be) to the aspiring writer of an ultimately failed development process of this kind is that the project was recognized as being worthy of an option in the first place. This gives her the beginning of a track record and a little credibility.

Treatment

A treatment is a condensed prose telling of your story (although see also **outline** below). A treatment is *not* a short story and it is *not* a screenplay (although see also **scriptment** earlier). Rather it is a kind of proof of concept document for sales and story development purposes. The treatment takes us on an accelerated ride through the structure of your story, moving from clear **beat** to clear beat so that the readers can "get it" fast and be able to collaborate as quickly as possible. Typically, treatments are the next stage in the studio development process after a successful **pitch**, but some writers use treatments when developing their **spec screenplays**. Many treatments are still written in **Courier font**, but this is not usually required.

Treatments are selling documents. The idea is to communicate the uniqueness and the brilliance of your expanded concept succinctly and engagingly. Many aspiring screenwriters think of treatment writing as a chore, something that gets in the way of writing an actual screenplay, and their bland writing style reveals their disinterest. This is never a good idea, because a treatment can be the one chance you have to hook potential buyers, investors and collaborators.

The opening paragraphs of a treatment typically sell the concept of the movie and establish the protagonist's dilemma or challenge. This is followed by a synopsis, focusing on key story and plot information. In this way the story is told both economically and dynamically. A good treatment draws the reader in and keeps her attention by removing detail without losing dramatic clarity. In the era of studio story departments the treatment was less a selling document and more like a detailed outline, Dore Schary once again: "you simply tell the story; who the characters are, what they want, what's blocking the way, and how they go about achieving their goals."[55]

When used in creative development, treatments are useful documents in that they provide a clear story summary in a few pages. That makes them much easier to unpick and revise than full screenplay drafts. With a treatment, you can cut and paste short paragraphs encapsulating story **beats** and map the result of the change easily. There is no set length for a treatment, although the clarity—and thus the utility—of the form tends to diminish after ten or so pages. As development progresses, treatments may get longer and more detailed, but then they are really becoming **outlines** (although in practice there is often slippage between these terms). Writers may be asked to produce treatments of different lengths, say a two page summary for a senior executive and eight or ten pages for development meetings.

Outline

An outline is less a sales tool and more a writer's own complete work-through of a story. Typically outlines are longer and more detailed than **treatments** as their purpose is to be something closer to a structural **blueprint** (although, as always, I use the term with care) for the screenplay-to-come rather than a persuasive document calculated to buy you the chance to be paid to write that screenplay. So outlines don't merely skip from **beat** to beat, they fill in those beats. An outline may be written just for the writer's own purposes or as another stage in collaborative development.

These terms shift, and sometimes an outline can refer to a much shorter synopsis of a screen story. In this context an outline is a couple of pages long, but is still more prosaic and less of a sales pitch than a treatment.

Breakdown

A script breakdown is a pre-production document that reduces a screenplay to a series of scene headings and lists to prepare for the budgeting and scheduling process. There are format variations, but typically the **slug line** of each scene is noted, along with an encapsulation of the key dramatic action,

---

[55] Schary and Palmer, *Case History of a Movie*, 27.

the location, a list of cast, extras, wardrobe and make-up needs, practical (on set) special effects and key props. Here's an invented example for a single scene:

```
INT. JIM'S BEDROOM - NIGHT        LOCATION:
SCENE NUMBER: 23                  CARSON HOUSE
JIM PREPARES FOR BED; FINDS ANNE  IN CLOSET

CAST:                             PROPS:
1. CAL BEST                       ANNE'S REVOLVER
3. SOPHIE TAYLOR                  JIM'S PHONE

EXTRAS/ATMOSPHERE:                SPECIAL EFFECTS:
NONE                              NONE

MAKEUP/WARDROBE:
M.U.: ANNE, SMALL CUT ABOVE LEFT EYE
```

A professional screenplay should be written in such a way that all the information required to prepare the breakdown will be available and *easy to find* in the script (see **screenplay format** above).

Pitch

Pitching is selling your movie idea, usually out loud, in a short, clear, dynamic statement that encapsulates the heart of your story and the height of your concept. Successful screenwriters need to moonlight as salespeople; the film scholar John Thornton Caldwell describes pitching as a kind of "industrial performance art." Since the 1980s spec pitching has become less important as a selling tool in Hollywood as more screenplays than pitches are now sold. However, the communication skills required to pitch ideas are still at a premium. In Hollywood, pitching is also the province of established writers giving their take on a studio job. In independent and microbudget film the ability to pitch and convince potential backers and collaborators is also still of vital importance.

Case Study: A Pitch Meeting

This is the way one of my ex-students described their first experience of a TV pitch meeting from the perspective of an assistant. (He gave me permission to use the story, but asked to remain anonymous.) I am very grateful for his detailed and entertaining narrative:

When you get to the production offices, the first words you hear are "who are you? What are you doing here?" You're here for a pitch, and you tell them who you work for and who you're meeting with. They check the list to make sure your name is on it, and point you in the general direction of the elevators. When you get upstairs, there's another check-in desk. "Who are you? What are you doing here?" Pitch, company, etc. They aren't sure you really belong there, but they call a courier anyway to take you to the floor where the meeting is taking place. You get to the waiting area outside the conference room, and a woman approaches you. "Who are you? What are you doing here?" You've been asked so many times at this point that it feels like a security checkpoint, and you start to have doubts. I'm not anybody. Oh God, what am I doing here? But you pretend like you belong there, and tell them who you are.

As soon as you walk into the conference room, everyone stops talking and just stares at you; you can practically hear a record scratch. They don't have to say it, because you can see it on their faces: Who are you? What are you doing here? You introduce yourself and they recognize that you're actually supposed to be there, so everyone relaxes. It's actually a fairly casual setting; you notice that no one is in a suit, and the executives are chatting about what they did over the weekend.

The pitch begins—your boss describes the characters, the storyline, and why the idea is exciting. It will be popular because it has one element from this show, and another from that. It has this celebrity attached to it as the lead. They have more energy in this presentation than they've had collectively over the entire course of the time you've known them. Throughout the presentation, executives spout questions and concerns, but your boss has an answer for everything. They can answer anything about the project ranging from marketing to legal issues. "We've thought of that, and we have a solution." Occasionally, they'll point at you to agree with them, and you nod. You don't dare open your mouth, because you're not there to have an opinion. After the presentation the executives start to spitball ideas and brainstorm which networks to approach. It doesn't mean anything yet, but this is a good sign—there's a dialogue going about the concept and they're getting excited.

The meeting ends, everyone shakes hands and smiles politely, hoping to see each other in the same room again soon. They're going to approach the networks to try and sell it, so now all that's left to do is validate your parking and wait for them to call you back.

Elevator pitch

If you had the time it takes to ride up in an elevator with an influential producer who might be interested in your screenplay, how would you pitch it before the doors opened? Producer Lloyd A. Silverman (*Snow Falling on Cedars*) often uses this one-line pitch for *Twins* as a perfect example of the high-concept elevator pitch: "Danny DeVito is Arnold Schwarzenegger's twin brother." That single sentence doesn't tell you what they will be doing throughout the movie, but it sells you a funny concept. You get the core of the pitch. Usually, however, an elevator pitch would treat with story rather than casting choices.

Logline

Similar to an **elevator pitch**, a logline is a one or two sentence outline of your idea. A good logline, which can also be an opening pitch statement, gives the reader a clear sense of the identity of the protagonist, their challenge and a little story world context if appropriate. Use adjectives sparingly to establish attitude and make sure your logline encapsulates, or at least hints at, the uniqueness or the unusual turn of your story. How is your western unlike other westerns?

Story consultant

Story or script consulting is a primary employment opportunity for many screenwriters. Often a writer is brought in during development to give a fresh pair of eyes to a script or even a treatment. Consulting is not necessarily the same thing as doing **rewrites** or **polishing**. The consultant may not be asked to write a single word of script. Rather they offer their analysis of what's working, what isn't and how things can be improved.

In independent and microbudget productions, writers are sometimes brought in during post-production to help a director find clarity during the editing process, or to help plan re-shoots. In my own professional experience, this tends to happen more frequently when directors go into a project without a conventional screenplay (see **scriptment** and **the transcended screenplay** above), or in other circumstances that have resulted in a lot of improvisation on set.

Rewrites

All scripts are rewritten by their authors, in the sense of being taken through multiple drafts. A writer who is brought onto a movie for rewrites, however, is working on a project that was written by somebody else. Sometimes this happens at the instigation, or at least with the knowledge of the first writer/s. I did rewrites on an independent feature some years ago which was being rushed into production because financing and a production window were suddenly in place (it often happens that way). The director, who was also one of the first writers, was suddenly incredibly busy with pre-production and needed help with a major rewrite of the script.

In the Hollywood development paradigm writers can be, and often are, replaced. This tends to happen if they kick too hard against the studio's analysis of where the project needs to go, or when they have taken so many passes at a script that they are creatively exhausted. In Hollywood speak, they are deemed to be "written out." Increasingly this is set up as a standard part of development through **one-step deals**. Sometimes, and this is a very much a Hollywood phenomenon, other writers are brought in without the first writer's knowledge. This shouldn't happen, strictly speaking, but it does. In this way, two—sometimes even more—versions of a script are being developed simultaneously. The original writers may never find out that anyone else worked on the project. Whatever the circumstances, the writer who is brought in has to navigate the process carefully. Not all writers feel comfortable reworking the writing of others, even in the best and most open of circumstances.

One-step deals

A one-step deal is a contract that guarantees a screenwriter only a single draft on a screenplay before he or she can be replaced on a movie in development. One consequence of one-step deals is that writers tend to avoid taking creative risks if they only have a single draft to prove their take on the movie. Billy Ray (*Flightplan, Color of Night*) explains: "When a writer is working on a one-step deal, he's going to be risk-averse because if he takes a flier on a wildly creative or inventive way of telling the story, he might wind up getting fired. He won't have another draft or two to make it work, so he's going to write it down the middle."

Variety quoted an unnamed agent in 2010:

> "The traditional seven-figure writers are so hit-or-miss for the studios. With the top-tier writers, the studios get one meeting with the guy and get one draft. The cheap writers often come from TV, where they are used to being super-collaborative and working in rooms with other people. These writers will give a studio exec 30 meetings on a project.... And they're super hungry."

This also speaks clearly to the bottom-line, according to a literary manager:

> "You don't need to hire [the highest-paid writers] anymore for the original draft because you're going to hire them later anyway for the uncredited rewrite or polish. It's simple math. Now, you see a studio pay a new writer rather than a high-paid veteran and save $5 million right there. And then the studio gets Koepp or [Lowell] Ganz and [Babaloo] Mandel on the rewrite."[56]

Increasingly, writers are also being asked to do free "pre-writes" and "producer's drafts," producing detailed outlines and rewriting specs before being given contracts.

Polishing

This is a Hollywood term for when a specialist writer is brought in to give an existing screenplay a final pass before it goes into production. This process often focuses on sparking up characterization and dialogue, hence the term "dialogue polish." There are writers who specialize in, and make very good money from, this kind of work. They are brought in because they have whatever version of the "Barton Fink feeling" the studio deems necessary to finish things up. Usually polishing does not involve significant changes to the story or its structure, the polisher is brought in once these are more or less set in stone. The term slips, however, and some writers make significant changes in polishing a script.

Part Three: The screenwriting industry

Screenwriting Software; Story Development Software; Lajos Egri; Aristotle's Poetics; Syd Field; Three-Act Structure

Sometimes also referred to as the para-industry, the term refers to the world of screenwriting classes, consultants, books (like this one), journalism and software development that works alongside (in *para*llel to) the film industry in support of established screenwriters and in the encouragement and development of aspirants. The para-industry sells the possibility of success—of "breaking in"—through the application of a certain definition of

---

[56] Tatiana Siegel, "Fast, Cheap and in Control: Franchises rely on newbies", *Variety*, March 29, 2010.

professional screenwriting method and through the revelation of "insider" knowledge on current trends in the spec market and so forth. While many screenwriters acknowledge the value of books on screenwriting, others are deeply suspicious. Shane Black is one of the latter: "...people respond to people who have passion and who like to play. They don't respond to plot point number twelve on page 32 a la **Syd Field**."

At their best, the products of the para-industry offer support for writers who can see beyond bland structural formulae, but find it helpful to have models on which to fall back if they get stuck. At worst it can feel like snake-oil for rubes. Chris Gore, editor of *Film Threat* magazine remembers the late 1990s thus: "...screenwriting turned into an industry preying on all these people from Michigan or someplace who think they're going to come out here and write a screenplay and make $1 million overnight. It became like the lottery."

It is important to remember that the para-industry did not emerge with the **freelance paradigm**, nor with the spec boom of the late 1980s. Aspiring movie writers have been offered models for professional practice and pathways to success throughout the history of cinema. In 1919, Frederick Palmer, a well-known early screenwriting "guru," offered a range of services, including correspondence classes to his readers. In his book he summed up what is in many ways still the basic pitch of the para-industry: the application of inside knowledge, explained clearly and practically, leads to the development of personal creative vision and the chance to break in.

We bring to you *knowledge*. The sum total of knowledge that it has taken the great writers, directors and producers years to acquire through experimentation, study and work, is condensed, compiled and presented for your benefit.

We shall give you *training*. You will be taught how to apply this knowledge in a practical way.

From your knowledge and training you will become possessed of *vision* – you will realize what a truly wonderful future is opened to you through the development and training of that most precious of all natural endowments – the creative imagination... The future lies in your hands. You are "master of your fate". Others have succeeded through studiously and persistently availing themselves of this same opportunity. Why not you?[57]

---

[57] Frederick Palmer, *Palmer Plan Handbook: Photoplay Writing Simplified and Explained by Frederick Palmer* (Los Angeles: Palmer Photoplay Corporation, 1919).

Screenwriting software

Screenwriters were early adopters of computer technology. Many writers began to transition from the typewriter to the personal computer in the 1980s. Companies like the Writers Computer Store in Los Angeles (now the Writers Store) serviced this transition for many writers and provided packages of hardware and software that helped us to format our scripts using the new technology. The first program that saw wide use amongst screenwriters was *Scriptor* from Screenplay Systems. This was followed by second generation packages, notably the *Warren Script Application* which was popular in the early 1990s when I was at film school. However, it was with the development of the third generation of formatting programs in the early 1990s, like *Final Draft* and *Movie Magic Screenwriter*, that screenplay software became standalone.

The more advanced programs allow writers to format their spec screenplays, but also to handle many of the common professional pre-production tasks, such as revision tracking, as a screenplay moves towards production and becomes a **shooting script**. These software packages certainly offered unheard of flexibility to writers, who could now easily save drafts and cut and paste. The programs also enforce their own standards of formatting, based on an interpretation of current industry practice. The default settings of screenwriting software encouraged new writers to conform and experienced writers to adapt their writing style to get the most from the programs. Screenwriting software also defaulted to or adapted the traditional **Courier font**, helping to ensure that it would continue to be the presentational font for screenplays written in the computer age.

Story development software

Alongside formatting programs (see **screenwriting software** above), the para-industry has also developed a range of story development programs to help writers flesh out and structure their ideas into scripts. These programs typically use variations on a question and answer interface to guide their users. Most work broadly under the rubric of **three-act structure** which has become the default organizing model of the contemporary screenplay in Hollywood. Some of these programs adapt story models developed by the authors of screenwriting manuals such as John Truby (*Anatomy of Story*) and Blake Snyder (*Save the Cat*). Others, including the popular and long established *Dramatica*, offer their own theories of story, but still fit into a broadly conventional structural paradigm.

As an illustration of how story development software presents its process, *Dramatica*'s website offers this concise explanation of its approach to story:

Dramatica is not all that complicated. It sees the central character of a story—the Main Character—entering with a predetermined way of doing things. Along the way they develop a relationship with their polar opposite, someone who challenges their way of thinking. Ultimately, this relationship leads the Main Character towards adopting or rejecting this new way of seeing things. The result of their decision determines whether they were on the right path or the wrong path.

This is a dialectical approach to story and character development. Thesis is tested in collision with antithesis, and development—perhaps even synthesis—emerges from the outcome of that collision. Story, here, is about the interaction and resolution of competing world views. This is a well established shorthand for dramatic storytelling, owing much to the writing of **Lajos Egri**.

The use of story development software is controversial even within the screenwriting industry, however. Robert McKee is a critic of *Dramatica*: "I came in, took a look and said, 'This is ridiculous. Only someone without talent, a computer nerd, would think it was useful.' They were not happy with me." For his part, **Syd Field** rejected these programs—despite subsequently being involved with a similar piece of tech for *Final Draft*: "It's all horrific. I don't understand a word of what they're saying."[58]

Lajos Egri

Still influential with some screenwriting teachers, Egri is best known as the author of *The Art of Dramatic Writing*, first published under that title by Simon and Schuster in 1946. He offered a dialectical theory of dramatic structure in which opposing principles collide, to prove a premise or theme and to impel character change. He also takes issue with one of the most important principles of **Aristotle's *Poetics*** in arguing that character drives story.

Aristotle's *Poetics*

The *Poetics*, written around 335 BCE by the Greek philosopher Aristotle, is the earliest surviving work of dramatic theory. Aristotle wrote the *Poetics* in two parts, but only the section on tragedy has survived. The second section, known to deal with comedy, has been lost. In his *Poetics* Aristotle defines

---

[58] Dana Kennedy, "Screenwriting @ Your Fingertips", *New York Times*, Jan 9, 2000.

types of "poetry," including tragedy, comedy, the satyr play and lyric and proposes a series of principles that make for effective dramatic writing in the context of his culture and period. In the Western canon, the *Poetics* has been one of the most influential treatises on dramatic form for centuries. Many of the techniques and assumptions screenwriters bring to their story structure derive at least in part from Aristotle's writing.

Although Aristotle's observations are both culturally specific and related to theater, writers within the modern screenwriting industry have attempted to adapt his precepts into a straightforward model of plotting for **three-act structure**. Notable contributions to the appropriation of the *Poetics* for screenwriters include Richard Walter's *Essentials of Screenwriting: The Art, Craft, and Business of Film and Television Writing* and Michael Tierno's *Aristotle's Poetics for Screenwriters: Storytelling Secrets From The Greatest Mind in Western Civilization.*

In the context of Greek tragedy, the *Poetics* analyses issues familiar to screenwriters such as the relationship between **character** and **story** (*ethos* and *mythos*), the nature of dramatic representation (*mimesis*), the power of dramatic revelation and reversal (*anagnorisis* and *peripeteia*), and the idea of the tragic flaw (a loose interpretation of the Greek term *hamartia*). One of the more controversial reformulations of Aristotle's thinking has been the transformation—some would argue cheapening—of the complex idea of *catharsis* (a powerful purging, or purification of emotions that Aristotle associated with the effect of tragedy on its audience) into the default Hollywood **redemptive ending**.

My own W model certainly bears the traces of this historical overhaul of Aristotle. Many of the most influential figures from the screenwriting industry were also influenced by Aristotle's work, including the late **Syd Field**.

Syd Field

Field was the first and probably still is the most influential of the contemporary group of screenwriting "gurus" whose ideas fuel much of the para-industry. His book *Screenplay* (1979) introduced the concept of **three-act structure** to many aspiring screenwriters, although it was a term that had some currency amongst writers before his book was published. Subsequently, the language of three-act form became the default for Hollywood movie development.

Like many proponents of screenwriting industry "formulae," when Field traveled to other countries to promote his ideas he was often treated with great suspicion, as his (somewhat self-serving) account of a trip to France indicates:

"In some other countries, like France, they call me the devil. When I went to France they were hooting, and they were shouting, and they were trying to disrupt the seminar. On the second day, a lot of people began understanding. By noon on the second day, they got it. Just because we have identified the structure, doesn't mean they have to change their content. They have to take their own ideas, their own problems, their own society and they have to weave that into a story, told with pictures."[59]

Three-act structure

One of the most influential products re-sold by the para-industry has been the three-act model of movie storytelling. Popularized by **Syd Field**, it has become the shorthand for how story is understood in much of the film world. Even most independent movies use some variation on three acts, and it is rare to find a conventional feature film that deviates significantly from its precepts.

Three-act structure is important to understand because it is the default common language of movie development. You may come to your own storytelling by other means but, as an aspiring screenwriter, you need to understand the three-act model because that is the language in which many of your future colleagues, employers and collaborators will "speak story." David Bordwell observes:

> Once the three-act template became public knowledge, development executives embraced it as a way to make script acquisition routine... Today most screenwriters acknowledge the three-act structure, and around the world it is taught as the optimal design for a mass-market movie.[60]

As noted above, three-act structure is a modernization of principles first outlined in **Aristotle's** *Poetics*, reoriented from a plot-driven to a character-driven model. The first **act** establishes the **theme** of the story expressed through character goals or objectives. The second act develops the protagonist's attempt to realize her story goals through conflict with an antagonistic force. The third act resolves both theme and objectives, thus completing the character's **arc**, usually successfully.

---

[59] Stephanie Argy, "Field exports the write stuff"" *Variety*, June 25, 1999.
[60] David Bordwell, *The Way Hollywood Tells It: Story and Style in Modern Movies* (Berkeley: University of California Press, 2006).

Redemptive ending

Most conventional movies resolve their stories through the actions of a character who restores balance where there was disorder. In this way, the restorative three-act structure can be seen to offer the comforting illusion that the world is somehow "solvable" and that flawed people can be redeemed through the application of a secular, storytelling equivalent of the Protestant work ethic. A common critique deployed against the redemptive ending is that it sells us fundamentally unrealistic fantasies.

Sometimes that kind of fantasy is entirely the point of the story, however it is possible also to use the classical story forms in subtly mimetic and complex ways. Our case studies of *Let the Right One In* and *Winter's Bone* both resist the simplicity of a purely redemptive ending for example. Dancyger and Rush offer a clear summation of the critique:

> The pattern of transgression, recognition, and redemption makes the restorative three-act structure a very comforting form. It allows us to identify with characters who have gone beyond acceptable behavior, while at the same time remaining aware that they will be forced to confront their behavior. The three-act structure privileges the individual over any social, historical, economic, and familial limitations. Although they may be underplayed, we cannot avoid the implications of the form altogether. If the feel of transgression, recognition, and redemption is what we want, then there is no better way to express this than by using the restorative three-act structure. But to create a different feel, to find a way to respond to the arbitrariness and indifference of the contemporary world, we have to look elsewhere.[61]

Part Four: Story structure

Ring Composition; Story and Plot; Narration; Narrative Voice; Beats; Acts; Midpoint; Scenes; Sequences; Inciting Incident; Parallelism

Ring composition

Anthropologists and experts in early literature have identified similar structures in some of the earliest written narratives produced by separate cultures around the world. These structures, called *ring compositions* are probably holdovers from oral storytelling. They are structured using simple

[61] Ken Dancyger and Jeff Rush, *Alternative Scriptwriting*, 38–39.

principles that are still central to how we tell, understand and take pleasure in stories in our contemporary cultures.

A ring composition splits a story into two parts, around a central turn or development that refers back to an opening premise. The second half of the story turns back and resolves material established in the first half through a series of "parallel" events. These parallels may be signaled by repeated, contradicted or transformed vocabulary, for example. At the end, the story resolves the premise or initial situation established at the start of the ring.

The narrative power of the ring lies in part in the creative use of **parallelism**. It cross-references material to show story development. Its power lies also in the idea that a good story "turns" and develops, often in unexpected or exciting ways. It lies also in the idea that exposition implies resolution to come and that the audience or reader enters a kind of contract in which she expects such resolution to be delivered at the end. Finally it lies in the understanding that storytelling has a ludic aspect—it enacts a kind of formal playfulness. The writer and the reader enter into a game of anticipation, revelation and puzzling out, controlled in part by the writer's skill in techniques of **narration**.

Story and plot

The distinction between story and plot is central to the interpretation of conventional movie storytelling. First one has to understand that in screenwriting the terms are not interchangeable. Every movie has *both* a story and a plot and they interact in a complex dance throughout. In this model, *story* refers to the emotional, or psychological track that follows the protagonist as she strives to change and to resolve her goals. It is an internal process that is manifest in her reactions to events and interactions with other characters, not in those events themselves. Events are the ingredients of *plot*: external markers and obstacles that the protagonist must confront, explore and overcome.

Plot manifests externally to characters; story is largely intimated from internal motivations. Plot is much of what we see on screen, story is how those events resonate in terms of character development.

The distinction between story and plot loosely echoes the distinction in formalist narratology between *fabula* and *syuzhet* (the raw material and the deployment of that raw material as narrative), but the two sets of terms are not precisely interchangeable. In either case, however, the distinction implies the importance of **narration** in establishing knowledge and, thus, power relationships between both elements. Sometimes plot is just a disguise for tone or **narrative voice**. The events we see on screen are important in establishing atmosphere as much as they are in driving the narrative forward.

Narration

As it relates to story structure, narration is the control of story information through story*telling*. Planning out who knows what and when they know it is one of the keys to establishing a pleasurable relationship between your audience and your film. Narration writes that contract, and it can change the terms at your will. Other terms are sometimes used to describe the work of narration. John Truby talks about controlling your "reveals," for example. The question of whether or not we can rely on the information you provide us— and your protagonist—adds another dimension to your storytelling. Is your narrator, or narration, unreliable? Is it always unreliable, or can we trust it sometimes—and how do we know when? Some movies—some genres, like mysteries, thrillers and horror films—play this game more overtly than others, but every movie works narration in its own way.

For example, some stories begin by positioning the audience ahead of the protagonist and the pleasure lies in watching and willing them to catch up. The TV detective show *Columbo* used to start by revealing both crime and criminal and the detective would work to uncover what we already knew to be the truth. Other stories position the audience with the protagonist in a position of relative ignorance, or even further behind the count. Think of the effect of memory loss on the story of *Memento* both for the protagonist and the audience. Whatever strategy you use, the play of knowledge, truth, and trust adds much to the engagement of your audience.

Playing catch-up can be as enjoyable as willing a character to catch up with us. However pleasure is not always happy fun. I am stretching the word to its broadest sense here. In this way it can encompass the very different pleasures of watching a comedy, a tragedy, and a horror movie equally.

Another way for screenwriters to think about narration is more technical, but no less creative. Here, narration is also how you write for the cinematic techniques that will be used to tell your story as a movie. Once again, the screenwriter's job, in Hollywood at least, is not to specify all of these technical solutions, but rather to imply them through compelling drama and situations.

How might light set the tone or emotional mood of a scene—how might light *narrate* the scene? The emotional context for that scene emerges from your dramatic writing. How might the creative use of sound add atmosphere or reveal important plot information—how might sound *narrate* the scene? You might specify an important sound effect, or your screenplay might establish the eerie context in a spooky movie that will make a good sound editor salivate in anticipation of bringing it to life. An extreme, but enjoyable example of this would be *Berberian Sound Studio* (2012, scr. Peter Strickland). Your words will be translated into film style, into the creative use of camera, lighting, sound, editing and so forth. Film style may be viewed as being largely the prerogative of the director, however it is also the interpretation of your narrative and your narration.

Narrative voice

Narrative voice is a term screenwriting has inherited from literature to describe the interpolation of the author's, or a particular character's, attitude directly into the storytelling. Independent filmmakers in particular value narrative voice as a tool through which they can express their creative purpose and attitude. However, it is somewhat problematic when removed from the context of literature and applied to a visual (not to say collaborative) medium like cinema.

Voice is not to be easily conflated with writing style. Despite their entertainment value in screenplays, Shane's Blackisms (for example) do not translate from page to screen. Rather, narrative voice is about adding a layer of meaning into the words and actions of your characters that implies an attitude in your story. The most obvious example of narrative voice in movies is voice-over narration. We have already learned from Hiccup how subjective narration speaks attitude.

Voice is about more than this kind of narration however. It can be discerned in different kinds of visual and structural patterning. A location used in an early scene might be returned to in very different circumstances later in a story. This return—this reinterpretation of the significance of the location—could strongly convey a political or emotional statement. In *Write What You Don't Know* I described the football ground colonized by racist skinheads in *This is England* (2006, scr. Shane Meadows). The interaction of historical or cultural context with the actions of your characters might also imply a similar kind of statement and so forth.

Beats

Story beats are building blocks of structure. They are moments when your story advances significantly. Something happens that changes things in your heroine's world, or that develops her **transformational arc** in some significant way. The term is fairly general and is often used to refer to elements of different sizes, from big **story** movements to subtle emotional shifts within a single scene, so the usage can be confusing. To clarify, we may talk about **scene** beats, character beats, story beats and even **act** beats.

To clarify, writers also insert the *word* "beat" in their scripts, to indicate a short pause in action or dialogue. This is not necessarily the same thing as a significant structural scene beat. Although it might also happen to mark one, you wouldn't type "beat" to do so otherwise. In this context, writing "beat" directs a moment of reflection, stocktaking, or hesitation on the part of one or more of your characters before they respond to an event or statement made in the story, thus:

```
Corporal Jones realizes there is no pin in the
grenade.

Beat.

He throws it as far as he can.
```

I use "beat" in this indicative way very occasionally in my own writing (indeed it turns up occasionally in the little dialogue interludes in this book), but I try to minimize it for the same reasons I try to avoid **parentheticals**. In short, writing "beat" is another way of asking the reader: "do you get me here?" It signifies a lack of confidence in your meaning, and its overuse is one of the most obvious *bad writer ticks* that a script reader will pick up on fast.

Acts

An act is a large unit of story structure that completes an important part of the overall storytelling. In the conventional, post-Aristotelian three-act model of screenplay structure the three acts enact the beginning, middle and end of the story:

Act One: *The beginning* introduces the world and the terms of the story, setting up the protagonist, their goals, the oppositional—antagonistic—force that will oppose them and following the process in which they make the initial choice to take action.

Act Two: *The middle* tests the protagonist and takes them through a process of development that prepares them for the final resolution of the story. The idea here is that your heroine may be willing to take action at the start of act two but is not yet capable of the kind of action—either in plot or story terms—that will lead to success. By the end of act two they should have learned, developed, changed, improved to the extent that at least they have a chance of doing so.

Act Three: *The end* resolves the theme and addresses your heroine's goals. She may succeed or fail but, either way, the premise of the story should be resolved. Of course resolution does not necessarily mean everything is tied up in a neat bow with no place for uncertainty. Resolution can often be messy, but it should still be thematically appropriate.

Midpoint

The Midpoint splits the second act (of three) and usually entails a second, deeper commitment to action and resolution on the part of your heroine. The first half of act two has taught her some hard truths about the task she took on at the end of act one and now she is able to make an informed choice to continue down a path that is only going to get harder.

Another common version of a story Midpoint is to give your heroine what she thought she wanted at the start of the movie. In doing so she comes to understand that what she has been given is not really what she wants after all. The second half of the story follows her new orientation, but should also follow the same theme as before.

Scenes

In a contemporary screenplay, a scene changes when time or location changes. So if we move from one location to another, or pick up action later in the day in the same location, we change scene.

Sequences

A sequence is a series of **scenes** that combine to enact an event or development (a story **beat**) that cannot be expressed adequately in one time or location. So a wedding, or a battle, or an important change in a character's awareness of their situation or their goals might play out in a sequence of linked scenes that all address parts of that story or plot element, or different perspectives on it.

Paul Joseph Gulino argues for a structural model of movie storytelling based on eight sequences. He notes that as movies extended beyond the length of a single reel of film, in the second decade of the last century, filmmakers learned creatively to acknowledge the beginning and end of a reel and to time their storytelling in relation to an approximate reel length of ten to twelve minutes. Reels would begin with fades in and out, for example, and sometimes with title cards indicating acts. Some early manuals actually advised aspiring writers to accommodate their storytelling to the length of reels.

Gulino suggests that consequently there is an underlying eight-sequence structure still discernible in screenplays today (it is not that different from my half-angle model). However, it is a stretch to suggest that the original technical reasons that may have artificially circumscribed sequence length before the widespread introduction of twin projectors in most movie theaters in the 1920s have defined their duration since. His link between sequence length and human attention span may have more weight.[62]

Inciting incident

Inciting incident is a term adopted by screenwriters from the manuals of the screenwriting industry to refer to the catalyzing event, in act one of a three-act screenplay, that sets the story in motion. In *Winter's Bone*, the inciting incident occurs when the sheriff tells Ree her father put their house up for bail bond and that he has disappeared. The obligatory scene or obligatory moment (per Robert McKee) is the future moment of resolution, implied by the inciting incident, where that event will be resolved. In *Winter's Bone* the obligatory moment is the interview between Ree and the sheriff when he accepts Jessup's severed hands as evidence of his death, releasing his bond. This sets up a pleasurable parallel for the audience who have been looking forward—both literally and metaphorically—to that unknown, but anticipated moment of structural payoff.

Parallelism

Parallelism is one of the simplest and yet most powerful structuring devices in all forms of storytelling, including screenwriting. Indeed many of the most influential models of screenplay structure speak in terms of parallelism. It is clear that parallelism is also one of the primary means through which an audience gets pleasure from storytelling—by making connections, recognizing patterns and anticipating or being surprised by plot revelations. Good writing plays to the power of parallelism in every way.

Part Five: Character development

Character; Theme; Wants and Needs; Transformational Arc; Through Line; Backstory; Protagonist; Antagonist

Character

In terms of story structure, characters are always constructions convenient to the requirements of a particular kind of narrative. Characters are not

---

[62] Paul Joseph Gulino, *Screenwriting: The Sequence Approach* (New York: Continuum Books, 2008).

real people and even the most complex and nuanced characters are different—more focused, more functional—than the people you know in real life. Movie characters are distillations of the way people present and behave in reality, refracted through the lens of your storytelling. They show only the traits you want or need them to show. Characters perform tasks for you in initiating or reacting to the patterning of structure.

Depending on the kind of story you are telling, characters can be more or less active—more or less in control of the progress of your story. In American genre movies characters are typically very active and energetic. The American paradigm is for characters to drive plot. This is not a universal, of course, and outside the American model other cinemas interpret the relationship between plot and character differently. In some character-driven American independent narratives, mumblecore movies being a recent example, characters can be more passive and reflective, appropriate to their sense of ennui or uncertainty.

Horror films sometimes play against the principle of genre characters driving plot. Slasher films offer us a community of complacent teens who can't see their danger because they are obsessed with their own immediate (narratively static) desires for sex, drugs and rock 'n' roll. The victims are reactive, apart from the survivor, or final girl, who is distinguished by her ability to externalize the threat she is facing and, thus, to take action to thwart it.

Theme

In screenwriting, your story's theme binds the internal logic of your structure together in the person of your protagonist. Their theme is constant, even if their attitudes to it change. The *meaning* of that theme to your characters at the end may be different from what it seemed to be at the start. So if your theme is loyalty you must be loyal to that loyalty throughout, even if your characters enact their own moments of betrayal in the course of events. If your theme changes, then the premise of your story changes and that doesn't work in any kind of conventional story type.

Wants and needs

Character goals exist in both story and plot. In screenwriting terms, plot goals are often called wants and story goals, needs. In the story, your heroine *needs* to prove herself capable of being independent from her over-possessive mother. In the plot, she *wants* to get an apartment. The theme of the story is independence, the plot is all about moving out and the new world of roommates and landlords—it's a gentle comedy of urban life, our movie—and the story is about a mother and daughter negotiating her move into adulthood. As in this simple example, your character's wants and needs should align thematically, even if they are different on the surface.

Transformational arc

This is a term used by some screenwriters to describe the track of change enacted by a significant character (not only the protagonist) in their scripts. A character's transformational arc should address the story's **theme** directly. It records the moments at which that character's view of their theme and purpose shifts. As we have noted, the theme of a conventional story does not change, however the attitude of your heroine to their theme might well change through experience and as the fight gets harder. The story will likely drive them away from their theme before bringing them back to it. Many conventional movies even require a kind of sacrificial relinquishment of the theme as part of the payment your character makes to ensure success.

Through line

A term appropriated from the work of Constantin Stanislavski, referring to the linked objectives which provide the emotional or psychological impetus to keep a character moving through her story and towards attaining her **goal**. Its original specific meaning has been appropriated and simplified and is now used in more general terms to refer to a character's arc or **transformational arc**.

Backstory

Backstory is a term screenwriters use to describe the preparatory work they do in developing a character for a screenplay. A character's backstory is all that happened to them before the start of the movie's story that has some bearing on their personality and their potential future actions once the movie's story opens. A writer who has developed a proper backstory for their characters will likely have a pretty good idea how their character will react in any given situation into which they might write them. All kinds of information may be germane to backstory, from childhood experiences to their medical history, or from their religious and political beliefs to their tastes in food and music.

It is easy for this kind of preparatory work to get out of hand, so as you develop material for a character's backstory keep asking yourself: a) how all the information you are generating helps form a usefully coherent picture of the individual; and (most importantly) b) how their backstory is relevant to the movie's story you are developing it to serve. In other words, don't waste time just inventing random information. Remember that all **characters** are constructs, so that gives you license to build them fit for purpose.

Protagonists

From the Greek for "first actor," we use the term protagonist to refer to the leading character in a screenplay. The protagonist is the character around whom the **story** develops and upon whose goals and struggles the story focuses. Not all protagonists are conventionally "heroic" because, in equally conventional movie storytelling, heroism requires transformative sacrifice. Many protagonists become heroes in the course of their stories even if they start out not being very heroic at all, like Cage in *Edge of Tomorrow*. Ensemble stories may not have a single protagonist, in which case each character in the group has his or her own, linked arc to play out. Many ensemble movies still tend to default to an implicit protagonist who helps us navigate the group, however.

The **Midpoint** is the key beat that enacts many of those transformations. In *How to Train Your Dragon* Hiccup wants to be a hero, but he is clearly not up to the task until he redefines heroism on his own terms and makes a choice to confront his culture with uncomfortable truths. In so doing he temporarily sacrifices his chance to be a hero in the eyes of his peers and becomes one in the eyes of the audience. Of course things work out in the end.

Antagonists

Antagonists are not necessarily villains, but villains tend to be antagonists. In a screenplay, the antagonist is best thought of as a force acting in opposition to the goals of the heroine (**Lajos Egri**'s opposition of forces). This force is usually personified in a character, but in some cases the antagonistic principle in a story may default to a more general manifestation of the story world. The antagonist of *How to Train Your Dragon* is Hiccup's father, Stoick the Vast. He represents a block in the path of cultural change that Hiccup has to move. Stoick means well, thinks his actions are for the defense of his people and, thus, resists change with every fiber of his being. That makes him a great antagonist, but in no way a villain.

Conclusion

This book has explored straightforward approaches to contemporary cinematic storytelling. It has offered a flexible helpmate-model of structure, illustrated through a wide range of examples, from the professional mainstream to the paradigm testing indie. It doesn't suit every movie type and that was never its intention—indeed, I don't follow it slavishly in my own writing and consulting. Neither the model, nor the examples, are intended to offer one-size-fits-all solutions. Its purpose has been to give you somewhere to go when you get stuck or are asking yourself what to do at any point in your own writing. The simple process and progress questions that I have included at the end of the discussion of each act and angle may sometimes be more useful in focusing your own thinking than any of the individual examples.

As I discussed in the Introduction, despite whatever help this book might give you, becoming a screenwriter is a very hard thing to do. My best advice to you is to think as laterally and creatively as you can about your possible future pathways and destinations while pursuing your writing goals. The new opportunities for writers and filmmakers and the ways in which media and platforms are converging and cross-pollinating are creating niches—spaces in which imaginative writers can insert themselves into the professional world. The good news is that there are more niches than there ever have been, but each niche will shape to the individual with the smarts and the cunning to find it and squeeze into it. What I'm telling you is that you have to shape your career ever more creatively nowadays, but there are more creative spaces into which you can fit.

I hope you approach this book with an appropriate degree of circumspection and creative distrust. That's how I would approach it if I hadn't written it. Of course I wouldn't have spent my time writing it if I didn't think it had some sensible advice to offer and some useful contexts to explore. On the other hand, I wouldn't be a writer if my own instincts didn't simultaneously kick against anyone telling me how to do the thing I love.

As I suggested at the start of the book, screenwriting manuals are selling you the unlikely prospect of making big money from Hollywood spec sales. However, remember that there is a great deal more to contemporary screenwriting than Hollywood. Even though we have spent much of the book considering relatively conventional storytelling,

I offer it as a point of reference only, a place of departure as much as a destination.

However you use this book I hope you have found it helpful. I also hope that it will ultimately become disposable, as your own confidence as a writer grows. Perhaps when you get to that point you will keep it on the shelf and refer back to it every so often, even if only to reassure yourself how completely you have transcended your need for its advice.

Here's to redundancy and transcendence then. Happy writing.

Implied You coughs politely.

                    FRIENDLY ME
          You still here?

                    IMPLIED YOU
          So, what should I do now?

                    FRIENDLY ME
          You're asking me for more advice?

                    IMPLIED YOU
          I've grown, I told you.

                    FRIENDLY ME
          Fair enough.

                    IMPLIED YOU
          So, my chances of selling my
          romantic comedy to Hollywood aren't
          so good?

                    FRIENDLY ME
          In the abstract, no. But I haven't
          read it yet, so I wouldn't want to
          say. Of course you haven't written
          it either. So, there's that.

                    IMPLIED YOU
          Yeah, but I really like the idea.
          Ever since we talked I've been going
          country; city; la la la. I'm filling

in details and beginning to really
find the story. There's a whole lot
of your bad ideas to cut out, of
course. "Let's put in a convenient
road-trip detour to Lucy's home
town." Come on.

Friendly Me holds up his hands in mock surrender.

>   IMPLIED YOU (CONT'D)
> But. No jokes. I want to do this.

>   FRIENDLY ME
> Then you should do it. Don't think
> about how hard it will be to sell.
> If you are inspired to write, then
> you should write. Listen, forget
> this book. Forget what anyone tells
> you about screenwriting. The best
> way to develop as a writer is just
> to write.

>   IMPLIED YOU
> Yeah. I should. I want to.

>   FRIENDLY ME
> Keep the budget low and you could
> even make it yourself. Microbudget
> style.

>   IMPLIED YOU
> Oh, I don't think I'm ready to
> direct a movie yet.

>   FRIENDLY ME
> You know, you might have a better
> chance selling it as a novel.
> Maybe it could be a Young
> Adult novel, in the perkier "Jane
> Levy version"? It's worth
> considering.

                    IMPLIED YOU
But, I want to be a screenwriter.

                    FRIENDLY ME
But remember what I said about
finding creative ways to approach
your career? In the current
climate it's easier to sell a
property as a potential movie if
it has a track record in another
medium - I'm not saying that's
easy either, only there are many
more novels published in a year than
spec screenplays are sold. If you
wrote a novel, and it got a good
following, then craven Hollywood
economics begin to kick in. A movie
adaptation would have a ready
audience. . .

                    IMPLIED YOU
I don't know if I can write a novel.

                    FRIENDLY ME
To be fair, you don't know if you
can write a screenplay either.

                    IMPLIED YOU
Ok, be a dick.

                    FRIENDLY ME
I'm just saying: now you're
exploring your desire to write,
why not explore it in prose as
well as script? You could self-
publish a novel if it came to that.
At least you would be getting it out
in the world. You can't do that with
a spec screenplay. You could even
draft it as a screenplay, to lock-in
the plot and the story structure,

then adapt it back to novel form.
Some writers have worked in that
way.

                    IMPLIED YOU
Yeah. OK, that's actually helpful.

                    FRIENDLY ME
Well, that's the idea.

                    IMPLIED YOU
I guess so. Listen, I know I can be
a pain in the ass.

                    FRIENDLY ME
If you don't come at the world
canted somehow then what do you
have to say?

                    IMPLIED YOU
Is this what they mean by a
redemptive ending?

                    FRIENDLY ME
Do you feel redeemed?

                    IMPLIED YOU
Not especially. Still. Hugs?

                    FRIENDLY ME
How about a polite handshake?

                    IMPLIED YOU
You're so English.

                    FRIENDLY ME
Yes. Yes I am.

Implied You and Friendly Me shake hands awkwardly,
then go their separate ways.
                         FADE TO BLACK.

Index